TUN . . . . TUNISIA
UGA . . . . UGANDA
ZAM . . . . ZAMBIA

CHA . . . . CHAD
CIV . . . . IVORY COAST
CMR . . . . CAMEROON
ETH . . . . ETHIOPIA
GHA . . . . GHANA
GUI . . . . GUINEA
KEN . . . . KENYA
LBY . . . . LIBYA
MAD . . . . MADAGASCAR
MLI . . . . MALI
MAR . . . . MOROCCO
NIG . . . . NIGER
NGR . . . . NIGERIA
RAU . . . . UNITED ARAB REPUBLIC
EN . . . . SENEGAL
LE . . . . SIERRA LEONE
UD . . . . SUDAN
AN . . . . TANZANIA

Asia

AFG . . . . AFGHANISTAN
BUR . . . . BURMA
CEY . . . . CEYLON
HKG . . . . HONG KONG
INA . . . . INDONESIA
IND . . . . INDIA
IRQ . . . . IRAQ
IRN . . . . IRAN
ISR . . . . ISREAL
JPN . . . . JAPAN
KOR . . . . KOREA (SOUTH)
LIB . . . . LEBANON
MAS . . . . MALAYSIA
MGL . . . . MONGOLIA
PHI . . . . PHILIPPINES

PAK . . . . PAKISTAN
SIN . . . . SINGAPORE
SYR . . . . SYRIA
THA . . . . THAILAND
TPE . . . . CHINESE TAIPAI
TUR . . . . TURKEY
VEI . . . . VIETNAM (SOUTH)

Oceania

AUS . . . . AUSTRALIA
FIJ . . . . FIJI
NZL . . . . NEW ZEALAND

THE OLYMPIC CENTURY
THE OFFICIAL 1ST CENTURY HISTORY OF THE MODERN OLYMPIC MOVEMENT
VOLUME 17

THE
XIX OLYMPIAD

MEXICO CITY 1968
SAPPORO 1972

BY
GEORGE G. DANIELS

WORLD SPORT RESEARCH & PUBLICATIONS INC.
LOS ANGELES

1996 © United States Olympic Committee

Published by:
World Sport Research & Publications Inc.
1424 North Highland Avenue
Los Angeles, California 90028
(213) 461-2900

1st Century Project
The 1st Century Project is an undertaking by World
Sport Research & Publications Inc. to commemorate the
100-year history of the Modern Olympic Movement.
Charles Gary Allison, Chairman

Publishers: C. Jay Halzle, Robert G. Rossi,
James A. Williamson

Senior Consultant: Dr. Dietrich Quanz (Germany)
Special Consultants: Walter Borgers (Germany), Ian
Buchanan (United Kingdom), Dr. Karl Lennartz
(Germany), Wolf Lyberg (Sweden), Dr. Norbert Müller
(Germany), Dr. Nicholas Yalouris (Greece)

Editor: Laura Foreman
Executive Editor: Christian Kinney
Editorial Board: George Constable, George G. Daniels,
Ellen Galford, Ellen Phillips, Carl A. Posey

Art Director: Christopher M. Register
Production Manager: Nicholas Pitt
Picture Editor: Debra Lemonds Hannah
Designers: Kimberley Davison, Diane Farenick
Staff Researchers: Mark Brewin (Canada), Diana
Fakiola (Greece), Brad Haynes (Australia), Alexandra
Hesse (Germany), Pauline Ploquin (France)
Copy Editor: Anthony K. Pordes
Proofing Editor: Harry Endrulat
Indexer and Stat Database Manager: Melinda Tate
Fact Verification: Carl and Liselott Diem Archives of the
German Sport University at Cologne, Germany
Statisticians: Bill Mallon, Walter Teutenberg
Memorabilia Consultants: Manfred Bergman, James D.
Greensfelder, John P. Kelly, Ingrid O'Neil
Staff Photographer: Theresa Halzle
Office Manager: Christopher Jason Waters
Office Staff: Chris C. Conlee, Brian M. Heath,
Edward J. Messler, Elsa Ramirez, Brian Rand

International Contributors: Jean Durry (France),
Dr. Antonio Lombardo (Italy), Dr. John A. MacAloon
(U.S.A.), Dr. Jujiro Narita (Japan), Dr. Roland Renson
(Belgium), Dr. James Walston (Ombudsman)

International Research and Assistance: John S. Baick
(New York), Matthieu Brocart (Paris), Alexander
Fakiolas (Athens), Bob Miyakawa (Tokyo), Rona Lester
(London), Dominic LoTempio (Columbia), George
Kostas Mazareas (Boston), Georgia McDonald
(Colorado Springs), Wendy Nolan (Princeton), Alexander
Ratner (Moscow), Jon Simon (Washington D.C.), Frank
Strasser (Cologne), Valéry Turco (Lausanne), Laura
Walden (Rome), Jorge Zocchi (Mexico City)

Map Compilation: Mapping Specialists Inc., Madison,
Wisconsin
Map Artwork: Dave Hader, Studio Conceptions,
Toronto
Film Production: Global Film Services, Toronto
Marketing Consultant: Robert George

Customer Service: 1-800-451-8030

Bookstore and Library Distribution:
Firefly Books Ltd.
3680 Victoria Park Avenue
Willowdale, ON M2H 3K1
(416) 499-8412

U.S. Offices
230 Fifth Avenue, #1607
New York, NY 10001

Printed and bound in the United States by R. R.
Donnelly Co.

ISBN 1-888383-00-3 (25-volume series)
ISBN 1-888383-17-8 (Volume 17)

Library of Congress Cataloging-in-Publication Data

Daniels, George G.
    XIX Olympiad : Mexico City, 1968, Sapporo, 1972 / by George G.
Daniels.
        p.   cm. -- (The Olympic century ; v. 17)
    Includes bibliographical references (p. 171 - 172) and index.
    ISBN 1-888383-17-8 (alk. paper)
    1. Olympic Games (19th : 1968 : Mexico City, Mexico) 2. Winter
Olympic Games (11th : 1972 : Sapporo-shi, Japan) I. Title.
II. Series.
GV722 1968D36 1996
796.48--dc20   96-28503
                                                            CIP

CONTENTS

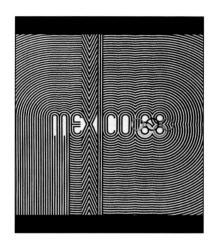

I

TO ANY LENGTHS
·7·

II

TO ANY HEIGHTS
·51·

III

CRUSADES AND COMMERCE
·93·

IV

THROUGH THE LOOKING GLASS
·117·

PEACEFUL BEGINNINGS

Political turmoil would beset the Games of the XIX Olympiad, but dissent was nowhere in sight as Mexico's president Gustavo Díaz Ordaz declared the festival open. The crowd, estimated at 100,000—well beyond the stadium's 80,000-seat capacity—cheered throughout the 80-minute Parade of Nations as a record number of delegations, 111, and more than 5,500 athletes marched by.

Loud cries of "Czech-o, Czech-o" greeted the Czechoslovakian contingent, the crowd voicing its solidarity with the nation that had been invaded by the Soviets only a month before the Games. Despite spectators' sympathy for the underdog, the Soviet team, its members waving tiny national flags, was favored with polite applause. Perhaps the crowd was awed by the sight of weight lifter Leonid Zhabotinsky, who carried the massive Soviet banner unbraced in his left hand.

After the Mexican delegation settled onto the infield, the Games' chief organizer, Pedro Ramírez Vázquez, and IOC president Avery Brundage welcomed visitors with brief speeches. The crowd watched quietly as the Olympic flag was raised. The stillness was broken by a blast from a conch shell that called everyone's attention to the stadium's north gate. There, Norma Enriqueta Basilio, a 20-year-old Mexican hurdler, emerged with the Olympic torch held high, making history as she ran: She was the first woman ever to bear the torch on the final leg of its long journey from Greece. She circled the stadium track, then mounted a stairway leading to the Olympic cauldron. As roars of "Me-hi-co" echoed through the stands, she ignited the sacred flame. The ceremony ended with the release of 10,000 pigeons into an afternoon sky that was darkening with storm clouds. The metaphor was apt: The traditional symbols of peace looked unusually frail against somber heavens that seemed to stress how fragile peace really is.

TO ANY LENGTHS

Never in his young life had Bob Beamon felt quite so good, so strong, so loose and limber. But he couldn't figure out why. He had spent the evening before with Gladys, his long-time love, dining quietly with her before retiring to a rented villa. At one point, making love in the night, Beamon had suddenly recalled the athlete's old shibboleth about sex on the eve of competition: It shouldn't happen; it weakened a man. It certainly shouldn't have happened on that particular night, since the next day shaped up as the most crucial of Beamon's existence. "Oh, my God, I've blown it," he had thought at the time, regret and apprehension washing through him.

Yet here it was the next morning, October 18, 1968, and Bob Beamon felt great. He felt relaxed and alive and in love. He felt that he could jump a mile—or at least as far as he had to to justify his presence in Mexico City this day, the day he would represent the United States in the long jump at the Olympic Games.

Beamon and Gladys enjoyed a late breakfast. Then he changed into his white track shorts and red-white-and-blue U.S.A. shirt and pulled a warm-up suit over the uniform. By early afternoon he was at the Estadio Olimpico. It was the sixth day of the Games of the XIX Olympiad, and 50,000 fans packed the former soccer stadium, most of them intent on the finals of the long jump. The event was scheduled to start at 3:30 p.m. and it promised brilliance, for rarely had such an array of champions contested an Olympic gold. Moreover, the site of the Games had experts in a froth of speculation. No one could be sure what effect Mexico City's 7,350-foot elevation would have on the athletes. But there was much talk that the rarefied air would offer less resistance to sprinters—and perhaps to jumpers as well.

Best known among the 17 qualifiers in the long jump were America's Ralph Boston and the Soviet Union's Igor Ter-Ovanesyan, both seasoned campaigners. Boston, 29, and Ter-Ovanesyan, 30,

Robert Beamon, Olympic Gold Medalist, Mexico City 1968

shared the world record at 8.35 meters, or 27 feet 4 ¾ inches. Yet neither was the current Olympic champion. At Tokyo 1964, Boston had finished second and Ter-Ovanesyan third behind a relatively unknown 26-year-old Welshman named Lynn Davies, whose winning jump was short of the record by almost a foot. But Davies was a good mudder, and he had achieved his Olympic gold in the pouring rain. And now, four years later to the day, with thunderheads looming over Mexico City, Lynn Davies was on hand to defend his title. He had to be the man to beat.

By some lights, though, that role should have gone to 21-year-old Bob Beamon. Physically, he was the living statue of a long jumper, carrying only 157 pounds on a 6-foot-3-inch frame that was spectacular for hugely powerful thigh and abdominal muscles. He was blessed with sprinter's speed to boot, and he had a way of attacking the takeoff board with a verve that bordered on ferocity. "You can hear it happen," he said, trying to explain that contact with the board. "It's a distinct sound, a rhythm you can't really capture in words. It's something like 'Ta-BOOM!'"

So far in 1968, Beamon had been virtually unbeatable, winning 22 of the 23 meets he had entered, jumping more than 26 feet regularly and twice exceeding 27 feet (8.23 meters). "I've come to win," he told reporters in Mexico City. But many experts dismissed that as so much bravado. For all his enormous talent, Beamon was still a novice, and he could be woefully erratic: He was prone to foul the board, and there were times when his form deserted him altogether. To unsettle matters further, he had been without regular coaching since mid-April, when he was suspended from the track team of the University of Texas at El Paso for refusing to compete against Brigham Young; the Mormon university was then under attack as racist by black protesters, and Bob Beamon was the sort of fellow who supported the brothers.

All in all, a lot of people in Mexico City were inclined to discount Beamon. And in the qualifying round, it looked as if they might be right. Twice he fouled. Only one jump remained when Ralph Boston strolled over to offer some friendly advice: Make a check mark well in front of the board, and be sure to hit that. Beamon nodded. He made the mark. Then he returned to the head of the Tartan composition runway, half-trotted down its length, took a couple of choppy steps before the safety mark—and gracefully lofted himself out to 26 feet 10 ½ inches (8.19 meters), almost 2 feet better than he needed to qualify.

Watching the jump in amazement, Boston thought Beamon had taken off at least 18 inches short of the board. "It looked like a foot and a half to me," he told Beamon. "I think it was 2 feet," said Bob. Unspoken, but on both their minds, was the certainty that if Beamon had hit the takeoff board, he would have pulled off history's first 28-foot jump.

The draw for the finals next afternoon had Beamon going fourth. Davies was 12th, Ter-Ovanesyan 13th, Boston 17th. The rain clouds were closing in and it was cool—74 degrees Fahrenheit, 15 degrees cooler than the day before—which made the Tartan runway firmer and faster. The change might have affected the timing of the first three jumpers: a Japanese, a West German, and a Jamaican. All three fouled.

Then, at 3:46 p.m., an official called No. 246, Robert Beamon, United States of America. A little earlier, still feeling terrific, the young jumper had murmured, half to himself, "I think I can jump 28 feet today." Ralph Boston overheard him and smiled wryly. "I'm always nervous when Bob goes down the runway," Boston later told newsmen, "because you know that someday he might put all his great talent together in one big jump."

Beamon stood at the head of the runway for perhaps 20 seconds. Boston graciously called encouragement: "Come on, make it a good one." Beamon lowered his head and closed his eyes. "Don't foul. Don't foul," he prayed. Then he

TRACKING COLUMBUS

The 1968 Olympic torch relay followed a route almost half a millennium old—a route that had changed the New World forever: Roughly, it traced Christopher Columbus's path on his first voyage to the Americas.

After the traditional lighting ceremony at Olympia on August 23, 1968, the torch toured Greece briefly before heading for Genoa, Italy, Columbus's birthplace. The Italian ship *Palinuro* carried the flame from there to Barcelona, where Columbus had returned with his skewed account of finding the Indies. After a short run through Spain, the fire sailed aboard a Spanish corvette, the *Princesa*, from Puerto de Palos, the point of departure for Columbus 476 years earlier. The *Princesa* retraced the explorer's inaugural crossing, landing in San Salvador on September 29. There, the tribute to Columbus was abandoned in favor of honoring another world-changing explorer, the Spanish conquistador Hernando Cortez. The fire traveled on the *Durango* along the course charted by Cortez on his 1519 maiden voyage to Mexico, landing at Veracruz. The relay traced Cortez's march to Tenochtitlán, then the Aztec capital, now Mexico City. A ceremony mixing elements of pre-Columbian and modern Mexico was performed on ancient Aztec ruins. The following day, October 12, the flame was carried to its final destination, the Olympic stadium.

Norma Enriqueta Basilio climbs toward the top of Mexico City's Olympic stadium. For Basilio, a student and the daughter of a Mexicali farmer, the torch ceremony was the highlight of the Games: She was eliminated from the 80-meter hurdles after finishing sixth in the first heat.

Organizers made 3,000 of these grooved, conical-shaped torches for the journey to Mexico City. The flame was conveyed on the 50-day trek from Olympia by ship and by relay runners, swimmers, and even water-skiers.

All eyes turn to the long-jump pit as American Bob Beamon finally lands. He was coming to rest in territory he would not reach again: Beamon would never come within a foot of his epochal jump for the rest of his career.

lifted his head, opened his eyes, and launched into his approach, legs driving, accelerating swiftly. Down the runway he raced, 19 strides, a fraction more than 130 feet, no safety check this time, eyes fixed on the white takeoff board rushing up at him. Spectators later remarked that he ran curiously upright, "more like a sprinting ostrich than a gazelle," wrote one reporter.

The jump was perfect. Ta-BOOM! At the end of a long final stride, the six-spike Adidas on Beamon's right foot pounded into the white board a few centimeters from the forward edge. Fair jump.

Up, up, up, the great, piston-like muscles propelled the lean body, fists clenched, arms out thrust for balance, torso erect, knees spread, feet

forward at waist level. Those who saw Bob Beamon on that day will never forget how high he soared: Some observers estimated his height above the ground at 5 ½ feet (1.68 meters); others, with a different angle, thought he cleared 6 feet at the apogee of his arc. He seemed to float forever, and when he finally glided into the pit, his forward momentum carried him up and out of the loose sand in one mighty bound.

"That's 28 feet," said Boston to Lynn Davies as they trotted over to the pit for a better look.

"With his first jump?" replied Davies. "No. It can't be."

"That's *more* than 28 feet," amended Boston.

Beamon was dancing around, arms clasped over his head. Like Boston, like everyone else in

the Estadio Olimpico, he knew it was good, maybe even a record. But the seconds passed, and no distance went up on the rotating electronic scoreboard.

At the pit, the officials were having a problem. The jumps were measured by a special optical device mounted on a rail. But the device wasn't built to record the impossible. The rail extended only 28 feet—and the scanner fell off before it got anywhere near Beamon's heel marks. "Fantastic. Fantastic," murmured a judge to Beamon, who by now was pulling on his sweats. "Get a tape!" someone shouted. And eventually, the distance went up in lights: 8.90 meters.

A gasp went through the crowd, then a thundering roar. But Beamon was no expert in metrics, and it took Ralph Boston to explain.

"Bob," he said quietly, "Bob, you've just jumped 29 feet."

To be exact, 29 feet 2 ½ inches.

In one incredible leap, Bob Beamon, not long out of his teens, had entirely bypassed the 28-foot level to lift the world record by an astonishing 21 ¾ inches (55.25 centimeters). It was by almost any standard the greatest single accomplishment in the history of track and field, and in the months and years to come, volumes would

be written analyzing all the whys and wherefores of Beamon's breakthrough.

The athlete himself was stunned. He turned to Boston, the man he called "the Master." "What do I do now?" he asked. "Ralph, I know you're gonna kick my ass."

"No, no," said Boston, shaking his head. "It's over for me. I can't jump that far."

"What about the Great Britain dude? And what about the Russian?" persisted Beamon. Then, as some realization of what he had done hit him, Beamon sank to the running track and held his head in his hands. Nausea burned his throat, and he thought he might vomit. Tears filled his eyes. "Tell me I'm not dreaming," he whispered. "It's not possible."

Igor Ter-Ovanesyan had been standing with Lynn Davies when Beamon's distance finally went up on the scoreboard. "After that jump, we are all children," the Soviet star muttered. Davies was devastated. "I can't go on," he said. "I can't go on after that. We'll all look silly."

But Davies did go on—champions always go on—although the best he could do in the rain that finally arrived was a ninth-place leap of 26 feet ½ inch (7.94 meters). Despite foul trouble, Ter-Ovanesyan managed a brave fourth with a

Beamon watches anxiously as officials use a tape measure to determine how far he'd jumped. Except for his miraculous leap, performances in the long jump were lackluster: Beamon was the only athlete to break 27 feet.

best-of-seven that measured 26 feet 7 ¾ inches (8.12 meters), while Ralph Boston salvaged a bronze medal at 26 feet 9 ½ inches (8.17 meters). The Olympic silver went to the European champion, East Germany's Klaus Beer, who stretched out a lifetime best one inch (2.54 centimeters) beyond Boston.

And Bob Beamon? When he got himself together—partway, anyhow—he lifted off in a second jump of 26 feet 4 ¼ inches (8.03 meters), then decided to sit out the rest of the afternoon. "I felt I was fairly safe," he would explain with a vast grin.

The jump of the century had scarcely been posted before controversy swirled up around it. The wind had been at Beamon's back; judges calculated its velocity at 2 meters per second, or 4.473 miles per hour, the exact maximum allowable. Debunkers suggested that the wind was actually well over the limit and that Mexican officials had deliberately misread their instruments for the sake of an astounding new record. Yet the naysayers had not a shred of proof.

Others tried to play down Beamon's feat by pointing to the thinner atmosphere, which offered less resistance to the human body, both while running and in the air. The carping continued for months, until *Sports Illustrated* magazine engaged a physicist to calculate as precisely as possible the effect of elevation on Beamon's jump. Taking into account the air density, Beamon's frontal area, his drag coefficient, approach speed, and all the rest, the physicist concluded that Beamon might have benefited a maximum of 10 inches from the elevation. So, subtracting the advantage of altitude—which every jumper of course enjoyed—Bob Beamon still ta-BOOMed it out there a full 12 inches—one whole foot—beyond what anyone in history had ever done.

Bob Beamon receives a congratulatory handshake from a Mexican judge for his record-setting exploit. Earlier in the meet, the press had labeled him a loudmouth for predicting he would jump more than 28 feet.

The sour grapes over Beamon's long jump was hardly an isolated incident at Mexico City 1968; discord didn't begin with his event, and it certainly didn't end there. Indeed, while every Olympics endures a certain amount of dispute, pervasive malaise and contention might be said to have characterized these particular Games—to the point where one writer titled his assessment "Altitude and Attitude." The fascination with Mexico City's elevation and whether performances were "real" or not, or "fair" or not, permeated the track and field competition. Yet that was the least of it.

The year 1968 was one of worldwide turmoil, the most chaotic 12 months since the end of World War II. And the attitudes of the athletes, judges, and spectators assembled for the Games

A building on the west side of Chicago goes up in flames during citywide rioting on April 5, 1968. Several American cities faced violent race riots following the April 4 assassination of civil rights leader Dr. Martin Luther King Jr.

quite naturally reflected the tempests lashing the outside world.

The time line for 1968 read like a circus of the mad. In January an unpopular war in Vietnam became all but unendurable for the U.S. when Vietcong and North Vietnamese forces unleashed a massive Tet offensive that eventually put another 1,100,000 South Vietnamese under Communist control; Washington reacted by stepping up the bloody conflict (25,000 American dead thus far) in desperate hopes of forcing the enemy to serious peace negotiations. Meanwhile, antiwar and antidraft riots erupted across the United States, further dividing a society already rent by swelling protest over the inequities suffered by African-Americans. So serious were the disaffections that in February, President Lyndon B. Johnson's National Advisory Commission on Civil Disorders warned that the nation was moving toward two societies: one white and one black, separate and unequal. Yet the U.S. Senate struggled through seven weeks of debate and filibuster before finally passing in March a civil rights bill aimed at closing the legal fissures—if not the spiritual and moral breach—that separated the races.

That month a beleaguered President Johnson announced that he would neither seek nor accept another term—as if his departure from power might somehow still the storm. It didn't. Calamity arrived on the evening of April 4, when a white gunman named James Earl Ray shot down Dr. Martin Luther King Jr., America's towering civil rights leader, as King stood on the balcony of a Memphis motel. Howling with horror and fury, black Americans took to the streets across the land—in Chicago, Baltimore, Washington, and other cities—in uprisings that prompted the U.S. Army to announce the establishment of a national riot control center in the Pentagon.

Suffering their own anguish, Europeans saw leftist mobs battle police in the cities of Germany and Italy. In May, France shuddered to a standstill when rebellious antigovernment students and workers by the hundreds of thousands occupied factories, mines, and offices. Further catastrophe visited the U.S. on the early morning of June 4, when Senator Robert F. Kennedy joined his brother John in death from an assassin's bullet; Bobby Kennedy had decided to run for president and had just claimed victory in the California primary when a deranged Tunisian Arab named Sirhan Sirhan cut him down as he departed a Los Angeles hotel.

There was more. July saw the U.S. Congress refuse first to mandate federal registration of firearms, then decline to require state licensing. That same month Cleveland, Ohio, reverberated to a violent gun battle between police and black nationalists. August was political convention month—and a time of still more bitter clashes between protesters and police, both in Miami Beach, where the Republicans nominated Richard M. Nixon, and in Chicago, where the Democrats chose Hubert H. Humphrey. Only the Youth International Party—the flaky Yippies—had any fun; they nominated a pig as their presidential standard-bearer.

Then, in mid-August, in counterpoint to the tarnish and madcap of American politics, Soviet tanks clanked into Czechoslovakia to crush the life out of a nascent liberalizing movement in that small satellite state.

Such was the condition of the world as the Olympic Games approached. As for Mexico, the first Latin American nation ever to host an Olympics, that unhappy land mourned the deaths of those caught up in a whirlwind of violence triggered by the very presence of the Games. Radical students had been protesting for months against the expenditure of so many millions on sport when so many countrymen lived in appalling poverty. The issue came to a head on October 2, ten days before the opening ceremonies, when troops backed by armored vehicles and helicopters confronted 10,000 demonstrators packed into Mexico City's downtown Plaza of Three Cultures.

Something led the soldiers to open fire. Before the conflict ended, between 40 and 300 people, depending on reports, had been fatally wounded, with another 1,200 injured and hundreds more jailed.

Cries of "Cancel the Olympics" went up on every hand. But the Olympic credo was the no-matter-what position of Avery Brundage, doughty president of the International Olympic Committee (IOC): Politics be damned, the Games would proceed. And so they did. With the Mexican government offering assurances of no further trouble—and the stunned protesters provoking none—athletes poured in from 111 countries across the face of the globe, more than 5,500 men and women of every size and color. Mexico, the host nation, fielded a team of 300; only the Soviet Union, with 324, and the U.S., with 387, sent more participants.

No fewer than 46 of the Americans were black, and they bore a burden beyond the mere competition for gold, silver, and bronze. All year long, fiercely determined activists had been trying to organize a black boycott of the Games to spotlight racial inequities in the world's greatest democracy. They had failed. With a few exceptions, America's premier athletes had decided to represent their country and themselves. But they retained the choice of how and whether to mount individual protests, in whatever manner a man or a woman might see fit.

Bob Beamon's choice was to demonstrate, in his own mild fashion. As he mounted the podium, the band playing "The Star-Spangled Banner," Klaus Beer below and on his left, Ralph Boston another step lower to his right, the crowd could see that Beamon's sweatpants were rolled up and that he was wearing long black socks—a symbol of black deprivation and black unity. "To protest what's happening to black people in the U.S.," he explained later. Boston

Czech dissidents carry their country's flag past a burning Soviet tank, protesting the invasion of their homeland on August 21, 1968. The Soviet incursion brought untimely winter to the "Prague Spring," the liberal reform movement led by Alexander Dubcek, head of the Czech Reform Communist party.

Flares float in the sky over Mexico City's Plaza of Three Cultures during a demonstration protesting Olympic expenditures in a nation plagued by poverty. Moments after this picture was taken, soldiers opened fire on the crowd.

The concentric-ring motif that was prominent on much of the promotional material for the Mexico City Games appears on the front of the winners' diploma and the back of the commemorative medal *(below, second from right)*. The front of the medal *(below, right)* shows the Aztec calendar with Tonatiuh, the sun god, at its center. The winners' medal uses a version of the Giuseppe Cassioli design that has been mandatory since Amsterdam 1928: The goddess Nike adorns the front *(below, left)*, while the back shows Diagoros of Rhodes, a champion of the ancient Olympics, being borne in triumph on the shoulders of his sons and grandsons, all champions themselves.

appeared barefoot at the ceremony, making his own statement about poverty in America. But that was all. Beamon stared resolutely ahead at the American flag during the ceremony. So did Boston. And Olympic officialdom, which had been coming down hard on the more aggressive African-American athletes, wisely decided to overlook the incident.

That evening Bob Beamon donned a favorite cream-colored suit, cut in the elegant Edwardian style he favored, and placed his Olympic medal around his neck. Then he and Gladys and another couple went out to dinner. Next day, without waiting for the end of the Games, Beamon packed his suitcases and left Mexico City. He never explained why. Yet the likelihood is that this young, essentially modest man was ill prepared for fame and that he fled home in embarrassment, to be alone while he attempted to assess the rewards and responsibilities attendant on history's greatest long jumper.

In many respects, Bob Beamon's life—his early travail, Olympic glory, and subsequent sorrow—could serve as a paradigm of the African-American athlete in the 1960s and 1970s.

He grew up in New York City's black ghetto of South Jamaica, where those who knew him labeled Beamon "the Clown" and "the Troublemaker." He started drinking when he was seven, then did marijuana and fought with knives in gang fights. He mauled girls in the coat closets at Public School 40. Whenever he got the chance, he danced—flop-floppity-flop—on the teacher's desk in shoes that purposely were a couple of sizes too large. He shoplifted outrageously, hauling on pants under his own pants in the dressing rooms, layering shirts under his own shirt, then tucking record albums under the stolen shirts before waddling out of the store. By the time he was 13 he had graduated to pushing nickel bags of marijuana, selling maybe $30 worth a day and putting the proceeds into sharp clothes and cheap wine. "No one knew what to do with me," Beamon recalled. "They all predicted that I would be in prison before I was 14."

That seemed a pretty decent bet, considering Beamon's background. All he knew of his mother was that she had conceived him in the spring of 1946 with a handsome lover while her husband was doing time in Sing Sing. She died when her baby was 11 months old—a slight, pretty woman in a faded photograph her son kept and treasured. His grandmother, Minnie, tried to bring him up, with a little help from her son—the man who had married Beamon's mother—now out of prison and going straight, mostly. But drinking turned the man into an abusive monster—"a werewolf," Beamon said. The results of this shaky home life showed soon enough: The boy started running with a zip-gun-waving gang. His school grades were in the 50s—on a good day. The New York City Board of Education put him in one of its "600" schools designed as holding pens for the hopeless.

P.S. 622, on Manhattan's 52nd Street just west of Eighth Avenue, lay in an area haunted by thieves, junkies, pimps, and prostitutes. Nevertheless, it was there that Beamon met with enlightenment on two fronts. First, he found that there were people in the world who would stand up to him. This discovery came at the hands of teachers—the kind who responded to disobedience with a thundering

left to the gut. Next, he found athletics. More to the point, he discovered how naturally gifted he was at running and jumping. For the first time, he started thinking about being somebody—somebody his mother would have been proud of.

Bob Beamon, with his pant legs rolled up to expose a pair of long black socks, shakes hands with a barefoot Ralph Boston. The oddities of dress protested racism and poverty in the United States, but at this point in the troubled Games, the gesture was comparatively mild.

Athletes stretch by the remains of an Aztec pyramid from the ancient ceremonial hub of Cuicuilco. Located just outside the center of modern Mexico City, Cuicuilco was buried under lava from an eruption of Xitle, a volcano whose cone makes up part of the mountain range surrounding the capital. The Aztec landmark was discovered during construction of the Olympic Village.

On the basketball court, only 15 years old and just 6 feet tall, Beamon could already uncoil and touch the steel rim of the basket. Competing in track and field for P.S. 622 in the Police Athletic League, he started out as a sprinter, then one day tried long jumping. Without benefit of instruction, he charged down the runway and sailed 19 feet—excellent for his age. A year later, in the Junior Olympics sponsored by the tabloid *New York Daily Mirror*, Beamon gave a hint of what was to come. The boy had never jumped 20 feet before. But on this night, he sailed an incredible 24 feet (7.32 meters)—almost out of the pit.

That was his ticket out of P.S. 622 and into Jamaica High School, notable for both outstanding academics and a fine athletic program. Jamaica High also was 80 to 90 percent white, with Jewish kids, Italian kids, kids from around the world whose parents worked at the United Nations. Beamon was assigned to the 10th grade—on probation. Prestigious Jamaica High had never enrolled a boy from a 600 school before, and Beamon's reading skills tested at fourth-grade level. But a couple of sympathetic administrators decided not to turn their backs on him—not on a 24-foot jumper.

Beamon was terrified. "I had never been around so many white kids in my life," he remembered.

Young gymnasts form human pyramids in front of the National Cathedral to welcome Olympic visitors. Begun in 1573, the cathedral is the oldest of its kind in the Americas.

But the clown and troublemaker were disappearing, to be replaced by a newly self-confident young man who made friends and impressed people. Some embarrassments remained, of course. When he went out for basketball, the equipment boy gave him a jockstrap with his uniform, and Beamon, never having seen one before, put it on backwards. No matter. He soon got that straight and earned a berth on the Jamaica varsity.

By 1965, his second year at Jamaica, he was 18 and had grown to his full 6 foot 3. He soon earned the status of a star athlete, but if he leaped on the track, he still limped in the classroom. Even so, he was making slow, determined progress, and his teachers told him he had the intellectual capacity for college. Thus in the fall of 1965, when he turned 19 and his high-school athletic eligibility ended, Beamon started taking extra credits so he could graduate in January and get on with the career he saw ahead.

But now, he faced one of those crises that scar as well as shape a man. Beamon's love life revolved around two girls: the stunning Gladys and a Honduran-born beauty named Bertha. Torn between the two, he found his mind made up for him when Bertha announced that she was pregnant. Wanting to do the right thing, he married her in late December 1965, only to be

A smiling Bob Beamon holds a trophy won in Kansas City during a National Association of Intercollegiate Athletics track meet in 1967. The award was for his long jump of 27 feet 1 inch (8.26 meters), which set an indoor world record.

told a month later that Bertha had suffered a miscarriage. Beamon, suspecting that he had been tricked into marriage, found his feelings for his new wife dying, and all his affections reverting—then and for years to come—to Gladys.

As if the turmoil attending his marriage weren't enough, the teenaged newlywed found himself facing yet another crossroads: college. The month after his wedding, Beamon graduated from Jamaica High. He stood 1,093rd in his class of 1,182. No scholar—but still a star—he was recruited by dozens of colleges, including the University of Southern California. But he passed up the big names—their size and standards scared him—for North Carolina Agricultural and Technical College, a small, largely black school whose recruiters

had promised him, among other things, a new car and wardrobe each year. The promises proved hollow, and after a single semester he transferred to the University of Texas at El Paso, where a young coach named Wayne Vandenburg and a bunch of generous businessmen were building a powerful track team.

Beamon blossomed. Shortly after entering UTEP in January 1967, he won his first national championship at the AAU meet in Oakland, California. He had never jumped 26 feet before—and now, just as he had gone from 20 feet to 24 feet in one swoop, Beamon obliterated his personal best with a prodigious leap of almost 27 feet—26 feet 11 ½ inches (8.22 meters). He beat runner-up Ralph Boston by 4 inches and came within half an inch of Igor Ter-Ovanesyan's indoor record. Practicing as never before, he went on to win a first, a second, and a third in three major international meets, topping 26 feet each time. He defeated Boston once and lost twice; he beat Lynn Davies once and lost once. Word went around acknowledging 20-year-old Bob Beamon as one of the four best long jumpers in the world.

Beamon only got better during the winter of 1967-68, reaching a zenith in March at the NCAA indoor championships in Detroit. He won the long jump with a world indoor record leap of 27 feet 2 ¾ inches (8.30 meters). But even now, he was no student of his craft. In training, he took off on the wrong foot—his left foot—from time to time, and he preferred to concentrate on sprinting rather than the actual jump. He made no marks on the runway, just zipped down the approach and took off—on one foot or the other. At least half the time he fouled. But if his technique was flawed, his native talent was awesome.

That spring, UTEP regarded Bob Beamon as a virtual one-man track team, listing him as a possible entrant in no fewer than seven events: 100-, 220-, and 440-yard dashes; 440-yard relay;

Four Flying Dutchman class yachts maneuver around a buoy in Acapulco Bay. Flying Dutchman yachts are 19 feet 10 inches (6.05 meters) long and carry a crew of two. They became a part of the Olympic program in 1960.

mile relay; long jump; and triple jump. Coach Vandenburg didn't register his star as a high jumper, but he might have: Beamon had casually cleared 6 feet 5 inches while hacking around with some of his buddies.

Then came the Brigham Young incident and the suspension of Beamon and seven other black athletes. Beamon competed as a member of the Houston Striders, a local independent track club, for which he racked up a dazzling string of 26-foot victories and one colossal leap of 27 feet 4 inches (8.33 meters), only three-quarters of an inch shy of the world record. The season done, he went home to spend the summer with Gladys in New York's Greenwich Village.

Trials for the U.S. Olympic track team were in mid-September at California's Lake Tahoe, which stands at an elevation of 6,200 feet. The thought was to give track and field athletes a foretaste of what it would be like in Mexico City. Beamon hadn't trained at all while enjoying the good Village life in July and August. Yet, with Gladys watching, he stepped out on his first jump of the finals and sailed 27 feet 6 ½ inches (8.39 meters), well beyond Boston's and Ter-Ovanesyan's record. It couldn't count because of a strong following wind, but it was—to date—the greatest jump of his life. Training or no, he was ready.

THE FLYING ENGLISHMAN

Olympic yachting events in 1968 were held in the cool Pacific waters off the coast of Acapulco, Mexico's world-famous resort city. October normally brings calm to Acapulco Bay, but sailors in the Olympic regatta faced stiff breezes. Captains had plenty of time, though, to adjust to whatever conditions prevailed: As usual, the lengthy yachting program for each of the five classes entailed a week-long series of seven races around a nine-stage triangular course. Points were awarded to teams according to how they finished; each yacht was allowed to drop its worst race.

United States crews overcame the tricky winds to win the Dragon and Star classes. Sweden's team of brothers Ulf, Jörgen, and Peter Sundelin sailed away with the 5.5-meter yachting gold medal. Valentin Mankin consistently finished among the top four in the Finn class races to give the Soviet Union its second yachting title ever. But the best seamanship at Acapulco was displayed by Great Britain's Rodney Pattisson, who teamed with Iain Macdonald-Smith to win the Flying Dutchman gold.

Pattisson and Macdonald-Smith won their first race but were disqualified for interfering with the start of the Canadian entry. Undaunted, Pattisson steered his boat *Superdocious* to five straight victories. A second-place finish on the last day clinched the gold medal.

Pattisson would successfully defend his title at Munich 1972, though with Christopher Davies as crew. In 1976 he would cap his Olympic career at Montreal with yet another shipmate, Julian Houghton, and the two would win a silver medal. Pattisson remains Great Britain's greatest Olympic yachtsman.

Ralph Boston, though hampered by a floating cartilage in his right knee, also got off a wind-aided leap of 27 feet 1 inch (8.26 meters). He was ready, too. So were the Europeans. Ter-Ovanesyan had done 27 feet 2 inches (8.28 meters) a few weeks before, and Lynn Davies had a 27-footer (8.23 meters) to his credit in 1968 as well.

But everything anyone had ever achieved, perhaps even dreamed of, became academic in those few seconds shortly after 3:46 p.m. on October 18 when Bob Beamon hurled himself aloft in Mexico City's Estadio Olimpico. Some idea of the feat's magnitude could be found in the past. In 1935 the exalted Jesse Owens had set a long-jump record of 26 feet 8 ¼ inches (8.13 meters). Over the next 33 years of intense competition, the record had advanced by only 8 ½ inches (21.6 centimeters). And here, in Mexico City, on his first attempt, Beamon had added almost 2 feet to the mark. What is more, Beamon's record would remain unbroken for 23 years—an entire generation—until in 1991 another gifted black athlete, Mike

Powell, would add 2 inches by soaring 29 feet 4 ½ inches (8.95 meters) at the world track and field championships in Tokyo.

After his moment of supreme, untouchable glory, was there anywhere to go but down for Bob Beamon? As he himself once wrote in an English class at UTEP, "Time runs out quickly for the athlete."

That, more or less, was how it happened for history's supreme long jumper. In another half-dozen years of competition, Beamon never again came close to 29 feet. He didn't leap 28 feet, rarely made 27 feet, and sometimes had trouble reaching even 26 feet. Yet in the end, in a different fashion, he made a success of his life.

When Beamon left Mexico City, he went home to El Paso and a gush of adulation. "Thirty feet?" he answered a reporter. "Yes, I might do it some day." He had no reason to think otherwise. In the voting for Track and Field Athlete of 1968, sponsored by *Track and Field News*, Beamon was the runaway choice of the experts, collecting 17 of 23 first-place votes.

Disaster overtook him in February when he flew to Washington, D.C., for a meet, missed connections, and arrived bone-weary at 4 a.m. Reporters consumed most of his day. That evening, on his first jump, Beamon heard the hamstring in his right leg go "pop" and felt a savage pain as he hit the sand.

For any athlete, particularly a jumper, a torn hamstring is a critical injury, one that must be left to heal without further stress. But Beamon was under ferocious pressure to keep competing. He was openly squiring Gladys around and now had two women to support; in celebration of his Olympic triumph, he had also acquired a new house and a flashy car—both with heavy monthly payments. All sorts of people had promised him all sorts of terrific jobs, but none had come through. The only way he could handle his

A detail from Diego Rivera's *A Sunday in the Alameda* was used in a promotional poster for Mexico City 1968. The mural's skeletal figures evoke images from the Day of the Dead, a holiday celebrated in Mexico every fall.

mountain of debt was by collecting the generous "expense" allowances handed out by promoters of indoor track meets. He was a headliner, to be sure. But sometimes he could manage only a token jump. Sometimes he couldn't jump at all.

Rumors spread that Beamon was faking the injury. Always reticent around strangers, he now withdrew further; that made him "greedy" and "conceited." Even his three-piece Edwardian suits and bowler hats came in for ridicule: "Flamboyant" the sportswriters called his mode of dress. Gladys pleaded with her despondent beau to take care of himself, and he eventually took her advice. The two of them holed up in New York while Beamon worked to get himself back into shape.

He started competing again at the end of April, and while he won a couple of meets, the hamstring still bothered him. He felt that the right leg was permanently crippled. So he started jumping off his left foot. And at the end of June 1969, at the AAU championships in Miami, Beamon performed what a number of experts regarded as the most extraordinary feat of his career, his Olympic 29-footer notwithstanding. Hitting the takeoff board with his left foot, this lifetime right-footed long jumper arched up and out to 26 feet 11 inches (8.20 meters). It was the longest jump by an American all year long. It was also Bob Beamon's last jump of major significance, left foot or right.

For many reasons, physical and psychological, his athletic career was winding down. He continued to compete halfheartedly and in 1973 joined the fledgling professional tour sponsored by the International Track Association. Some of the big stars got five-figure bonuses for signing up; Beamon received $2,000. And though he could jump normally again, hitting 26 feet regularly, he never managed 27 feet as a pro and won only $3,600 in prize money all that first season. Amateur track had been a lot more profitable.

Other things were ending, too. As 1969 waned,

BROTHERS IN ARMS

Four brothers from Sweden's Pettersson family hold close formation in cycling's team time trial. Some years after the Games, the brothers all changed their surname to Fåglum to honor the town where they'd grown up.

Frenchmen dominated the cycling competition at the velodrome at Mexico City. Pierre Trentin was the individual star, taking home two gold medals and a bronze. Teammate Daniel Morelon claimed the sprint event for the second consecutive Games and with Trentin also took the tandem title.

In the team time trial, brotherhood abounded on the Swedish squad, composed entirely of four siblings from the Pettersson family of Fåglum: Gösta, 27; Sture, 25; Erik, 24; and Tomas, 21. The three older brothers had competed together at Tokyo 1964, and in the four years since, Tomas had completed his military service and joined the team. The Petterssons had won the team time trial at the 1967 world cycling championships, boosting their Olympic hopes. Their form held in the early going at Mexico City: They were leading, but then Tomas's bike got a flat tire and they fell back. Sture later dropped out of the race, but the three remaining brothers pedaled on to finish in second place. (Times for only the first three riders count.) The Netherlands' team finished first.

The Petterssons remain the only all-brother team ever to compete in an Olympic cycling event.

he and Gladys had broken up. She was weary of waiting for Beamon to get a divorce. Ironically, he and Bertha did divorce, in 1972. (He would marry again, twice.)

Oddly enough, Beamon found success at last where he had always had the hardest time—in school. In December of 1968 he enrolled at Adelphi University in Garden City, New York, as a junior. In 1972, at the age of 25, he earned his bachelor of arts degree.

When Beamon's biographer, ace sportswriter Dick Schaap, went for a series of visits that led to the book *The Perfect Jump* in 1976, Beamon could still talk wistfully about how he might like to own a vintage Rolls-Royce and open a fashion boutique for men. "The best boutique around. The most flamboyant clothes around," he chuckled. In fact, though, the great athlete's life had taken a far more productive turn: He had found his true calling in helping underprivileged kids. In a succession of jobs and projects, first in California and then in Florida, Beamon devoted himself to aiding disadvantaged youngsters with athletics, with jobs, even with academics. By all accounts, he was very good at his work—a natural talent.

The seeds of Beamon's calling were of course sown in his own South Jamaica childhood, and they had undoubtedly germinated at Mexico City. For the Games of the XIX Olympiad were nothing if not a consciousness-raising experience. Everyone there, competitor or spectator, all those who watched worldwide TV or read about the Olympics, understood that they were witnessing the emergence of a new, socially motivated black athlete.

Theretofore, African-Americans had largely accepted whatever the white athletic establishment chose to dole out to them. That was little enough. Blacks might win accolades on the playing field, but off it they were subjected to the same galling racism and ghetto conditions as members of their race everywhere. And while black athletes could say that they were going to college, the majority never graduated; when they had used up their athletic eligibility, they were allowed to flunk out—having learned little of value for a future life.

"A white kid tries to become president of the United States," explained one African-American educator, "and all the skills and knowledge he picks up along the way can be used in a thousand different jobs. A black kid tries to become Willie Mays, and the tools he picks up on the way are useless to him unless he becomes Willie Mays." With such inequities in mind, an exceedingly angry young man named Harry Edwards set out to boycott the Olympic Games and thereby bring black athletes into the vanguard of the civil rights movement.

A 6-foot-8 giant of a man, Edwards had the attributes that once led a white coach to call him "a terrific animal." As a track star at California's San Jose State College, he approached 200 feet with the discus and contemplated playing professional football or basketball. Yet he couldn't join a fraternity, buy a meal at an upscale restaurant, or rent a decent place to live off-campus. Edwards forgot about a career as an athlete; instead, he got a master's degree in sociology at Cornell University and began working on a doctoral thesis called "The Black Muslim Movement and Malcolm X"—"Saint Malcolm" to Edwards. In 1966, at the age of 24, Edwards returned to teach sociology at San Jose State and mobilize a rebellion among black athletes.

With the rhetoric of Malcolm X resonating in his words, Edwards explained the aim of his movement: "Black dignity. The black athlete was always expected by the honkie to play the role of the responsible Negro, the good Negro, no matter what else was going on in the black world. The black athlete was the institutionalized Tom, the white man's nigger."

In September of 1967, Edwards announced the

USOC, and finally, the desegregation of the New York Athletic Club, whose doors had long been closed to both blacks and Jews.

It was unclear whether Edwards would call off the boycott if all the demands were met, but his oratory didn't leave much room for maneuver. "We are not trying to lose the Olympics for the Americans," he said. "What happens to them is immaterial. We are not Americans. We are black people." It was time, he said, for blacks "to stand up as men and women and refuse to be utilized as performing animals for a little extra dog food." To one degree or another, a lot of African-American athletes sympathized with Edwards' view. Said sprinter Bill Gaines: "I'm fully prepared to do anything necessary to dramatize the plight of black people." Lee Evans agreed: "There is need for anything that brings about unity among black people." And Ralph Boston declared: "If we decide on some kind of protest, I'd be less than a man not to participate. I'd be letting myself down, my family, my race."

But Boston stopped short of endorsing a boycott. "I've put too much time and effort into track and field to give it up," he said. Nor could Charlie Greene, world-record holder at 100 meters, come to grips with the notion that he was other than American. "It comes down to a matter of whether you're an American or not. I'm an American and I'm going to run." John Thomas, who set an Olympic high-jump record at Tokyo 1964, offered a further perspective. "How much pride can you lose by emerging an Olympic champion?" he asked. Black athletes also were hearing from the revered Jesse Owens, winner of four gold

formation of the Olympic Project for Human Rights (OPHR). Soon afterward, he convened a strategy session in Los Angeles attended by a number of activists. Perhaps 60 athletes were there, among them basketball star Lew Alcindor—soon to be known as Kareem Abdul-Jabbar—world-class high jumper Otis Burrell; and two renowned sprinters, Lee Evans, world-record holder at 400 meters, and Tommie Smith, tops at 200 meters. After the meeting, Edwards issued a statement saying that the attendees had "unanimously voted to fully endorse and participate in a boycott of the Olympic Games of 1968."

Through the OPHR, Edwards issued a series of demands to the United States Olympic Committee and a number of other sports governing bodies and organizations. Primary among them were the dismissal of crusty old Avery Brundage as head of the IOC, the continued exclusion of apartheid South Africa from the Olympics, the hiring of two black coaches for the Olympic track team, the appointment of two blacks to the executive committee of the

Olympic boycott instigator Harry Edwards, with militant activist H. Rap Brown at his side and a bodyguard looking on, announces to the press his plan to picket the New York Athletic Club's 100th anniversary meet at Madison Square Garden on February 16, 1968. That effort would prove more successful than the boycott planned for Mexico City. Nevertheless, Edwards' challenge to the Olympics did focus attention on the inequities facing African-American collegiate athletes.

medals at Berlin 1936. Advised Owens: "There is no place in the athletic world for politics."

Harry Edwards responded by hanging a picture of Owens in his office with the bitter caption: "Traitor (Negro) of the Week." He did the same with photos of Willie Mays and 1960 Olympic decathlon champion Rafer Johnson, both of whom also deplored the boycott.

Prevailing opinion seemed to support Owens and the antiboycott faction. In a poll of black athletes, *Ebony* magazine found that only 1 percent supported a boycott, while 71 percent came out against and 28 percent declared themselves undecided. The openly discriminatory New York Athletic Club was another matter, however, and in February 1968, Edwards had considerable success with a

boycott of the track meet celebrating the NYAC's 100th anniversary. Bob Beamon and eight teammates from UTEP crossed the picket lines thrown up by 2,000 unruly protesters— Beamon acting out of both competitive desire and a powerful urge to see Gladys in New York. But Lee Evans, Tommie Smith, Bill Gaines, and scores of others refused to compete; numerous high-school and college teams withdrew; the service academies stayed home; so did the Soviet national team. The NYAC Games went off as scheduled, but the performances were lackluster. Score one for Harry Edwards.

Simultaneously, the IOC made a decision that gave the incipient boycott of the Games another boost. At its Session just before the 1968

Olympic Winter Games in Grenoble, the IOC voted by secret ballot to readmit South Africa to the Olympic movement. The South Africans had promised to integrate the team they would send to Mexico City, explained Avery Brundage in announcing the vote, though they still planned to hold segregated trials. Harry Edwards' response was swift. "They've virtually said the hell with us," he raged. "Now, we'll have to reply, 'Let Whitey run his own Olympics.'" Within hours both Ethiopia and Algeria withdrew from the Games, and a wave of indignation rolled through Africa. In the U.S., many prominent Americans, white as well as black, came out in favor of the boycott. The murder on April 4 of Martin Luther King Jr. added further impetus to Harry Edwards' cause; he immediately dedicated the boycott to King's memory.

By now, 32 African nations were threatening to keep their athletes home, and the absentees would include a dozen or so stellar distance runners the world was aching to see compete. On April 20 a badly rattled Brundage and the IOC announced another change of course: South Africa's invitation to Mexico City 1968 would be withdrawn after all. With that, the African nations relented—and when they decided to attend, the steam started leaking out of Edwards' U.S. boycott.

Olympic officialdom was still so nervous about black protest that it canceled all victory ceremonies at the California selection trials in July. An insensitive Brundage rekindled black ire when he was quoted as saying: "It seems a little ungrateful to attempt to boycott something which has given them"—meaning blacks—"such great opportunities." Yet most of the athletes felt that Harry Edwards had made a large point in a short time, and they were content to let individuals express themselves without a formal boycott. As Lee Evans put it: "We voted on the boycott at Los Angeles, and it was almost unanimous that we go. But it was also 100 percent that we make some kind of

protest at the Games. What that will be I don't know." He would know soon enough—he and the rest of the world.

Monday, October 12, dawned clear and crisp in Mexico City, and by 11 a.m. more than 100,000 spectators had found somewhere to sit or stand in the handsome Estadio Olimpico, originally built to hold 80,000 soccer fans. Magnificent opening ceremonies went off without a mishap. Toward the end, the huge scoreboard flashed, "We offer and desire friendship with all the people of the world," and Mexican runner Pablo Garrido recited the Olympic pledge: "In the name of all competitors, I swear that in taking part in these Olympic Games we will respect and comply with the official rules as true sportsmen, for the glory of sports and the honor of our teams."

For a time it seemed the Games might keep those promises: amity and respect and honor, a brief haven of peace and glory in a storm-tossed world. It certainly seemed that way through the first great glamour event of track and field, the men's 100-meter dash, the run for the traditional title of "world's fastest human."

At Mexico City, interest in the event was magnified by two factors. Never before had every one of the eight finalists been black—three Americans, a Jamaican, a Cuban, a Canadian, a Frenchman, a Madagascan. And every man among them had proved himself capable of running the 100 in 10 seconds flat, just 0.1 of a second off the world record. As for Mexico City's altitude, Nebraska's 23-year-old Charlie Greene, one of the three record holders, doubted its effect. "We're a different breed of cat," he grinned. "We don't need a lot of time or space or air. One gulp and it's all over."

Greene and Jim Hines, a 20-year-old flash from Texas Southern, had been trading victories all year—to the point where *Sports Illustrated* called them "the fastest four-legged sprinter ever

THE GAMES AT A GLANCE

	Oct 12	Oct 13	Oct 14	Oct 15	Oct 16	Oct 17	Oct 18	Oct 19	Oct 20	Oct 21	Oct 22	Oct 23	Oct 24	Oct 25	Oct 26	Oct 27
Opening Ceremony	■															
Athletics (Track & Field)		■	■	■	■	■	■	■	■							
Basketball		■	■	■		■	■	■			■	■	■			
Boxing		■	■	■	■	■	■	■	■	■	■	■	■		■	
Canoeing											■	■	■	■		
Cycling					■		■	■	■	■		■				
Diving							■	■	■	■	■	■	■	■		
Equestrian					■	■	■	■	■	■		■	■			■
Fencing					■	■	■	■	■	■	■	■	■			
Field Hockey		■	■	■	■	■	■	■	■	■		■	■	■		
Football (Soccer)		■	■	■				■		■		■				
Gymnastics											■	■	■	■	■	■
Modern Pentathlon		■	■	■	■	■										
Rowing		■		■		■	■	■								
Shooting								■	■	■	■	■	■			
Swimming									■	■		■	■	■	■	■
Volleyball							■	■	■		■		■		■	
Water Polo			■	■	■	■		■	■	■	■	■	■	■	■	
Weight Lifting		■	■	■	■	■	■									
Wrestling								■	■	■		■		■	■	■
Yachting			■	■	■	■		■	■	■	■	■	■	■	■	
Closing Ceremony																■
Demonstration Sports																
Fronton		■	■	■	■	■	■	■	■	■	■	■	■	■		
Tennis		■	■	■	■	■	■	■	■							

sent to the Olympics." Both had won their semi-final heats, and now at the gun for the finals they blasted out of the blocks, both with beautiful starts—but not as beautiful as that of U.S. Army captain Mel Pender, practically an old man at 30, but still blessed with astonishing acceleration. Pender led for 30 meters before Greene and Hines drew even. Then, at 40 meters, Hines powered ahead. "I felt good because I knew I had another gear," he said later, "and when I switched it on, I just went away."

Charlie Greene made his move at 50 meters. "But at 60, I felt a little pull on the outside of my left knee, just like somebody tapped me," he recalled. For a split second, Greene considered pulling up rather than risking serious injury. Then he drove on. "I decided I'd come this far, and I was going to get one of those medals," he said, "but I couldn't go with Jimmy the way I normally did." Jamaica's Lennox Miller inched ahead as they blazed across the line—Jim Hines' appropriately gold shoes flashing first, Miller a yard back, Greene a step behind. Showing his age just a little, Mel Pender faded to sixth. Hines' time: 9.9 seconds, shattering the Olympic record and equaling the world mark.

Jimmy Hines and Charlie Greene embraced in bear hugs and danced deliriously around the

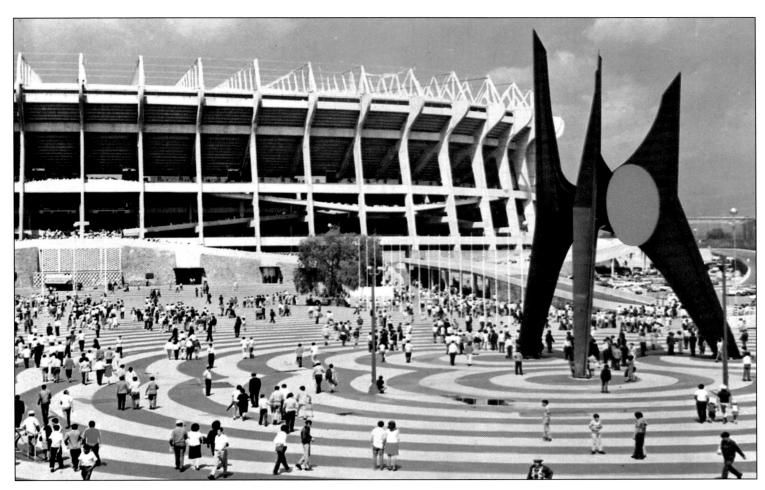

track. On the podium, their gold and bronze medals around their necks, both Americans waved jubilantly at the crowd. No politics from these two. "It was—and still is—the greatest feeling of my life," said Hines years later. "You are No. 1 and nobody can take that away from you. There will never be anything to surpass it."

Six days later, on the final day of track and field competition, Hines, Greene, Pender, and Ronnie Ray Smith went looking for gold in the 400-meter relay. The team to beat was Cuba. The Cubans were hot; they had beaten the U.S. team in both the heats and the semifinals. Charlie Greene was competing with heavily bandaged legs, but he ran as if they were fine. The real problem for the Americans in the preliminaries had been sloppy baton passing, and some awkward passes would persist in the final.

With a 5-foot lead going into the anchor leg, Cuba looked unbeatable. The U.S. lagged in third place. But Jimmy Hines grabbed the baton and, in what surely rates as one of the great dashes of all

time, blew past the field to win by a full yard. The Americans' time of 38.23 chopped almost 0.4 of a second off the record. It was not recorded how fast Hines ran the final leg; he had to have eclipsed the world mark by a sizable margin. What did make the chronicles was how he joyfully hurled his baton to the cheering crowd.

The United States relay victory was glorious, certainly—but it took place in a bitter backwash of protest and punishment and discord. The trouble had started two days earlier, on the fourth day of competition.

The class of the 200-meter dash was two almost evenly matched black Americans from California's San Jose State: Tommie Smith, 24, and strapping at 6 feet 3 inches, 180 pounds; and John Carlos, 23, and even bigger at 6 foot 4 and 198 pounds. Between them, Smith and Carlos held virtually every indoor and outdoor record worth mentioning at distances from 220 to 440 yards. Equally to the point, both had been charter members of San Jose professor

America's Jim Hines rushes to a victory in the first electronically timed Olympic 100-meter final. Hines' record of 9.95 seconds would endure as the world standard until 1983. The times for the top eight finishers in 1968 would remain the fastest in Olympic history until Barcelona 1992.

ABC sportscaster Howard Cosell interviews the members of America's winning 4 x 100-meter relay team *(from left)*: Mel Pender, Charlie Greene, Ronnie Ray Smith, and Jim Hines. The Mexico City Games were the first to provide extensive live television coverage worldwide.

couldn't get a beer in a bar in Austin, in the Texas state capital. I wanted to change it." But, like so many of his race, he found that change came hard. At East Texas, he said "the football coaches called a black receiver who'd dropped the ball 'nigger' or 'nigra' or 'boy.'" When black athletes protested, the athletic department told them, according to Carlos, "'You don't like it here, you can leave.'" "I am leaving," he answered, and he did. Back in New York he met up with Harry Edwards and Martin Luther King Jr. They persuaded him to enter San Jose State with the help of student loans. He enrolled there in the spring of 1967.

At East Texas State, Carlos had already run the 100 yards (yards, not meters) in 9.2 and the 220 yards in 20.2. San Jose State, known as Speed City in those glory days of coach Bud Winter's great track squads, nurtured his talent, cutting slack for his abrasiveness, his jive, his casual and chronic flouting of the rules.

"I'll save you niggers a piece of the tape," Carlos liked to tell the competition before a race, the bombast all the more ominous in his characteristic low, hoarse croak. He was difficult, but he was also extraordinarily talented.

So was Tommie Smith, although he tended to be as shy and obedient as Carlos was cheeky and intractable. Smith was born in Clarksville, Texas, on June 6, 1944—D Day—the seventh of 12 children of a black sharecropper and his American Indian wife. Smith adored his father, a strong, self-taught man who somehow managed to protect and feed his large brood through bleak, backbreaking years, first in Texas cotton fields and later in the migrant labor camps of California's San Joaquin Valley. Schooling was spotty, and Smith, as a sixth grader, could barely read. He was so ashamed of his bad English that he hardly ever talked. But he worked hard. He wanted to learn. And he could run.

By the eighth grade in LeMoore, California, Smith had almost reached his full 6-foot-3 height,

Harry Edwards' Olympic Project for Human Rights and his failed boycott of the Olympics. The odds were 99-to-1 on some sort of demonstration.

Carlos and Smith were emblematic of the black experience in America in those days, although they represented different aspects of it. Like Bob Beamon, Carlos was a big-city kid, street smart and brash. He was a product of Harlem's P.S. 90, Frederick Douglass Junior High, and Manhattan Vocational and Technical High. He was married and a father while still in his teens. And, like Beamon, he found that his strong legs could walk him out of the ghetto. Mostly to get his wife and daughter out of Harlem, Carlos accepted a track scholarship at East Texas State, assured by the recruiter that race relations in Austin were just fine.

"When we hit the airport," he would recall years later, "I realized my mistake. A black man and he weighed 155. Coaches noticed his lean, athletic build, and soon he was the rising star of LeMoore High's basketball team. He ran the 100-yard dash in 10.9 seconds that year. The next year, in the ninth grade, he knocked off a full second—maybe because, for the first time, somebody introduced him to running shoes with spikes. By 1963 he had run the 100 yards in 9.5 and the 220 in 20.1. He had managed 24 feet 6 inches (7.47 meters) in the long jump and 6 feet 5 inches (1.96 meters) in the high jump. Inevitably, he was on his way to San Jose State on a track scholarship.

At Speed City, Smith kept all the rules that Carlos broke. "I always made it a point to follow the rules," Smith would recall. "Write me a rule and I follow it." He was still quiet. Sometimes he ran wearing sunglasses, not because he was hip or flashy, but because he was still so painfully shy. But whatever he ran in, he ran fast: In 1967 he ran the 400 meters in 44.5, the 440 yards in 44.8—two world records. In fact, during his college career he either tied or broke or rebroke 18 world marks, relays included.

Smith wasn't the collegiate golden boy of the sort that would become common in later decades. There was no money, aside from the basic scholarship; to take up slack he helped his father swab out hallways at a local hospital. And, enrolled in the Army Reserve Officers Training Corps, he was hardly a flaming radical. But he was a diligent and intelligent student, and his former speechlessness was evolving into a vivid verbal acuity that gave shape to his perceptions.

Smith took note of what was going on in his country—the burgeoning civil rights movement, the white backlash that followed it. He knew that four little girls had died in their Sunday school class when their church was bombed in Birmingham, Alabama, in 1963. He knew of the riots that erupted when young blacks tried to integrate white universities in the South. He knew how often he had been called "nigger" himself and how he couldn't seem to rent an apartment in San Jose

once the landlord saw his black skin. "I could read the Constitution," Smith would say. "I could compare the writing of this land with its reality."

So superficially different in style, John Carlos and Tommie Smith had a lot in common: Both were prodigiously talented. Both had been bruised by bigotry, early and often. Both had gone to San Jose State, to be snared there by the compelling rhetoric of Harry Edwards. They had declined, in the end, to take part in his boycott. But would they, from Olympian heights, make some kind of protest? Anyone who knew them could hardly have thought otherwise.

First, though, Smith and Carlos would have to earn a spot on the winners' podium.

Each had handily won his semifinal heat in the 200-meter in the identical time of 20.1 seconds, just 0.2 of a second off the world record then held by Carlos. But as Smith crossed the finish line, he felt a pang that might signify a pulled adductor muscle in his left thigh. He limped off the field. "I was 80 percent certain I was out," he recalled. But two and a half hours later, after ice packs had been applied and Smith was taped from his waist to just above the left knee, he was ready to settle into the blocks.

John Carlos blasted away first, zipped into the turn, and had a one-and-a-half-yard lead at 120 meters going into the straight. Then Smith kicked in what he liked to call his "Tommie-jets" and with phenomenal acceleration caught Carlos before they passed 140 meters. At the finish, Smith was far enough ahead to allow himself the luxury of easing off just a hair and throwing up his arms in victory. That might have cost him 0.1 or maybe 0.2 of a second. As it was, the electronic scoreboard read 19.83 seconds—a new world record by better than 0.1 of a second. Carlos might have had the silver medal save for an unaccountable schoolboy error. He had turned slightly to look as Smith powered past, and that was enough for a fast-improving Australian named Peter Norman to

SURE FOOTING

The track at Mexico City's Olympic stadium was the first artificial running surface ever used at a Games. Made of 3M's new Tartan surfacing, it was tinted red to combine with the white lines and green infield grass, suggesting the color scheme of the Mexican flag. Tartan was one of a wave of synthetic tracks developed during the 1960s that promised stadiums rugged, uniform running surfaces. Praise for the artificial tracks was universal. Groundskeepers liked them because they didn't need raking or relining. Athletes appreciated the fact that they didn't get sloppy in rain or develop ruts. Moreover, the spongy surfaces prevented injuries such as shin splints.

The synthetic tracks spawned a secondary revolution when, predictably, shoe companies reacted to them. In 1968, Puma and Adidas both came out with shoes designed for the new surfaces, but athletes couldn't use them at Mexico City. International Amateur Athletic Federation rules required equipment to be available at least a year in advance of the Games. In addition, the shoe's many spikes far exceeded the IAAF maximum of six.

Even without the innovative shoes, the Tartan track delivered as advertised. In spite of frequent rains, records fell steadily at Mexico City.

Decathletes Bill Toomey *(left)* and Dr. Tom Waddell dash across the Estadio Olímpico's rainswept red Tartan track. They probably would have had better traction in Adidas's Tartan shoe, shown above, at left, in a 1968 advertisement extolling its virtues in comparison with those of an ordinary track shoe. Adidas's 42 tiny "quill" spikes were designed for improved performance on synthetic running surfaces, but international track federation officials didn't approve the innovative shoe in time for use at the Mexico City Games.

America's Tommie Smith flings his arms up in joy as he crosses the finish line of the 200-meter dash. A decisive surge in the last 60 meters assured him of victory over his chief rival, teammate John Carlos (No. 259).

overhaul him on the other side. John Carlos had to be content with the bronze.

The moment had come. The two Americans mounted the podium with their sweatpants rolled up to reveal long, black socks. OPHR buttons shone prominently from their U.S.A. sweatshirts. Smith wore a black scarf around his neck, Carlos a string of colored beads. On the platform, both men took off their shoes. Smith's wife, pentathlete Denise Paschal, had

brought a pair of black leather gloves to him just before the medals ceremony. He pulled on the right glove and gave the left to Carlos.

"What do I do with it?" Carlos asked.

"Just do what I do," Smith said.

Then, as the band played "The Star-Spangled Banner," gloved hands shot up in the clenched-fist black power salute as Smith and Carlos stood with bowed heads, refusing to look at the American flag. The crowd was shocked into silence, then

the booing started. Whatever Mexicans might think of the United States, their huge, often-arrogant neighbor to the north, they did not like this.

Neither did the press, although Smith and Carlos tried to explain: The unshod feet and black socks symbolized black poverty. The scarf and beads memorialized lynchings of blacks. The raised fists signified black unity and strength. The bowed heads meant that the freedom professed by America's national anthem applied, in their view, to whites only. "It was not a gesture of hate, it was a gesture of frustration," said Smith, so long the silent one. "This was going to be a silent gesture that everyone in the world would hear."

The world did hear. For better or worse, the picture of the two great black athletes standing on their platforms, their raised arms and gloved fists forming a U of grievance and outcry, became the lasting afterimage of Mexico City 1968.

The clenched fists and bowed heads of Tommie Smith *(top step)* and John Carlos provide the Games' most controversial moment—and most enduring image. Australia's Peter Norman, the bronze medalist, shows quiet sympathy for the protest by wearing an Olympic Project for Human Rights pin.

Olympic officials also heard, and they were outraged.

The morning after the protest, the U.S. Olympic Committee held an emergency meeting, then apologized to the world for the "discourtesy," the "untypical exhibitionism," and the "immature behavior" of its athletes. "I am embarrassed. All of us are embarrassed," said acting executive director Everett Barnes, his eyes brimming with emotion. "It makes our country look like the devil." Many people thought that the USOC would reprimand Smith and Carlos and leave it at that. But they reckoned without the IOC, whose nine-man Executive Board, headed by Avery Brundage, was bent on severe punishment. There were indications that Brundage himself didn't force the issue but was pressured by the eight other elderly sport statesmen on the board. The Marquess of Exeter, representing Great Britain and a long-ago Olympic champion himself, had awarded the medals to Smith, Norman, and Carlos. He was furious. "I will not countenance such action again," he raged. "I'll refuse to hold a victory ceremony if any such attempt is made again."

The Executive Board summoned Douglas F. Roby, president of the USOC, and commanded him to suspend Smith and Carlos. It was said that the IOC might banish the entire U.S. Olympic team if the two remained at the Games. The USOC responded by ordering Smith and Carlos to surrender their credentials and leave the Olympic Village. Within 48 hours they were on their way out of Mexico. "I'm going home," snarled Carlos, shouldering past reporters. "Do you mean the United States?" shot back one of the journalists.

In the uproar that followed, a lot of athletes expressed sympathy for the ousted black sprinters. Certainly many African-American members of the U.S. team were distressed and dismayed—and furious at the officials who had sent Smith and Carlos home.

No one felt the incident more keenly than Lee Evans, world-record holder and favorite in the upcoming 400-meter dash. Evans was a friend and teammate of Smith's and Carlos' at San Jose State. He and Smith were especially close; their backgrounds had been dismally similar. In fact, Evans was pretty sure he had seen Smith when both of them were children, little migrant laborers picking grapes in California's vineyards. Like Smith and Carlos, Evans had joined Harry Edwards' OPHR at the start, and he now wrestled with a powerful desire to join his comrades on the plane out of Mexico.

Tears staining his face, the 21-year-old Evans first announced that he wouldn't run. He relented only when Carlos personally asked him to stay and compete. From a purely athletic point of view, it would have been a shame for him not to stay: The top dozen 400-meter men in the world were American, and the U.S. Olympians—Evans, Villanova's Larry James, Arizona State's Ron Freeman—were expected to give America its first sweep of the Games.

Though they call the 400 the longest dash, the human body isn't built to go flat out for such a searing distance. It's a race of strategies, and Lee Evans was a master strategist, often hanging back just a hair, husbanding his strength, reacting to the field. But in Mexico City, Larry James had an inside lane; he could see Evans when Evans couldn't see him. There was nothing for Evans to do but go for an unbeatable time.

He burst from the blocks in a perfect start. "I didn't hear the gun when I went," he said. "'Now' and 'Pow' were the same instant." Evans and his coach had planned a 21.4-second 200 meters. He hit it exactly, running not quite full bore. Then he took off. When he hit the straight, Evans thought he was 5 yards ahead. But he wasn't. As the staggered lanes straightened out, he could see Larry James to his left, scarcely a stride behind. "I felt the bear clawing at my legs," said Evans. "I felt faint." Now the champion in him took over. "OK, relax," he thought. "High knees

Sentiment against IOC president Avery Brundage showed at the Olympic Village *(right)* following the expulsion of Tommie Smith and John Carlos from the Games. Far less subtle in their support of the ousted athletes were students at Howard University, who cheered Carlos *(wearing the beret)* at a rally on the Washington, D.C. campus a week after his forced departure from Mexico.

. . . relax . . . arms straight ahead . . . relax." Three steps from the finish, James conceded; out of the corner of his eye, Evans saw him drop his head. "I knew I had it then and powered through," said Evans. "Larry ran 395 meters. I ran 401. That was the difference."

Evans flashed across the line in 43.86 seconds, James in 43.97, Ron Freeman a couple of strides back in 44.40. The U.S. had its sweep and another world record: All three had smashed the listed world mark of 45 seconds held by Tommie Smith.

There remained the matter of protest. The trio mounted the podium wearing black berets and giving the clenched-fist salute. But they were smiling, and when the band struck up "The Star-Spangled Banner," they whipped off the berets, stood at attention, and, with heads held high, gazed steadfastly at the flag. "We wanted to show respect for the flag," said Evans, adding that he hoped white people "will honor our respect." A reporter asked about the berets, mainly associated in those days with the militant Black

Panthers. "It was raining," Evans smiled. "We didn't want to get wet."

As a heroic postscript to the fabulous 400, Evans, James, Freeman, and another ace named Vince Matthews went out and obliterated the 4 x 400-meter relay on the final day of track and field. Unofficially and with a running start, Ron Freeman contributed an incredible 43.20 leg, and anchor man Evans was 30 yards ahead of the pack at the finish. Time: 2:56.16, more than 3 seconds better than the world record. Like Bob Beamon's long jump, it was a mark that would stand for a generation.

The mark made by the protests in Mexico City would also last for a long time, and the young men who had made their controversial gesture would be long in paying for it. Even before they returned home, Smith and Carlos

Almost too fast for the camera, America's Lee Evans sprints to victory in the 400-meter dash. Evans and silver medalist Larry James both broke the 44-second barrier in the final, establishing times that still rank among the fastest ever recorded for that distance.

were notified that they had been banned from Olympic competition for life. There were death threats. Their marriages foundered. (Carlos' wife, Kim, would commit suicide in 1977. "It had a lot to do with 1968," Carlos would say.) Their careers were, for a time, derailed. Smith finished college and later played on the taxi squad of the Cincinnati Bengals for three years, but it wasn't a happy time. His football teammates, remembering Mexico City with disapproval, avoided him.

John Carlos, who never got his college degree, continued running track, mostly on the European circuit, then played football for a while in Canada. He was at the 1972 Olympic Games in Munich—representing a shoe company. Afterward, in Los Angeles, he took odd jobs, once as a bouncer in a bar. There were lean, sad times.

But time and age and history have a way of altering perspectives, and in the end, the Speed City contingent to Mexico City 1968 fared pretty well. In 1977, Carlos founded the John Carlos Development League to work with disadvantaged kids. It didn't pay much, but he liked it. He stayed with it until 1983, when he went to work as a community organizer for—of all things—the Los Angeles Olympic Organizing Committee. That post evaporated when the committee was dissolved following the Games. Carlos bounced around some more, reaching his nadir in 1986 with an arrest for cocaine possession. But he came back, and in 1988, by then remarried, he began coaching high-school track in Palm Springs, California.

Tommie Smith, the kid who at one time could hardly read, dedicated himself to education. He took a master's degree in sociology in the Goddard-Cambridge Graduate Program for Social Change in Cambridge, Massachusetts. Then he taught sociology and coached track at Oberlin College in Ohio for six years before moving back to California to become track coach at Santa Monica College.

As for Lee Evans, he traveled a very long way from his farm-labor boyhood in the vineyards. Applying himself to developing athletics in the Third World, he was named Nigerian National Coach of the Year in 1978. He held a Fulbright professorship to Cameroon from 1986 to 1988. In 1990 he began coaching track and field in the little Persian Gulf country of Qatar, and in 1991 he received the Nelson Mandela Award for his contributions to African rights.

Evans was also inducted into the United States Olympic Hall of Fame. For Carlos and Smith, however, Olympic memories would always be tinged with some bitterness.

"It's ridiculous to feel you can fight the dragon for so long and not be scarred," Carlos, by then a grandfather of three, would say in the 1990s. "I've said enough and done enough. And it's not like we've made progress."

Smith said he had kept his gold medal—"at home with all the other hardware. It's one of those things you can't eat."

Protest may have permeated the ranks of America's track and field team at Mexico City 1968, but it didn't necessarily extend to other venues. It didn't extend to boxing, for instance. Pappy Gault, the first black coach of an American Olympic boxing team, absolutely wouldn't hear of it. Gault wanted everybody to

Years distant from the cheers and tumult of Mexico City, Tommie Smith demonstrates a move at a 1991 water-fitness class at California's Santa Monica College. When not at poolside, Smith coaches the school's track team.

NO DIVING

NO SURRENDER

Courage and strength are hallmarks of good wrestling, and there was no shortage of either at the Pista de Hielo, the ice rink that served as the venue for the freestyle and Greco-Roman tournaments at Mexico City.

The Soviet Union's Aleksandr Medved displayed the requisite grit in his freestyle heavyweight bout against West Germany's Wilfried Dietrich, winner of gold medals in two previous Games. At the height of the match, Dietrich heard an odd crunch. Later, at a break, he looked on in amazement: Medved was calmly setting his own broken finger. Unfazed as the bout resumed, the Soviet attacked, winning the match to claim his second consecutive gold medal. Dietrich himself had showed the heart of a champion in wrestling Medved despite a groin pull. The injury would keep the German from fighting for the silver medal, and he would unhappily settle for the bronze.

No less courageous was Japan's bantamweight freestyle champion, Yojiro Uetake. In his penultimate bout, Uetake suffered a separated left shoulder. Undaunted, the defending Olympic champion squared off against America's Donald Behm in the final. Even with only one good arm, Uetake managed to secure the championship and another gold medal.

The surprise of the tournament was the team from Mongolia. Never a factor in earlier Games, the Mongolians won a silver medal and three bronzes. The Soviets proved to have the strongest team, though, taking nine medals. The American wrestlers made a disappointing showing, leaving Mexico City with only two silver medals.

understand from the start about his boys' attitude. "There are no big shots on this team," snapped the 46-year-old retired Air Force sergeant. "I'm the big shot. I built this team on unity and desire. None of my fighters have been involved in any of this demonstration stuff. We're proud to be fighting for the United States."

Of Gault's 11 boxers in classes from the new light flyweight (106 pounds) division to heavyweight, nine were black, two Hispanic. And under Gault's eagle eye, no one so much as left the Olympic Village during the two weeks of competition. In talent they couldn't match the squad that had won five championships at Helsinki 1952, and Gault himself didn't rate them as highly as the 1964 team that had managed only one gold medal (heavyweight Joe Frazier) in Tokyo. But dedication could take a fighter a long way, and in the end Gault could say, "I think we've surprised a lot of people."

With the growing popularity of boxing in Asia, Latin America, and Africa, 67 nations sent 312 boxers to Mexico City. Some underdogs displayed remarkable teeth. Venezuela's Francisco Rodriguez whipped a South Korean for the light flyweight title and then wept

Iran's Shamseddin Seyyedabbasi bridges desperately as Japan's Masaaki Kaneko tries to pin him to the mat. Kaneko, a featherweight, was one of four Japanese wrestlers to win gold medals at Mexico City.

uncontrollably into his country's flag. Host nation Mexico came away with a pair of gold medals with Ricardo Delgado in the flyweight and Antonio Roldan in the featherweight class, although Roldan's victory was a little dubious. And no one at all was ready for a curly-haired, 24-year-old Cockney named Chris Finnegan to become the first British boxer to win an Olympic gold medal since Melbourne 1956.

But Finnegan loved the sun and warmth of Mexico City from the moment he landed. "It was my sort of place," he said, and the altitude bothered him not one whit. "I had great stamina," he allowed. "I was a hod carrier, running up and down a ladder eight hours a day with half a hundredweight on my back. We were only boxing three-minute rounds. No problem." Fighting as a 165-pound middleweight, Finnegan jabbed and danced his way past five opponents, including America's Al Jones, who nailed him for two standing counts in the semifinals before losing a close decision. In the finals, Finnegan measured the Soviet Union's Alexei Kiselyov and decided that his opponent might be a little short on conditioning. So he attacked the more skilled Kiselyov with a ferocity that one observer described as "almost tigerish." It was very close, but the Russian faded just enough for the Englishman to win a 3-2 decision.

Otherwise, the Soviets and East Europeans plodded through the divisions with their inelegant but wearing hold-and-hit, clinch-and-wrestle style. The USSR's Boris Lagutin, defending Olympic light middleweight champion, outlasted a Cuban for a repeat gold; Soviet boxers won the bantamweight and light heavyweight classes, while a Pole and an East German took the light welterweight and welterweight titles.

Pappy Gault's "bunch of untested guys," as he tabbed them, got to five of the semifinals, and three of them made it to the finals. Fighting as a 132-pound lightweight, Ronald Harris easily outpointed his Polish opponent for a 5-0 decision.

Robert "Pappy" Gault ruled as coach of America's overachieving Olympic boxing team. Though the squad would win only two gold medals, more American fighters reached the semifinals at Mexico City than in any previous Games.

And Albert Robinson was on his way to a second U.S. gold in the 126-pound featherweight class when the Soviet referee simply stepped in and took it away from him. The officiating had been appallingly poor throughout the bouts, with 32 judges and referees dismissed for one reason or another. Now, as Robinson whaled away at Mexico's Roldan, blood suddenly spurted from the Mexican boxer's left eyebrow. Instantly, the referee stopped the fight, disqualified Robinson for head-butting, and awarded the victory to Roldan.

Observers saw no butting, and the fight films showed none. Robinson actually had been pounding away at arm's length when the referee made his controversial call. Roldan, with a long history as a bleeder, appeared apologetic about it all. Yet even on appeal, the best the USOC could do for Robinson was a silver

Flowers and the flag make for a patriotic demonstration as America's George Foreman celebrates winning the heavyweight boxing gold medal. Not a single fighter managed to stay three rounds with Foreman, who was heralded as the next Cassius Clay.

medal—which he received after the Games were over.

If that was the low point for U.S. boxers, there was plenty to cheer about in the performance of George Foreman, only 19 and fighting as a 218-pound heavyweight. Foreman was still awkward, but he packed a jackhammer jab and had put away by devastating knockouts all four of his opponents. In the finals, Foreman

splatted maybe 200 jabs into the face of the Soviet Union's Inones Chepulis, chopping it into such hamburger that the referee halted the fight in the second round.

Foreman walked over to Pappy Gault and picked up a small U.S. flag. He kissed it and waved it at the cheering crowd as he walked around the ring. No protest from this blue-collar son of a railroad worker. "That's for college

kids," he snorted. "They live in another world." In fact, many of them had lived at least part of their lives in much the same world he did: Foreman had come up the hard way in a Houston ghetto. He had also managed to become an alcoholic and a street mugger before he even reached his teens—all before boxing and a yen for a better future helped him clean up his act.

Foreman would defeat Joe Frazier in Jamaica in January of 1973 for the professional heavyweight crown, losing it in turn to yet a third Olympian, Muhammad Ali, in Zaire in October of 1974. Foreman would retire after that, only to return—in his 40s—in the late 1980s. The sports world was still laughing when, in 1994, Foreman got a title shot at champion Michael Moorer. The beefy old-timer, then 45, knocked out Moorer and became the oldest heavyweight champ in modern annals.

While the nonpolitical Foreman was salvaging U.S. honor in the ring in Mexico City, the American basketball team was supplying its own share of noble surprises at the Games. To say that the U.S. had dominated the sport since its inclusion in 1936 wouldn't be entirely accurate; in fact, Americans had owned the game, reeling off an astounding 74 victories without a loss. But not in 1968, said the smart money.

Black protest had deprived the U.S. team of Lew Alcindor, Elvin Hayes, Wesley Unseld, and a dozen other stars. The lure of the professional game, academic problems, and other woes had further weakened the squad to the point where reporters labeled it "ragtag," "pickup," a "smorgasbord outfit that probably will have trouble beating Sweden." Tallest of the Americans was 6-foot-9-inch Spencer Haywood, only 18 and a junior college student. The fast-improving Soviets, with a couple of 7-footers, were the clear favorites. The U.S. might get a silver, if it could handle the Yugoslavs, not to mention the Brazilians, who had their own 7-foot-6-inch center to control the rebounds.

Yet the scoffers, as so often happens, were wrong. Though young Haywood and his mates struggled at times, they got by eight opponents to play for the gold. And their opponents would not be the Soviets, but the Yugoslavs, who had defeated their Communist comrades 63-62 in the semifinals. The championship game was not very artistic. The Americans were lucky to lead 32-29 at the half. But 64-year-old coach Henry Iba said a few fatherly words in the locker room, and the team came roaring out with a fire-horse offense that ran off 17 straight unanswered points. At the buzzer the U.S. was ahead 65-50. Haywood had 22 points all by himself.

However much the Mexicans and their guests had applauded the runners and jumpers, however extraordinary they found the boxing and basketball, the spectators' hearts belonged to the women gymnasts. It seemed to be in the national blood; Mexican tumblers and acrobats graced the circuses of the world. And here in the Games of the XIX Olympiad, the fans were about to witness one of the most dramatic competitions—some might call it confrontations—in the history of the sport. A highly vocal crowd of 16,000 packed downtown Mexico City's Auditorio Nacional to watch tiny Czechoslovakia take on the Soviet Union, its gargantuan oppressor, and to pray for petite Vera Čáslavská against a number of supremely well-trained Russian women.

By any measure, the 26-year-old Prague secretary was Queen of the Gymnasts. Blonde, poised, charming, and talented, Čáslavská had won her first gold medal at 17 for beam exercises in the European championships of 1959. But she hadn't captured her Olympic laurels until Tokyo 1964, where, at 22, she won three gold medals and one silver to beat two Soviet women for the overall championship. With exquisite grace and agility, she won the horse vault, uneven bars, and balance beam, losing only in the floor exercises. Čáslavská

America's Spencer Haywood snares a rebound during the basketball final against Yugoslavia. Haywood was the standout of an undersized and unappreciated American team that nevertheless managed to keep the U.S. Olympic winning streak alive.

had since won two European and one world championship. She was looking forward to Mexico City 1968 when politics almost defeated her.

Two months before the Games, in furious response to the Soviet invasion of her homeland, Čáslavská had been among the prominent Czechs who signed the Manifesto of 2,000 Words, bitterly condemning the aggression. Warned afterward by friends that the secret police had her on their list, she fled into the mountains. There she trained by swinging from tree limbs and tumbling in grassy meadows. Eventually the authorities relented; Vera Čáslavská was too great a national sports figure to persecute. And now she was in Mexico City to defend her Olympic championship.

The fans erupted with shouts of "Ver-a! Ver-a! Ver-a!" whenever she took the floor and, like a Greek chorus, took part in the proceedings as much as observed them: When judges awarded Čáslavská an unusually low 9.6 for an optional exercise on the balance beam, the crowd reacted with such an inferno of boos, hisses, and whistles that the judges reconferred and boosted the mark to 9.8. A Russian eventually won the beam, but Čáslavská was unbeatable on the vault, the bars, the floor exercise, and over all. She shared the gold medal in the floor exercise with the Soviet Union's Larissa Petrik. As the two young women stood on the podium, the band made sure that the Czech national anthem rang out first. Čáslavská averted her head at the playing of the Soviet anthem; she couldn't bear to look at the red banner.

Czechoslovakia's Vera Čáslavská nimbly assaults the uneven bars in a championship performance. Čáslavská's routines, executed with grace and style in front of a worldwide TV audience, helped popularize women's gymnastics.

High above the horizontal bar, Japan's Sawao Kato soars into a swan dive of a dismount. Kato won three gold medals at Mexico City, including the first of two consecutive individual all-around titles.

Altogether in those stirring days, Czechoslovakia's Vera Čáslavská won four gold medals and a silver to retain with ease her championship. Her four golds equaled those of Jesse Owens at Berlin 1936, Dutch runner Fanny Blankers-Koen at London 1948, and U.S. swimmer Don Schollander at Tokyo 1964.

Two days after the gymnastics competition, Vera Čáslavská and her fiancé, Czech 1,500-meter runner Josef Odlozil, were married in Mexico City's magnificent El Zocalo Cathedral while 10,000 adoring fans filled Zocalo Square. Then she and her husband flew home to Prague, where she presented her cherished medals to Czechoslovakia's embattled political leaders as a gesture of strength, solidarity, and faith in the future.

Wrapped in a Mexican blanket, Vera Čáslavská enjoys a moment at her wedding reception with Czech runner Josef Odlozil. The marriage would end in divorce in 1987, and worse tragedy would follow: Odlozil was fatally wounded during a fight with his son, Martin, in 1993.

TO ANY HEIGHTS

When they first met in early 1967, Jim Ryun didn't quite grasp immediately what the young physiologist was telling him.

"You know, Ryun," said Jack Daniels, a doctoral candidate at the University of Wisconsin, "that altitude in Mexico is going to be a serious problem, and you'd better get used it." The world's premier middle-distance runner merely shrugged. He was only 20, after all, in extraordinary health, a world-record holder unbeatable in the mile.

"I'll work hard," Ryun said. "I'll be sure to arrive in top condition." But Daniels was writing his doctoral dissertation on how altitude affected athletic performance, and he persisted.

"Being in shape won't matter, and you can't acclimatize yourself," he advised. "All you can do is reduce the impact of the problem, get used to how it feels."

"My coach doesn't think there's anything to worry about," Ryun said, and it was Daniels' turn to shrug. He explained about oxygen debt, the debilitating deficit that occurs when the body burns more oxygen than it can take in.

"There just won't be enough oxygen at 7,000 feet for sea-level runners to perform anywhere near optimum levels," a concerned Daniels said. "It will affect the 5,000, 10,000, steeplechase, and marathon. The times will be slow and the recovery horrendous." The metric mile, the 1,500 meters, would probably be the worst. "In the 1,500 you have speed and stamina converging at a very concentrated point. In the longer races, because the speeds are slower, the oxygen debt won't be as severe. But in the near-sprint pace of the 1,500, it's going to be unbelievable."

Ryun wasn't particularly worried. Nevertheless, in early June he accepted Daniels' invitation to visit Alamosa, Colorado, for a one-mile time trial at 7,400 feet, almost exactly the altitude of Mexico City. Ryun dropped out after a lap and a half. "I felt awful," he remembered. "My chest was heaving and I couldn't get my breath. I simply could not continue." Ryun had just

Jim Ryun, Olympic Medalist, Mexico City 1968, shown training in Colorado before the Games

Physiologist Jack Daniels records the breathing of American runner Bob Williams at a practice session in South Lake Tahoe, California. Pre-Games concern over Mexico City's thin air had the United States, the Soviet Union, and France rushing to build high-altitude training camps to study the effects on athletes of an oxygen-poor environment.

come from a brilliant 3:53 mile at a meet in Los Angeles, and he couldn't believe his body would fail him this way. He took a 30-minute break and started off again—and tottered on numb legs through a 4:32 mile. "I felt about ready to die," he said later.

Jim Ryun spent a couple of weeks with Daniels and some other runners. At one point they set out on a seven-mile jaunt along a road that climbed from 8,500 feet to 11,000 feet. "That run was unlike anything I'd ever experienced," remembered Ryun. "My ears were shot through with pain, my lungs had a thousand little knives stuck in them, and as I gasped for air, there just

didn't seem to be any relief. By the time we staggered toward the finish, I was moving at about a nine-minute-mile pace." By now he fully grasped, in mind and body, the meaning of oxygen debt—as other great runners had before him. Dr. Roger Bannister, the sports physician who had made history in 1954 by breaking the four-minute barrier in the mile, was once asked how a runner could deal with altitude. "There are two ways," he coolly replied. "Be born at altitude—or train there for 25 years."

About the same time that Jim Ryun was learning about altitude the hard way, the world's second greatest middle-distance man was stunning

the track world by breezing through a 3:55 mile at Nyeri, Kenya—elevation 6,000 feet. He was Kipchoge Keino, a 26-year-old Kenyan policeman who had been loping around the African highlands since childhood and had recently blossomed into a national hero for his prowess at races from 3,000 to 10,000 meters. Starting to compete on the international circuit, Keino occasionally tried his legs at the mile and 1,500 meters, but he felt more comfortable in the longer distances. "The mile is fast becoming just a sprint, and I am really more of a distance runner," he suggested. But after that astounding mile at Nyeri, Kenyan officials persuaded Inspector Kipchoge Keino to challenge Jim Ryun's supremacy at 1,500 meters.

The 1,500 meters at the Mexico City Games, when it finally played out on the last day of track and field, would bring down the curtain on a personal drama of unparalleled intensity. It would make prophets of Wisconsin's by-now-Dr. Jack Daniels and some others, and it would usher in a tremendous new cadre of competitors at every distance beyond 800 meters. In the women's dashes, as in the men's, altitude would play a more or less benign role. It would neither impose a penalty nor offer much of a boost in the men's pole vault or high jump: In the one, a new fiberglass pole would be the thing; in the other, an amazing technique would amuse the world and capture the gold. Yet altitude would remain an element in the heavy field events: the shot put and the discus, hammer, and javelin throws. It would prove a critical factor in that already supremely taxing event, the decathlon. It would powerfully affect cycling, the walking events, men's and women's swimming. And in rowing, Mexico City's thin, smoggy atmosphere would come close to killing. Where they could, athletes would take advantage of the conditions. Where they could not, by and large they would overcome.

Concern over the host city's 7,347-foot elevation—indeed, over Mexico itself—had marked preparations for the Games ever since the sprawling Mexican capital had entered its bid for the Olympics six years before. Avery Brundage and the IOC were inclined to look favorably on the offer. After Tokyo 1964, it seemed appropriate to follow the first Olympics in Asia with the first to be held in Latin America. But at an elevation that might endanger the athletes?

The five-man committee presenting Mexico's bid to the IOC dismissed the altitude issue as "a problem that has been artificially created, undoubtedly in good faith, but due to a lack of familiarity with the facts." The Mexicans earnestly offered testimony by the pneumology unit of the capital's general hospital that altitude "does not impair in any way the capacity to carry out sporting events and does not cause a pathology of any kind in human beings." Dr. Louis Mendez, the head of the country's Cardiac Institute, added that after two or three days' stay, athletes would be able "to effect every kind of physical effort, obtaining the same records previously reached in their own cities."

The Mexicans reminded the IOC patriarchs that their capital had hosted the Central American and Caribbean Games in 1954, the Pan-American Games in 1955, the world modern pentathlon championships in 1962, along with Davis Cup tennis, major golf and international soccer matches, and top equestrian events—all without fatality or serious health problems. It was a good presentation. The IOC was convinced.

Yet the issue of altitude would not go away. Dr. Ernst Jokl of the University of Kentucky stated that it would take at least two and a half months of training at altitude "if athletes were to maintain their standards. And even then I fear that we may have cardiac difficulties in the 10,000 meters and the marathon." Coaches, trainers, and athletes traveled to Mexico City to check out the altitude for themselves, and in October of 1967 the Mexicans staged a "Little Olympics" that included the

WHERE THE GAMES WERE PLAYED

Virgilio Uribe Rowing
and Canoeing Course

Juan Escutia Sports Palace

Francisco Márquez
Olympic Pool

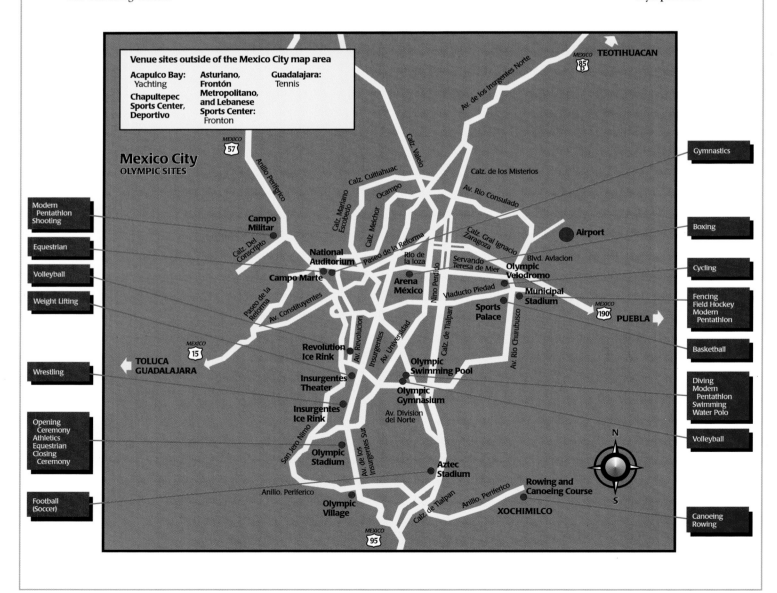

Venue sites outside of the Mexico City map area

Acapulco Bay:
Yachting

**Chapultepec
Sports Center,
Deportivo**

**Asturiano,
Frontón
Metropolitano,
and Lebanese
Sports Center:**
Fronton

Guadalajara:
Tennis

Mexico City
OLYMPIC SITES

TEOTIHUACAN

MEXICO 85 D

Av. de los Insurgentes Norte

MEXICO 57

Anillo Periferico

Calz. Vallejo

Calz. Cuitlahuac

Calz. de los Misterios

Ocampo

Calz. Mariano Escobedo

Calz. Melchor

Av. Rio Consulado

Gymnastics

Modern
Pentathlon
Shooting

Campo
Militar

Calz. Del Conscripto

National
Auditorium

Paseo de la Reforma

Rio de
la loza

Calz. Gral Ignacio Zaragoza

Blvd. Aviacion

Airport

Boxing

Equestrian

Campo Marte

Paseo de la Reforma

Servando
Teresa de Mier

Olympic
Velodromo

Cycling

Volleyball

Av. Constituyentes

Arena
México

Nino Perdido

Viaducto Piedad

Municipal
Stadium

MEXICO 190

PUEBLA

Fencing
Field Hockey
Modern
Pentathlon

Weight Lifting

Sports
Palace

Calz. de Tlalpan

Av. Rio Churubusco

Basketball

MEXICO 15

Revolution
Ice Rink

Av. Revolucion

Av. Universidad

Av. Insurgentes

TOLUCA
GUADALAJARA

Olympic
Swimming Pool

Diving
Modern
Pentathlon
Swimming
Water Polo

Wrestling

Insurgentes
Theater

Olympic
Gymnasium

Volleyball

Insurgentes
Ice Rink

Av. Division
del Norte

N

Opening
Ceremony
Athletics
Equestrian
Closing
Ceremony

San Jero Nimo

Olympic
Stadium

Av. de los Insurgentes Sur

Aztec
Stadium

Rowing and
Canoeing Course

S

Football
(Soccer)

Anillo. Periferico

Olympic
Village

Anillo. Periferico

Calz. de Tlalpan

XOCHIMILCO

Canoeing
Rowing

MEXICO 95

marathon. Belgium's veteran Gaston Roelants won a slow, careful race without ill effect.

But a Japanese runner who finished fourth collapsed after crossing the line and took 20 minutes to come around; he later was quoted as blaming the heat, not the height, for his problem. That led Dr. Griffith Pugh, the physiologist attending British runners at the preview, to emphasize that athletes needed "to adjust not only to the altitude but also to the time changes, the different food, the sometimes intensely hot sun combined with cold air, and the extreme humidity. We are still not sure how an athlete could strain himself here if unacclimatized."

The chorus of concern about geography was matched by fears in some quarters that Mexico, as a Third World nation, might not be up to the Games. "These people can't do it," snapped a European observer, demonstrating an ethnic bias all too common in more developed nations. He was very wrong.

The Mexicans not only successfully organized the world's greatest sports show, they turned it into a grand and glorious "Fiesta of the Whole Man" that for the first time in the modern era truly melded the arts with athletics. That had been a goal of the founders of the modern Games—although a goal seldom realized. Other host cities had arranged for peripheral performances of operas, ballets, and symphonies. But the Mexicans brought the dream to life by staging a cultural extravaganza.

Led by Pedro Ramírez Vázquez, Mexico's ranking architect, the Mexico City Olympic organizing committee invited a pantheon of greats from five continents: Evgeny Evtushenko, Robert Graves, Maurice Chevalier, Salvador Dali, Eugene Ionesco, Martha Graham, Dave Brubeck, Arthur Miller, Duke Ellington, and Alexander Calder were among the hundreds of guests who shared their talents with the Mexicans and 170,000 visitors. World-renowned ensembles and soloists performed in music; scores of nations joined in film and folklore festivals; modern dance groups, ballet troupes, and theater companies graced stages throughout the city. The festival commenced in January with the New Year and by the end of the Games in October had seen no fewer than 145 separate cultural events and 2,500 performances of one sort or another.

The preparations for the Games themselves involved all of Mexico City. Organizer Ramírez Vázquez and his people opted for a decentralized plan in which Olympic sites were separated by as much as 14 miles, the routes ablaze with color and graphic symbols, the destinations marked by gigantic balloons or whimsical figures distinguishing the various sports. Spectators were whisked to and fro in fleets of special buses, taxis, and private cars. Anchoring the plan was the Olympic Village, a 5,000-unit brick tower complex built to house the athletes, their coaches, officials, and a press corps of 1,500—everybody rubbing elbows in a self-contained world of cafeterias, lounges, a discotheque, and an outdoor theater, along with a vast array of training facilities.

Three miles away stood the magnificent Estadio Olimpico, first built in 1953 and now refurbished, expanded, and decorated by Mexico's renowned Diego Rivera with murals depicting pre-Columbian sport. A mile northeast of the stadium rose the new Juan Escutia Sports Palace, its copper geodesic dome glowing in the sun, with seats for 24,000 people to enjoy basketball. The Mexicans built a triple-tiered Aztec Stadium for soccer, a fine new velodrome for cycling, an elegantly designed natatorium, the Francisco Márquez Olympic Pool, holding 10,000 spectators. This was joined to a gymnasium where 5,000 enthusiasts could enjoy the volleyball competition.

The cost of it all came to something like $150 million—more than enough to send radical university students on a rampage. But the Mexican government was determined to showcase before the world its international good will, its art and architecture, its organizational ability, its energy

ARTS AT LAST

Mexico City throbbed with activity during the 1968 Games, and not all the vibrations were sports-related. Arts of all sorts and from every corner of the globe were on display in the theaters, in the stadiums, and on the streets. They were part of the Cultural Olympiad, a year-long celebration that established an international aesthetic component to the Games as no other Olympic arts festival had ever done before.

Founders of the Games had included art competitions in early programs, but the contests were so anemic that they were abandoned after London 1948. There were noncompetitive cultural events at every subsequent Games, but most were small and unimpressive, featuring talent from the host country alone. At Mexico City, though, organizers sought to give art parity with Olympic athletics and to showcase the best talent in the world.

There were 20 cultural disciplines, reflecting the number of sports at the Games. Folk dancers and classical dance troupes performed. There were recitals by orchestras and contemporary music groups. Sculpture, paintings, and crafts were gathered from collections worldwide. The cultural festival opened with a ceremony at the Palace of Fine Arts on January 19, 1968, and the final event, a jazz concert, closed the celebration on December 15, 1968. By that time, Mexico had hosted performances and exhibitions representing 97 countries in a long-running extravaganza that easily eclipsed all previous efforts to link art and sport.

Poet Evgeny Evtushenko *(seated)* watches as Mexican actor Ignacio López Tarso reads the Russian's work. Crowds of 25,000 flocked to recitals of Evtushenko's politically charged verse.

A Mexican Indian performs a ritual dance as part of the World Folklore Festival. Ensembles of native peoples from 25 countries took part.

A sculpture by America's Todd Williams was one of 19 monumental pieces positioned on Mexico City's Route of Friendship during the Games. The abstract works were spaced along an 11-mile stretch of the beltway that connected the Olympic stadiums.

A member of the famed Ballet Folklórico de México flares her skirt in a dance inspired by carnival celebrations in Panama. Along with participating in the arts festival, Folklórico dancers graced the opening and closing ceremonies at Mexico City.

This carved gourd featuring burned-in scenes of village life was a Peruvian contribution to an exhibit of folk art of the Americas. The show emphasized the beauty of indigenous crafts, both before and after European contact.

The Mexican government commissioned an 11-stamp commemorative issue for the Games. Three of them, all featuring the concentric-ring motif, are shown at right.

and perseverance. Construction crews worked around the clock as deadlines approached. Nothing was overlooked that might make the Games a success; so thorough was the work that rumors circulated of venues with oxygen-pumping systems to help offset the effect of the thin air. The Mexicans repeatedly denied that canard: There was no problem with the air, they maintained, and thus no need for oxygen.

But there was some truth, anyway, to the buzz about the vast basin created at Xochimilco, the Virgilio Uribe Rowing and Canoeing Course. The rumor spoke of ecological tampering and disastrous results: It was said that an excess of tiny frogs made a gumbo of the waters, which naturally led to the introduction of frog-eating carp, which—being so splendidly fed—grew to a size and number that interfered with the sports, which in turn brought on the introduction of fish-egg-eating turtles, which then became so numerous that their shells played havoc with delicate oars and paddles. Only an all-out assault by fishermen, related the informants, finally remedied the problem. Organizer Ramírez Vázquez smiled at the tale. Yes, they had imported carp from Israel to deal with an abundance of frogs, and the fish did become a problem: Being bottom feeders, they disturbed the layer of gravel laid down to floor the basin, and that gave a foothold to annoying, long-stemmed aquatic plants. The solution was midget trout, which ate the carp eggs. End of problem. No turtles.

Being country boys, Jim Ryun and Kip Keino could appreciate such vagaries of nature, even though neither had ever really been a farmer. Growing up in Lawrence, Kansas, Jim Ryun could not remember wanting to be anything but an athlete. But he was tall and gangly, and he had to wear glasses. Worse, a high

fever at an early age had affected his middle ear, leaving him with a 50 percent hearing loss and causing occasional dizziness.

Watching Superman on TV, however, sickly young Jimmy got this terrific idea about how to overcome his handicaps. "I'll mix myself an incredible drink," he thought. "I'll drink it just once and it'll supply me with enough permanent energy to become a boy superman." So he raced to the kitchen. Pickle juice, Coca-Cola, mustard, ketchup, orange juice, chicken gravy, milk, a little iced tea, vinegar, Worcester sauce all went into the glass. Then came the spices, from cloves to cayenne pepper. He managed to gulp down the concoction without throwing up.

He was fortunate enough to survive, but the drink didn't work. Nothing worked until one day in physical education class when 15-year-old Jim Ryun saw some classmates lining up for a 440-yard race—one lap around the junior high track, the first two finishers to be on the track team. He decided to try out. At 6 foot 1, Ryun loomed over the other kids, and his long legs quickly put him in front. "Hey, this is great," he thought. Then he tired and wound up with a dismal 58.5 quarter, nowhere near good enough for the team. But he started to think about bringing down his time, and a fantastic thing happened: Scrawny, bespectacled Jim Ryun became an athlete.

His coach, Bob Timmons, noticed that Ryun had a high tolerance for the pain that comes with extra-hard work. So he put Ryun to running 15 miles a day, and the times got better and better. In his sophomore year at East High, Ryun ran against a field that included the state schoolboy champion in the mile; Ryun came in second, mainly because he kept focusing so hard on keeping up with the champion that he failed to sprint at the end. Two weeks later, in what was to develop as his famous kick, he blasted past the

erstwhile champ to set a new meet record. Then he found a quiet place and did what he would often do after a race: He lost his lunch.

"Let's talk about goals," said Coach Timmons. Well, mused Ryun, maybe he could run the mile in 4:10. Timmons set him straight. "I'm talking about the four-minute mile, Jim," he said. "No high-school boy has ever run one. I think you can be the first."

That happened in May 1964, shortly after Ryun had turned 17. Timmons entered his youngster in a big meet in Los Angeles. The best milers in the U.S. were on hand, and some people wondered what a mere high-school junior was doing there at all. Ryun thought he ran a poor race, suffering an attack of dizziness at an early stage, just trying to keep up after that. He finished next to last in the nine-man field. Then the times were announced. The winner, Dyrol Burleson, had run a 3:57.4 mile, about 3 seconds shy of the world record. And Jim Ryun—finishing back in the pack—had run it in 3:59.

At that announcement, the crowd erupted. For the first time in history, eight men had broken the four-minute mile in a single race. Said Burleson: "There was nothing unusual about my victory. The entire story was back in eighth place. There is simply no way to imagine how good Jim Ryun is or how far he will go after he becomes an adult." That September, Ryun astonished a few more people when he turned in a 3:41.9 time for the 1,500 meters, good enough to win him the No. 3 slot on the U.S. Olympic track team headed for Tokyo. And he had started running only 18 months before. "What a distance I'd come," he exulted.

But Tokyo proved a terrible bust. Ryun came down with a debilitating virus and finished dead last in his semifinal heat. Back home, swallowing disappointment, he returned to East High for his senior year, and when spring rolled around he got ready to run against New Zealand's great Peter Snell, winner of the Olympic 800 and 1,500 meters in 1964 and record holder in the mile at 3:54.1. They met at Compton, California, on June 4. Ryun planned to stay with Snell all the way, but he was flabbergasted by the New Zealander's explosive kick. "In an instant he was

Three-time Olympic champion Peter Snell *(third from right)* toes the line against lanky Jim Ryun *(fourth from left)* and other stellar milers at a San Diego meet in 1965. Ryun's athletic talent blossomed early, enabling him to compete against the world's elite distance runners before he turned 18.

The Soviet Union's Leonid Zhabotinsky (*below*) shifts his 359-pound body into its lifting motion. The defending heavyweight champion, Zhabotinsky was never threatened by the competition at Mexico City. Spectators for the weightlifting events knew they were in the right place when they saw the fiberglass strongman statue near the entrance to the Teatro de los Insurgentes, where Zhabotinsky and the other lifters competed. There were statues for all 20 sports contested at Mexico City.

6 yards in front," said Ryun, and there was no way to make up that sort of deficit late in the race. Ryun finished third in 3:56.8, his best mile to date, but still not good enough.

The reigning champ and the young challenger met again in the 1,500 at San Diego, three weeks later. Ryun and Bob Timmons had a new strategy: Ryun would make his move first and force Snell to run wide to catch him. Before the race, Snell told newsmen that he felt good enough to achieve a new record. "What about Ryun?" someone asked. "Oh, I doubt that he'll be a factor," replied Snell. Thinking about it later, Ryun suggested—charitably—that Snell simply reflected prevalent opinion Down Under that 18-year-olds shouldn't try to compete with their elders and betters.

In the race, Ryun's legs made their own commentary. Coming out of the last curve he spurted into the lead, keeping to his plan, running hard, but not quite all out. The partisan crowd roared encouragement. Sprinting down the stretch, Ryun could see Snell in the corner of his eye—just to the right, driving for all he was worth. Ryun's legs felt like lead as he reached for his final reserves. Then, at last, he felt the blessed tape across his chest. He had beaten Snell by a stride and 0.1 of a second. Time: 3:55.3, an American record.

The muscular New Zealander threw an arm around the lanky American youngster as they slowed to a walk. "Ryun ran a perfect tactical race," Snell told reporters. "He's got it—that quality which goes to make a champion."

Ryun entered the University of Kansas in the fall, ran well in some indoor meets during the winter, and then prepared for the 1966 season, running as much as 120 miles a week. His kick grew so powerful that he was blazing through the last lap in around 55 seconds. On June 4 he ran a 3:53.7 mile, just 0.1 of a second off the world record held by France's Michel Jazy. A week later he dumbfounded the sports world by ripping off a half-mile in 1:44.9 to shatter Snell's world record. "I just had the feeling of all this tremendous strength," said Ryun later. Over in New Zealand, Snell commented: "Now that Ryun has reeled off this half-mile, the 1,500 meter and the mile must be his for the asking."

Ryun made his bid for the mile at Berkeley on July 17. He had eased off the training a little and felt wonderful. The weather was perfect. So was the clay-and-granite track at the University of California; it felt firm and fast. And Ryun would have help from three other runners—"rabbits," in track parlance—who had volunteered to act as pacesetters. "I told them I thought I'd be fine after the half if they could get me there close to 1:56," said Ryun. They did better than that. Ryun hit the first lap in 57.7, and a ripple of excitement went through the seats. The crowd started to cheer when Ryun passed the half in 1:55.5, and everyone was screaming when the announcer called 2:55.3 at the gun lap. Ryun envisioned a 3:50 mile. But he was tiring; he felt his legs gradually tightening up.

Around the curve, the past four years came into focus for Ryun—"all those miles, all those cold, lonely morning runs, all that sweat in the heat of the Kansas summers." Down the straight the tired legs pounded, clay flying up behind the spikes, head rocking, mouth gasping. Then he hit the tape, and there was a sustained roar from the crowd. The news came over the loudspeakers: 3:51.3. Jim Ryun had done it. He had his world record—and by the unbelievable margin of 2.6 seconds.

Watching the news on CBS that evening, Ryun sat astonished when Walter Cronkite paused in his broadcast. "We have just received this late

SHAKY HANDS

Drug testing began at Mexico City 1968 and brought with it the first drug-related disqualification of an Olympian. The drug in question was alcohol and the sport was the modern pentathlon. A competition that consists of riding, fencing, shooting, swimming, and running, the modern pentathlon allows its participants to drink alcohol (it steadies the shooting hand), but they can't have a blood alcohol level above .07 percent. Theirs is the only Olympic sport that entails testing for alcohol.

The modern pentathlon has been dominated by Sweden and Hungary since it joined the Olympic program in 1912, and it looked as though the Mexico City Games would continue the tradition. Athletes compete as individuals with their scores also counting toward a team title, and Swedish and Hungarian pentathletes were leading in the individual and team events when the contest turned to shooting. Hungary's István Móna finished 12th in marksmanship—not great, but good enough to move him past Sweden's Björn Ferm in the challenge for the individual title and ensure that the Hungarian team maintained its lead over Sweden at that point.

Ferm remained consistently good in the final two events, holding off a charge by East Germany's Karl-Heinz Kutschke to claim the individual gold. Móna did poorly in the swimming and running and faded to seventh place. Even though Móna slipped, Hungary's depth gave it the team gold. Sweden, despite Ferm's fine showing, fell to third behind the Soviet Union—but only until the alcohol tests came in.

The lab results showed that Sweden's Hans-Gunnar Liljenvall (above) had too much alcohol in his system after the shooting event. He and the Swedish team were disqualified, though the ouster didn't affect Ferm's individual award. France moved into third in the team standings and took the bronze medal. Liljenvall suffered the ignominy of being the only athlete disqualified at Mexico City for failing a drug test.

Snowy Mt. Kenya looms behind Kip Keino as he runs in his homeland's highlands. Keino's training routine was marginal by European standards. He reportedly ran only twice a day, three times a week, never covering more than 6 miles at a time.

story from Berkeley, California, where just a few hours ago, young 19-year-old Jim Ryun broke the world's record for the one-mile run." Ryun asked himself: "What have I done? Is this really me?" Then it sank in. "Why, I'm part of history."

The next June, Ryun knocked another 0.2 of a second off his record, and he said he seemed to be adjusting to the pace. "I wasn't nearly as tired as I was last year at Berkeley," he reported. He thought he had a real crack at the world record of 3:35.6 for the 1,500. That mark had been set seven years before by Australia's Herb Elliott at the Rome 1960 Olympics and rated as the greatest feat in all of track. Jim Ryun entered the 1,500 at the U.S.-British Commonwealth Games to be held at the Los Angeles Memorial Coliseum on July 8. But he changed his plan from an assault on the record to a tactical confrontation when he learned that the man he would have to beat was Kenya's Kipchoge Keino, whose campaigns in Europe and Africa had led a Swedish sportswriter to label him "the new wonder runner."

By the masochistic standards of Americans and Europeans, the distance runners of Kenya seemed hardly to train at all. Instead of agonizing through 150 or even 200 miles a week, the Africans might do only 5 miles daily, maybe 40 miles a week, and in such relaxed fashion that one observer was led to call their sessions "haphazard and desultory." Yet that was an illusion. Kenyan athletes had been walking and running over vast expanses of their mountainous homeland ever since they were toddlers. Mere survival in a harsh world demanded it, and by the time a youth matured, if he did, he possessed immense endurance to go with the tremendous lung capacity that was the birthright of those who lived at high altitude.

When Kip Keino, the son of a Kipsigis herdsman, was a boy helping his father tend goats, he might walk and trot 35 miles behind the herd between sunup and sundown. There were things to run after and things to run from: He remembered once running away like the wind after surprising a leopard at its kill. Another time, his legs saved him from a band of bloodthirsty enemy tribesmen. He ran 18 miles back and forth to school—the few years of it available to him—and at 13 he won a bar of soap by placing fourth in a cross-country race against much older boys. Keino was on his own by the time he was 16, living in a shack, growing a few vegetables, and often walking 40 miles to the train for Fort Tern An, where he searched unsuccessfully for work. Eventually, at 19, he joined the police, which gave him room and board, a little money, a bit of status—and a chance to do what he did so well: run.

Kip Keino was still a corporal in 1962, running rather unevenly and starting to compete outside of Africa. Lean and wiry at 5 feet 10 and 145

A Bible and a photo of Kenya's prime minister Jomo Kenyatta are among the treasured objects in Kip Keino's home in Kiganjo. Keino became the first black African runner to set a world record when he broke the mark for 3,000 meters at a 1965 meet in Helsingborg, Sweden.

Jim Ryun and Kip Keino duel for the first time in a 1,500-meter race at Los Angeles in 1967. Moments after the turn, Ryun would use his awesome kick to win in a world-record time of 3:33.1. It was their only head-to-head meeting before Mexico City.

pounds, he liked to start out fast, with long, loping strides, simply to see how long he could hold up. "I just figure to run as hard as I can as fast as I can for as long as I can," Keino once said. He learned about tactics, pace, and a finishing kick at the 1962 Commonwealth Games in Perth, Australia. Running the three-mile race, he had a 200-yard lead going into the last lap. "We came to the stretch," he recalled, "and then *shhhh*, one is by me. *Shhhh*, two is by me. *Shhhh*, three comes. I am thinking they are all coming by me. Four, five, six. *Sh, shhhh*. They are all sprinting. I was annoyed. I could do nothing." Keino finished an exhausted 11th. "I thought to myself that I must cut my stride in order to accelerate," he assessed. "It was about eight feet. I cut it to six feet."

Keino lost a year because of injury and spent another couple of years gathering experience. Then, in 1965, he sent up such a dazzling star

burst of performances that Kenya's proud president Jomo Kenyatta bestowed the Order of the Burning Spear and Distinguished Conduct Medal on his "flying policeman." In a matter of months, Corporal Keino became Chief Inspector Keino.

It had started at Turku, Finland, when Keino defeated the great Australian champion Ron Clarke at 5,000 meters in the startling time of 13:26.2, just 0.4 of a second off Clarke's world mark. Returning to the All-Africa Games in the Congo, Keino ran an amazing 1,500 heat in 3:39.6, his personal best, then followed that with history's fastest 5,000 heat: 13:38.0. Such a typically extravagant display of energy dropped his winning times in the finals to 3:41.1 in the 1,500 and 13:44.4 in the 5,000. Hurrying to Sweden in August, the Kenyan cop trounced Gaston Roelants in the 5,000 with a good

13:29.4, then two days later destroyed the world record at 3,000 meters by nearly 6 seconds, posting a time of 7:39.6.

In London, on August 30, Keino ran the mile in 3:54.2, tossing away his trademark orange cap on the last lap, his green-clad figure sprinting irresistibly for the tape. Next came a visit to Auckland, New Zealand, and a world record of 13:24.2 in the 5,000, erasing Ron Clarke's mark by 1.6 seconds.

Kip Keino, now with two world records under his orange cap, felt very good as he prepared to test Jim Ryun at 1,500 meters in the 1967 U.S.-British Commonwealth Games in Los Angeles. And why not? Only two weeks had elapsed since the Kenyan's sensational 3:55 mile at Nyeri's 6,000-foot elevation. Keino and Ryun had competed once before—at 2 miles in the Los Angeles Coliseum Relays of 1966. Ryun won. Keino finished third. Now, Keino was challenging Jim Ryun in the 1,500, the metric mile, on Ryun's turf, at Ryun's altitude, at Ryun's best distance.

July 8 dawned hot and grew hotter, until it was sweltering on the floor of the Coliseum. The field started out slowly. But by the second lap, Keino—a vision in maroon jersey, green shorts, and blue shoes—and, of course, the orange cap—grew characteristically bored and raced into the lead with a 56-flat quarter. Ryun was right behind him. The crowd stirred.

Around they went, hitting the 880 mark in 1:57.0, surging into the final lap at 2:39.2. The pace was so fast that Ryun needed only a final quarter of 56.3 to better Herb Elliott's 3:35.6 performance of Rome 1960. The crowd knew it and started yelling. Keino ran on, still ahead, still powerful. In the backstretch Ryun moved alongside, psyching himself up for the kick. Then his sixth sense told him something. "I knew I could get the record because I was feeling strong, especially in the legs," Ryun said later. He accelerated inexorably into his drive, racing away from Keino, gaining a yard in every 10. Ryun looked

back twice and hit the tape after running the final 100 meters in 13.5—the fastest finish of all time in this event. The crowd shrieked when they heard Ryun's overall time: 3:33.1, 2.5 seconds faster than Elliott's record.

Ryun ducked the trackside interviews. The sudden release of tension had nauseated him, and his head was splitting. Keino, who had finished far back at 3:37.2, said little publicly, but was heard to tell a Kenyan teammate: "Oh that Jim Ryun. He run too fast." He did inform a reporter: "I learned more of tactical running in the two times I have raced against Jim Ryun than any other way. Ryun is very strong." True enough, but then Kip Keino went home for a regional African meet at Kisumu, Kenya—altitude 3,720 feet—and ran a 3:53.1 mile, third fastest in history. Later that day, he completed a double by winning the grueling three-mile race in a fine 13:31.6. He, too, was strong.

The Olympic year 1968 brought woes to both runners. In March, Jim Ryun popped a hamstring and was out of action for a month. When he started practicing again, he felt weak and lethargic, a condition doctors eventually diagnosed as mononucleosis. That set him back another month. Next he twisted an ankle, following that mishap with a nasty case of flu. "It was the most depressing time of my life," he would recall. But he eventually came around, and in mid-July he went up to nearly 8,000 feet at Flagstaff, Arizona, where he showed his post-recovery mettle. First he ran a 12-mile course in the remarkable time of 1:12:0, then tore off a half-mile at 1:47.9, one of the fastest times ever run at that height. "I'm no longer afraid of altitude," he said. He was feeling so confident, in fact, that he revived an old dream: to try for an Olympic double, to win both the 800 and 1,500 meters.

The dream died that September at the Olympic trials at Lake Tahoe. Ryun ran what he

A steady hand keeps Yevgeny Petrov's aim perfect during the inaugural Olympic skeet shooting competition. The Soviet marksman didn't miss a target in a three-way shoot-off for the gold medal.

STRAIGHT SHOOTER

Milestones marked the shooting competition at the Campo Militar range at Mexico City. A record number of countries, 64, sent a record 458 competitors. Skeet was included on the program for the first time. Women were allowed to compete alongside the men—another Olympic first—and three female sharpshooters took part in the seven-event program. Top team honors went to the Soviets, who captured two gold medals, a silver, and two bronzes. Five other countries shared first-place honors in the remaining events. The standout for the United States was Gary Anderson, who won his second consecutive gold medal in the 300-meter free rifle match. His score of 1,157 out of a possible 1,200 beat his own world record. A rare left-handed shooter, the 29-year-old Anderson was a lieutenant in the U.S. Army and a divinity student. He thought there was nothing unusual about combining ministry with marksmanship, explaining that any sport would help keep a preacher in touch with his flock. But shooting and guns would become his ultimate calling: Anderson would become executive director of general operations for the National Rifle Association.

called "a dumb race," attempting too fast a pace, and failed to qualify for the 800. The 1,500, though, remained his meat; he won the final easily and was on his way to Mexico.

Meanwhile, Kip Keino was encountering difficulties of his own. Competing against Ron Clarke in the 5,000 at Oslo on July 10, Keino was running nicely when he doubled up with violent stomach cramps. It took a herculean effort to finish third. The next day, in the 10,000, the same cramps hit him, but he struggled valiantly on, again finishing a distant third. A meet in Leningrad was fraught with the sort of harassment the Soviets habitually inflicted on visiting athletes: Their plane was fumigated with the Kenyans on board, dinner was denied ("too late," said the hosts), and Keino's gear was stolen. He still won the 5,000—in borrowed, oversize track shoes. But they blistered his feet, and in the 10,000 he finished second, his face working in agony. Then it was time for Mexico City.

The Games had scarcely begun when athletes, coaches, trainers, officials, journalists, spectators—everybody—riveted their attention on the first of the major endurance races, the 10,000 meters: Here the answers about athletes at altitude would begin to emerge.

The class of the field over many years had been Australia's 31-year-old Ron Clarke, who since 1963 had set 18 world records at distances from 2 miles to 20,000 meters, including 13:06.6 for the 5,000 and 27:39.4 for the 10,000. Experienced mainly at sea level, Clarke had long been openly apprehensive about the altitude. He predicted a time of between 13:5 and 14:0 for the 5,000 and perhaps 29:0 for the 10,000. "Everyone may be affected differently," he said, "but most will feel they are going in slow motion." Clarke himself was said to have done the 10,000 in 29:1 while practicing at Mexico City. That might be good enough, if his prediction held. He remained the favorite.

Ranged against the Aussie star that Sunday afternoon, October 13, was a quartet of African runners, all of whom reflected Roger Bannister's comment about dealing with altitude: either be born there or train there religiously.

Before escaping to the army, Tunisia's tireless little Mohamed Gammoudi had spent a childhood in the high, rocky central desert of his North African land, where, it was said, the kids hunted jackrabbits by chasing after them in relays until the animals dropped from exhaustion. He started competing in 1959 as a recruit and three years later impressed the European sports world by winning a double—10,000 and 3,000 meters—at a military meet in Amsterdam. In 1964, Gammoudi had failed to win the 10,000 at Tokyo by a whisker; both he and America's Billy Mills, the upset winner, had broken the Olympic record in an electrifying finish. Now Gammoudi wanted his own gold medal so badly that he had spent two full years running an average of 500 miles a month at high altitude in the French Pyrenees. "No one," said Ron Clarke, "prepared better for the Games in Mexico than Mohamed."

Ethiopia's sprawling capital of Addis Ababa lies at elevations ranging from 7,775 to 8,100 feet, and the Imperial Palace Guard is good duty for aspiring distance runners, with plenty of spare time for coursing over the hills. Haile Selassie's guard, in fact, had produced one of the greatest marathoners of all time in Abebe Bikila, who brought glory to his country by running off with the gold at both Rome and Tokyo. Trotting behind the great man all the while was fellow guardsman Mamo Wolde, a wispy 117-pounder whose enormous endurance had gradually established him as one of the best 10,000-meter men in Africa. But Wolde had managed only a fourth-place finish in the Tokyo 10,000, and no one gave him too much of a chance at Mexico City. He seemed destined for perpetual twilight.

The same might be said of Kenya's 24-year-old Naftali Temu, who had beaten—by an astounding 150 yards—the renowned Ron Clarke over 6 miles at the 1966 Commonwealth Games in Kingston, Jamaica. But Temu had never really emerged from the shadow of his more famous countryman, Kip Keino.

And Keino? That blazing competitor—stomach cramps be damned—had entered the 10,000 and the 5,000 as well as the 1,500 meters. Kenyans hoped he would win all three.

Rain clouds loomed over the Estadio Olimpico at 5 p.m., making it so dark that the lights were on when the gun sounded for 37 entrants in the 10,000. They would go 25 times around the 400-meter track. A Colombian led first, then a Hungarian, next a Soviet runner. Coming into lap 14, Mexico's Juan Martinez jumped into the lead, triggering an explosion of cheers until he faded on lap 19. All the favorites—Clarke and the four Africans—remained with the leaders.

The serious running began on the 22nd lap, 1,600 meters from the end. Ethiopia's Wolde picked up the pace with a 1:08.4 circuit, and attention settled on Keino, everybody expecting him to counter with a burst of his own. But a horrified gasp went up as the runners pounded into lap 23. There was Keino staggering, reeling from the track and collapsing onto the grass with another attack of stomach cramps. Medics rushed to him, but he bounded to his feet and dashed after the field, disqualified yet still dazedly competing.

Now the order was Wolde, Clarke, Temu, and Gammoudi, the Africans running easily, Clarke showing the first signs of struggle. Temu surged into the lead on lap 23, then whipped through the 24th lap in 1:04.4, trying to shake off the field. He succeeded—except for Wolde, who shot ahead as the bell rang for the last lap. Down the backstretch they sprinted, Temu slowly creeping back up until they were shoulder to shoulder 50 meters from the finish. With a final, supreme effort, Temu inched past Wolde—and hit the tape perhaps a stride ahead. Gammoudi coasted home third.

An emotional Dr. Brian Corrigan administers oxygen to Australia's Ron Clarke, who collapsed at the finish of the 10,000-meter final. Among the greatest distance runners in history, Clarke nonetheless never won a gold medal.

Kenya's novice steeplechaser Amos Biwott tries to keep his feet dry as he sails over the water jump. Poor technique failed to keep Biwott from leading Kenya to a one-two finish in the race.

But back in sixth place, Ron Clarke was fighting desperately with oxygen debt. Ashen-faced, rubber-limbed, the world champion dragged himself across the finish line and toppled unconscious to the track. Australian team physician Brian Corrigan ran to him. Someone brought oxygen. "I remember thinking he was going to die," said Corrigan. People standing around the form beneath the blanket started to weep. At last, after a nightmarish hour and 60 liters of oxygen, Ron Clarke came around. "There was an awful tiredness in all my limbs, a difficulty even in seeing," he later recalled. "But I had to finish. It was a matter of pride."

There was pride on the podium, too, when Naftali Temu, Mamo Wolde, and Mohamed Gammoudi were awarded their medals for giving Africa its first 1-2-3 sweep in Olympic history. As might be expected, various critics complained that the victory had been tarnished by Mexico City's geography. But that did a disservice to three magnificent athletes. And for those who had forgotten, young Temu reminded them of the 1966 Commonwealth Games. "Now tell me," he said, "I beat that Clarke they were talking about in Jamaica, and tell me . . . were there any mountains in Kingston?"

If Temu had been obscure, Amos Biwott was totally unknown outside Kenya prior to the Olympics. But everybody knew the name shortly after 5:30 on the afternoon of Wednesday, October 16. Actually, eyebrows started shooting up on Monday, in the third elimination heat for the 3,000-meter steeplechase. The willowy (5 feet 11, 146 pounds) Kenyan did everything wrong.

Biwott started out with a heedless sprint that put him 30 meters ahead after half a lap. Exacerbating his lack of strategy, his form was nonexistent. So ludicrous was his style that *Track & Field News*, bible of the sport, chortled, "He cleared the hurdles like he feared they had spikes embedded on top and leaped the water hazard as if he thought crocodiles were swimming in it." When Biwott won the heat in 8:49.4, eight seconds faster than anyone had ever run the event at such an altitude, Kenya's coach told reporters: "This boy hasn't run six steeplechases in his life. He says he's 21, I'd place him around 19. With little real running

behind him, he didn't realize you don't kill yourself off in the heats."

The coach must have spoken to young Amos because in the final, Biwott dutifully hung back just behind the leaders until after the last hurdle. Then he blasted past them all, including his better-known countryman Ben Logo, to give Kenya its second gold. Logo brought home the silver. Biwott's time of 8:50.0, though well off the 8:24.2 world record, was impressive enough for George Young, America's bronze medalist, to remark that Biwott had more potential than anyone he had ever seen in the steeplechase. Roger Bannister, however, was fuming over the consequences of altitude. While acknowledging Biwott's possibilities, Bannister wrote that the novice had won by chance, the happy happenstance of having been born in the highlands.

Nevertheless, reporters were filing stories about how tiny Kenya had blossomed into a

track power. They might have added that not only Kenya but all Africa was parading to the podium. The 5,000 meters the next day produced a second African sweep of the gold, silver, and bronze; all told, five of the first eight finishers were Africans.

Australia's Ron Clarke had recovered sufficiently to run in the 5,000 and led briefly on an early lap, but he never really proved a factor. This was Mohamed Gammoudi's moment of glory. The red-shirted Tunisian glided into the lead with 1,000 meters to go and fought off determined charges, first by Naftali Temu and then by Kipchoge Keino, to win a very close race by about 4 feet. The only disappointment was the time. Gammoudi's 14:05.6 came nowhere near Clarke's 13:16.6 world mark, nor did it even come close to the 13:39.6 Olympic record. As in all the distance races thus far, no one ran especially fast at altitude.

A trio of African runners—Tunisia's Mohamed Gammoudi and Kenya's Naftali Temu and Kip Keino—lead in the 5,000-meter race. The ascendance of African athletes at Mexico City had experts searching for explanations. Most attributed the excellent performances to the Africans' living at high altitudes. Phenomenally consistent success in later Games would suggest that tactics and a culture predisposed to running also factored in their success.

In a curious way, the slower times suited Jim Ryun as the hour for the climactic 1,500 meters against Kip Keino drew near. His physiologist friend Jack Daniels had advised him that his best chance was to take it slow, to avoid the oxygen-debt problem that had debilitated Ron Clarke. Daniels prescribed a first quarter of 60 seconds or more, and some experts thought it possible that Keino might accept a slow pace. After all, in the previous five days the Kenyan had run a brutal 10,000 meters, a hard-fought 5,000 meters,

plus a heat and a semifinal in the 1,500. He ought to be just a little weary. "How I prayed for a slow pace," said Ryun.

But it was not to be. At the gun, Keino's teammate, Ben Jipcho, set himself up as the rabbit. Jipcho shot off the mark and ripped through a dismaying 56-second quarter. Keino followed on his heels, and the other 10 contestants chased after them. By 800 meters the field was split into two groups, Jipcho and Keino leading one bunch of four runners,

Ryun leading the other eight, about 40 yards back. Around they raced, Keino accelerating, Ryun struggling to stay within striking distance. "I realized that oxygen debt or not, I had to do something quick," he would recall later. "It was now or never."

At the bell signaling the last lap, Keino was 2:53—a phenomenal 5 seconds ahead of Ryun's world-record pace in the mile. Ryun moved up between the front-runners and the stragglers and summoned his celebrated kick.

He passed Jipcho and the other two runners in Keino's group. But he could sense the onset of oxygen debt: "My thighs felt like they had 50-pound weights attached to them," he would remember, "my lungs were stabbed through with intense, wracking agony." At 1,200 meters—300 to go—Ryun was still 14 yards back. He made up another 2 yards, hoping against hope that Keino would crack. He didn't. Overwhelmed by fatigue, Ryun at last gave it up and slowed until he was a full 20 yards behind

staggered up a steep ramp out of the stadium and slumped into a wooden folding chair. "Oh, God . . . it hurts," was all he could say.

As the American champion sat gasping for air, the marathon runners came trotting into the stadium after a race of 42,195 meters—26 miles 385 yards—under a blazing sun. At their head, 3 minutes ahead of his closest pursuer, jogged Ethiopia's redoubtable Mamo Wolde, following proudly in the footsteps of his famed compatriot and fellow palace guardsman, Abebe Bikila.

The marathon made it five out of five golds for Africa in the distance races—and another five of the 10 silvers and bronzes in those events. An inheritance of legs and lungs had a lot to do with the fabulous showing, as the experts concluded. But so did heart.

Heart was a quality not confined, however, to the male track stars at Mexico City. Heart was a legacy and tradition for an exclusive group of fleet-footed women who called themselves the Tigerbelles. They came from Tennessee State University, and they were perhaps the most competitive female track team anywhere, anytime.

Starting in the 1950s, Coach Ed Temple had scouted high-school meets throughout the South: A promising prospect would be invited to Temple's summer camp in Nashville, and if she minded her studies and graduated, she might be offered a work-aid scholarship at Tennessee State. Wilma Rudolph, the peerless sprinter who won three Olympic golds at Rome 1960, was a celebrated Tigerbelle. Another dazzler was Wyomia Tyus, who assumed Rudolph's crown at Tokyo 1964—and at Mexico City became the first athlete, male or female, ever to successfully defend an Olympic title in the 100-meter dash.

The wonder was that Tyus could walk, much less run. As an infant she had polio, or something like it, and her problems were compounded when she suffered leg injuries in a car accident at

Keino as the Kenyan flashed across the finish in an Olympic record 3:34.9, a time second only to the 3:33.1 world record that Ryun had set at sea level in Los Angeles.

"I knew Ryun had a very good kick," Keino told the newsmen swarming around. "So I prepared myself to have a big lead going into the final quarter." He confided that he had felt twinges of stomach cramps—later diagnosed as a gallbladder infection—in the final 200 meters. "But I said to myself that I must finish." Ryun

age four. But she grew up with three brothers, which meant a lot of running—"both to keep up with and away from them," she allowed. Tyus caught Ed Temple's eye as a high-school sophomore in Fort Valley, Georgia, and by the time she was 19 she was winning regularly the 50-, 75-, and 100-yard dashes. Coach Temple thought she would be unbeatable by the 1968 Olympics. He had it wrong by four years.

In the qualifying heats for the 100 meters in Tokyo, Tyus set an Olympic record and equaled Wilma Rudolph's world mark with a blazing 11.2 time. Then, in the final, she edged a fellow Tigerbelle and a Pole for the gold in 11.4, streaking into the tape with the wide-armed dip that was her trademark. Tyus and her teammates had to settle for a silver in the 4 x 100-meter relay. But the winning Polish quartet needed a world-record 43.6 to win, and if it was any consolation, the U.S. team's 43.9 also bettered the record.

Back home, Wyomia's mother suggested that she give up running. "Too unladylike," thought Mrs. Tyus. But her daughter burned to compete,

and by the time the 1968 Games rolled around, she held a world-record 11.1 for the 100. She did not, however, hold it alone. The record was shared with four other women—two Americans, a Pole, and a Russian—and all of them were at Mexico City, uncorking scary heats of 11.1 and 11.2. Tyus herself got off a wind-aided heat of 11 flat.

In the final she false-started once, then blew away exactly with the gun. "Gosh, you got a good start," she recalled telling herself. "Now you gotta go. Stay relaxed. Keep your knees up. Don't tighten up at 90 because Szewińska will be coming. She always comes on at the end." That would be Poland's tall, dark-haired Irena Szewińska, co-record holder in the 100 and the absolute class of the world at 200 meters. Szewińska was known for making up for a slow start with incredible speed at the end. But on this day, in the 100 meters, Wyomia Tyus held on, winning gold and resetting the world mark at 11.08 seconds. Her U.S. teammate, Barbara Farrell, finished second, Irena Szewińska third. Five days later, Tyus led the

Finalists in the women's 100-meter dash streak to the tape. America's Wyomia Tyus *(third from left)* topped a field that included four of the five coholders of the world record.

American women to a world-record 42.87 in the 4 x 100 relay. And then, with three Olympic golds and one silver in her trophy case, the swiftest Tigerbelle of them all retired from competitive running to get married and raise a family.

Irena Szewińska's triumph arrived in the 200 meters, where the longer distance gave full play to her extraordinary acceleration. This was her second of what would prove to be five consecutive Olympics, yielding a brilliant harvest of seven medals. At 18 she had won silver medals in Tokyo in both the long jump and the 200 meters, then contributed to Poland's record-breaking 4 x 100 team. Now, four years later, Szewińska seemed to have lost it in the long jump, failing to qualify for the finals. But not in the 200, where she already held the world record at 22.7. Revving up her long legs, she rolled to a couple of 23.2s in the heats and then ran a whistling 22.5 in the finals. So fast was the track and sharp the competition that the runner-up, Australia's 17-year-old Rae-lene Boyle, equaled the old 22.7 record.

And the women's assault on the record books continued without letup. In the 400 meters, a little-known French beauty named Colette Besson came from far back in the pack to nip Britain's highly favored Lillian Board at the tape. The 52-flat time for both women equaled the Olympic record. Besson's gold was France's only one in track and field, and it prompted a

Poland's Irena Szewińska breaks the tape at the finish of the 200-meter dash. Szewińska was competing in the second of her five consecutive Games. During her long Olympic career, she would win seven medals in five different events.

French sportswriter to observe that because of it "Colette Besson became, together with Brigitte Bardot, the most celebrated of all French women."

But such celebrity was a two-edged sword. At Mexico City—as at so many of the Games—the pressure to excel, to become famous, was crushing. At the Olympic Village the press corps totted up the daily medal scores nation by nation and devised elaborate point values to see who was ahead, who behind. Any athlete suspected of less than maximum effort found himself or herself on the sharp end of jabbing stories. Jim Ryun knew about such pressure. "If you don't make it, you are nothing," he said, shortly before the 1,500. "They're only interested if I win. If I lose, forget it."

Yugoslavia's 20-year-old Vera Nikolic, world-record holder in the women's 800 meters, also knew about the pressure. In the end, it was more than she could bear. Nikolic, her Communist country's only hope for a medal, was rated by oddsmakers a 10-to-1 favorite in the 800. She easily won the first heat in 2:05.7, but the time was well off her 2:00.5 record. The pressure mounted. After 300 meters of the semifinals, young Vera Nikolic simply halted, stepped off the track, and jogged out of the stadium. Lurid stories went around that her coach had saved her from suicide, that she was flown home in disgrace and stripped of her numerous privileges. As might be imagined, the incident and the play it received proved a further sensation at the troubled Games. And it obscured an admirable, Olympic-record 2:00.9 victory in the 800 by Madeline Manning, another of Tennessee State's phenomenal Tigerbelles.

The pressures of high expectations and media hype often focused on individual duels between well-matched athletes. The Keino-Ryun face-off in the 1,500 was one example, and some observers thought that the men's 800 meters might be a replay in a minor

America's Madeline Manning pulls away from the field in the 800-meter race. Manning, a member of the heralded Tennessee State Tigerbelles, gave the school's runners their third gold medal of the Mexico City Games.

key of that dramatic event. The distance was shorter, with less time for oxygen debt to afflict sea-level runners. But no one was inclined to dismiss altitude altogether, or say that a highland-born-and-raised athlete wouldn't have a significant advantage—especially if he were Kenya's Wilson Kiprugut. A seasoned campaigner, the 30-year-old soldier had won the bronze at Tokyo and had signaled his intentions at Mexico City with a warm-up 800 in 1:45.9, only 1.6 seconds off the world record. He had to be the favorite.

Kiprugut's strongest competitor looked to be Australia's Ralph Doubell, a fast-improving 23-year-old with excellent times to his credit, as well as a victory over Kiprugut at 1,000 meters during the 1966-67 indoor season. Moreover, Doubell was both cool and canny: The night before the finals he got 10 untroubled hours of sound sleep—a sign of a confident man.

At the gun, Kiprugut flashed out to a typically withering start, charging around the first 400-meter lap in 51 seconds. Doubell let him go, content to run fifth or sixth, keeping the Kenyan within range but not expending too much effort in the thin air. The Aussie started to make his move as the bell rang for the second lap, easing up to within 8 meters of Kiprugut and hanging there. "I made sure I was on Kip's shoulder with 200 meters to go," he said. Up in the stands a couple of teammates were hollering, "Wait! Wait!" He couldn't hear them over the crowd. Nor could he hear when they yelled "Go!" But at that moment he went. "I came up to him with 80 meters to go and for the first 30 he was still with me," recalled Doubell. "As I finally passed him, I was screaming to myself, 'Christ, I can win! I can win!'"

His time was 1:44.3, equaling the world mark and good enough for a new Olympic standard.

Kiprugut finished only 0.2 of a second behind. *World Sports* magazine rendered this salute: "None of the great champions in the Mexico City Olympics won his title in more classical style than Ralph Doubell."

The British Commonwealth had another hero to celebrate, this one in the 400-meter hurdles—though Americans tried hard to claim him because he had spent 10 of his 24 years in the United States and was attending Boston University. After the race, the press even proclaimed that he was planning to become a U.S. citizen. England's David Hemery just smiled and said, "That's news to me."

On paper, the Mexico City 400 hurdles stacked up as one of the great contests of the Games. The hurdles have their home in the United States, and in 1968 an overwhelming 19 of the world's 25 top hurdlers were Americans. This contingent included the two favorites, world-record holder Geoff Vanderstock, and Ron Whitney, ranked No. 1 in the world in 1967. Italy's Roberto Frinolli, the European champion, was on hand as well.

Yet as it turned out, the race was no match at all. Frinolli and Vanderstock got the better starts and led to the third hurdle. Then the tall, blond Hemery, his shaggy hair flying, powered ahead with such a display of grace and speed that he gained at least a yard over each of the last seven hurdles. At the finish he was ahead by 8 full meters, so demoralizing Vanderstock and Whitney that they fell back to fourth and sixth respectively, leaving the silver to West Germany's Gerhard Hennige and the bronze to John Sherwood, another Briton.

When it lit up the scoreboard, Hemery's time brought a gasp from the crowd: 48.12, almost

Alone at the last hurdle, Great Britain's David Hemery competes only against the clock. Until Mexico City, Americans had won all but two Olympic 400-meter hurdling titles. The last non-American victor before Hemery was Ireland's Robert Tisdall at Los Angeles 1932.

America's Bob Seagren soars more than 17 feet during a pole vault competition that ended under the stadium lights. Seagren, along with two German vaulters, reached the winning height of 17 feet 8 ½ inches (5.4 meters). Fewer misses gave the American the gold medal.

0.7 of a second better than Vanderstock's world mark. "He didn't just beat them, he paralyzed them," whistled an observer. The medal ceremony put icing on the cake: The IOC official who placed the gold medal around David Hemery's neck was his countryman David Lord Burghley, Marquess of Exeter, winner of the same event at Amsterdam 40 years before.

America got back a measure of lost glory in the 110-meter high hurdles when Willie Davenport and Ervin Hall skimmed to a 1-2 victory, Davenport in an Olympic-record 13.33. And there was further gold to mine in the field program.

For unremitting tension, few events could match the pole vault. At Mexico City the competition went on for seven and a quarter hours. At the end, a newsman belabored the obvious by asking America's Bob Seagren if he was tired. Seagren regarded him wryly. "The thing that tired me out the most," he said politely, "was all the trips back and forth to the john."

The era of the fiberglass pole had recently dawned, and heights were soaring dramatically, from 15 feet (4.57 meters) before 1962 to almost 18 feet (5.49 meters) five years later. The popular view held that the light, springy fiberglass simply catapulted vaulters over the bar. That was not quite accurate. Unlike rigid aluminum poles, the new composite material stored and then released the energy imparted by the athlete himself: Pole vaulting thus became less of a test of upper-body strength and more a measure of coordination, timing, and speed down the runway. It was tricky, though. "You can be the best in the world," said Seagren, "but have a bad day and not make our Olympic team."

Seagren himself had almost missed out on the Games—not because of a lapse in form, but because of excruciating pain from a cracked vertebra that immobilized him for several days at the Lake Tahoe trials. The 21-year-old Californian was ready to quit when the agony miraculously subsided. After that he went out and demolished

the competition with a world-record vault of 17 feet 9 inches (5.41 meters).

But he wasn't alone; the field at Mexico City was loaded with 17-foot vaulters. After three hours, the bar rested at 17 feet ¾ inch (5.20 meters), and nine athletes were still in contention. Five remained after another three hours when the bar reached 17 feet 8 ¾ inches (5.40 meters), almost a foot higher than the existing Olympic record. At this point, Seagren was in last place under a complex scoring system that took into account missed jumps, along with a competitor's option of sitting out a turn at various heights in the gamble that rivals would fail. "Like poker or Russian roulette," Seagren called the strategy.

Each athlete got three tries. American John Pennel failed on his third attempt. Next to go was Greece's Chris Papanicolaou, who a year later would be the first human to exceed 18 feet (5.49 meters). East Germany's Wolfgang Nordwig, West Germany's Claus Shiprowski, and Bob Seagren all cleared 17 feet 8 ¾ inches with soaring vaults. Seagren made it over the bar on his second vault, while the two Germans only succeeded on the third try. Thus Seagren won the cherished gold, but all the vaulters could feel

tremendously proud: In the competition, eight of the top 11 men had gone to heights they had never before achieved.

Assessing appearances alone, things went from the sublime to the ridiculous in Mexico City on the final day of track and field. The ridiculous—at least, at the time, he looked ridiculous—came in the form of America's Dick Fosbury, making a bid for gold in his international debut as a high jumper. No gracefully striding run-up or classic forward scissors and straddle for this 21-year-old Oregonian. Fosbury took off like a terrier spying a rat, planted his right foot, spun 180 degrees and launched himself backward—yes, backward—into the air. If all went well, he cleared the bar, jerking his legs up after his torso, and landed smack on the back of his neck. The style became known immediately and immortally as the Fosbury Flop. It looked so wacky, and Fosbury was such an engaging youngster, that everybody loved it. Wild cheers accompanied his every jump. "Only a triple somersault off a flying trapeze with no net below could be more thrilling," burbled one German writer.

What was more, it worked. "I've studied physics and engineering," said Fosbury, "and jumping my

His aptly named flop looks awkward, but Dick Fosbury's signature leap worked perfectly for him in the high jump. Fosbury developed the technique, now universally popular, without the benefit of modern landing pads.

way, I'm less likely to hit the bar with my head, arms, or legs." He could, however, break his neck: He had, in fact, suffered a couple of compressed vertebrae while perfecting his method.

That happened back in high school. In 1963, Fosbury, then in the 10th grade, found that he couldn't master the traditional scissors leap over the bar. He started tinkering, trying to lower his center of gravity, and came up with his backward approach. Practically overnight his jumps went from 5 feet 4 inches (1.63 meters) to 5 feet 11 inches (1.71 meters), and by the time he graduated he was jumping 6 feet 7 inches (2.01 meters)—but at some cost. "When I jumped in high

school, none of the schools could afford foam rubber landing pits," he told an interviewer in 1968, "so I would have to jump into sawdust pits." It was the regular hard landings on the back of his neck that resulted in the compressed vertebrae.

In 1967, Fosbury's best jump, 6 feet 10 ¾ inches (2.10 meters), barely put him among the world's top 50 high jumpers. But he was refining his radical style. In 1968 he was clearing 7 feet on a regular basis, and that put him among the elite of the sport. Going into Mexico City, in fact, he had topped 7 feet 2 ¼ inches (2.19 meters) to win the national collegiate title. Now, with 80,000 spectators urging him on, he jumped flawlessly,

clearing 6 feet 8 inches (2.03 meters), 6 feet 10 ¼ inches (2.09 meters), 7 feet ¼ inch (2.14 meters), 7 feet 1 ⅞ inches (2.18 meters), 7 feet 2 ⅝ inches (2.20 meters), and a personal best 7 feet 3 ⅜ inches (2.22 meters)—mastering each height on his first attempt. Only two jumpers were still with him—his teammate Edward Caruthers and the Soviet Union's Valentin Gavrilov—when the bar went up to an Olympic record 7 feet 4 ¼ inches (2.24 meters). Caruthers and Gavrilov jumped three times and missed three times.

Dick Fosbury missed twice. One last time he stood ready for the run-up, rocking slowly back and forth on his heels, hands clenching and unclenching, psyching himself up. Two minutes were allowed for preparation; they passed. Then Fosbury raced for the bar, jackknifed absurdly up and cleanly over. The stadium shook with acclaim as he leaped to his feet, grinning hugely and flashing a V-for-victory sign, the first American to win the high jump since Melbourne 1956. In another dozen years, at Moscow 1980, 13 of the 16 Olympic finalists would be doing the Fosbury Flop.

Americans had a brighter history in a couple of other field events. In fact, the U.S. "whales," as such massive athletes were known, practically owned both the shot put and the discus throw, winning the shot put in 14 of 16 modern Games and the discus in 12 of them. The tradition would hold in Mexico City.

Watching Randy Matson put the shot for Texas A. & M., a rival coach once exclaimed, "His foot explodes, his calf explodes, his thigh explodes, his hip, his back, his shoulder, his triceps, and right out to the very tips of his fingers. It's like a whole string of firecrackers going off." And when all that action was generated by a 6-foot-6 ½-inch, 265-pound mountain of muscle, the 16-pound (7.26-kilogram) brass and iron ball went places. As a 19-year-old college freshman, Matson had won the silver medal at Tokyo with a put of 66 feet 3 ¼ inches (20.20 meters), just 5 ¼ inches

short of the Olympic record set by teammate Dallas Long. A year later, Matson became the first man ever to hurl the shot more than 70 feet (21.34 meters). Since then he had pushed it out to a world record of 71 feet 5 ½ inches (21.78 meters) and had registered 23 of the 25 longest puts in history. "He is so fantastic," said Hungary's Vilmos Varju, the European champion, "that we have no motivation left."

At Mexico City, now out of college, married, and thinking about a job, Matson got off a first effort of 67 feet 4 ¾ inches (20.54 meters)—not great by his standards, but good enough to boost the Olympic record by more than 6 inches. Nobody else came close, and the gold was his.

The discus proved to be another matter altogether. The defending Olympic champ was practically an old man of 32, an aircraft company computer supervisor participating in his fourth Olympics. Al Oerter did not rate as the favorite. He had never been the favorite—not when he won the gold medal as a 20-year-old at Melbourne 1956, not when he won it again at Rome 1960, not when he collected his third gold at Tokyo 1964, despite the agony of a slipped cervical disk and torn cartilage in his rib cage. But the 6-foot-5, 260-pound Oerter was one of those consummate competitors who never choke, never falter. "He's all heart and guts," said U.S. head coach Payton Jordan.

The strong favorite at Mexico City was America's Jay Silvester, who a few months earlier had added 8 feet to the world record with a prodigious heave of 224 feet 5 inches (68.40 meters). Oerter figured that he himself had thrown the discus something like 33,000 times in his life, and he had never come within 17 feet of Silvester's throw.

In the preliminaries Oerter looked unimpressive.

TRY, TRY AGAIN

Discus champion Lia Maniolu of Romania had one of the longest Olympic careers of all time—and one of the more checkered. She debuted at Helsinki 1952, reaching the final and finishing sixth. Maniolu improved through the seasons leading to Melbourne 1956, but the competition had gotten better, too: She came in a disappointing ninth. Rome 1960 was her breakthrough. The discus field had two former gold medalists, both of them able to hurl the disk several feet farther than Maniolu could. Nevertheless, she was good enough to win Romania's first track and field medal, a bronze. She was third once more at Tokyo 1964.

Complaints that she'd passed her peak grew every year, but even though she was 36 in 1968, no one in Romania could unseat her for a place on the team. She made it to Mexico City for her fifth Olympic Games. And, finally, she won.

Maniolu's lifetime best was 194 feet (59.13 meters)—good but well short of the record of 205 feet 2 ¼ inches (62.54 meters) set by West Germany's Liesl Westermann, her chief rival at Mexico City. Westermann and an elbow injury made Maniolu's prospects for a gold seem dim indeed. So she decided to put everything into her first try, figuring her arm wouldn't hold up for subsequent tosses. She hurled the discus 191 feet 2 inches (58.28 meters). Rain came shortly thereafter, and the rest of the field, including Westermann, struggled with their footing. No one could match Maniolu's first throw.

Munich 1972 was her last appearance; there, at 40, she finished out of the medals—but not out of the Olympic movement. Maniolu would go on to become president of Romania's national Olympic committee.

Silvester uncorked a 207-foot (63.09-meter) throw that topped Oerter's lifetime best by several inches. But then the final was delayed for an hour by torrential rains that filled the concrete throwing ring with water and greatly annoyed the competitors, especially Silvester. Oerter coolly waited out the deluge without even bothering to put on his sweat suit. Then he made his third attempt, unleashing a towering throw of 212 feet 6 ½ inches (64.78 meters), his best ever by 5 feet. The throw seemed to demoralize Silvester. He fouled three times out of six, could not get past 202 feet (61.57 meters), and wound up fifth, behind a Czech and a pair of East Germans. "I didn't think I had a chance," smiled the only athlete in Olympic history ever to win four times in the same event.

Scorekeepers in the United States could add another tick to the tally when Bill Toomey of California hurled, jumped, and ran away with the grueling decathlon. Americans had dominated that event as well, triumphing in eight of the 11 Games since Jim Thorpe won at Stockholm in 1912. But at Tokyo 1964, West Germany's Willi Holdorf had earned the right to the title "World's Best Athlete," the accolade traditionally reserved for the winner of the grueling 10-part event. Now Toomey wanted that title, partly for his country and mostly for himself.

"You know what it takes to become a good decathlon man?" Toomey once rhetorically asked. "It takes the upper body of a weight man, the lower body of a sprinter, and the brain of an idiot." Now 29 and an English teacher, Toomey had settled on the decathlon a decade earlier when it became evident that he would set no records as a quarter-miler. At Mexico City he brought the crowd to its feet with a flabbergasting 45.6 for the 400 meters, faster than he had ever run in his life, scarcely 1.8 seconds off Lee Evans' brand-new world record. That, along with a 10.4 time in the 100 meters and a long jump of 25 feet 9 ¾ inches (7.87 meters) gave Toomey a huge lead, with 4,499 points after five events on the first day.

But on the second day, the heat and the altitude began to tell. Toomey ran a fine 110-meter high hurdles. But mediocre discus and javelin throws and a badly flawed pole vault brought everything down to the 1,500-meter run. At this point in the competition, Kurt Bendlin was in second place. If Bendlin could beat Toomey by 10 seconds or more, he would succeed his countryman, 1964 gold medalist Willi Holdorf, as the world's best amateur all-around athlete. At the finish both Toomey and Bendlin were gasping and staggering. But Toomey had won by 30 yards over Bendlin, who faded to third in the competition behind another West German, Hans-Joachim Walde. Toomey's score of 8,193 points gave him an Olympic record as well as the medal. On the point of collapse, he rasped: "I've never had to endure anything so intense. They shouldn't call this the Olympic Games. It's not a game out there."

Overall, the Americans had performed about as expected in track and field, and the Africans had added a splendid new dimension to the distances. Yet in their own specialties, the men and women from the Soviet Union and Eastern Europe dominated the Games as they had for years. The Soviet Union's outstanding Viktor Saneyev won the triple jump with a world-record 57 feet ¼ inch (17.39 meters) to begin a reign that would continue through three Olympics and taper off with a silver at Moscow 1980. A pair of mighty Hungarians bracketed a Soviet in the hammer throw, all three eclipsing the Olympic record. In the javelin, another Soviet, a Finn, and a Hungarian shared the honors, and again, all three men bettered the Olympic mark. The agonizing 50-kilometer walk belonged to an East German and the 20 kilometers appeared to be 1-2 for the Soviets—until 200 meters from the finish. There Jose Pedraza Zuniga, a 31-year-old Mexican soldier, caught one of the Russians and came within 3 yards of nailing the leader. The host country's joyful fans screamed approval as Zuniga took the silver, his nation's only medal in track and field.

The rarefied air of Mexico City helps triple jumper Viktor Saneyev toward a prodigious leap. The Soviet became the first jumper to break 57 feet (17.4 meters) when he launched himself a half inch beyond that on his fifth attempt in the final.

A pair of Australian women and a Taiwanese all bettered the Olympic record in the 80-meter hurdles. But when it came to the women's field events, the show was strictly an East European extravaganza. Romania's Viorica Viscopoleanu won the long jump with a world-record leap of 22 feet 4 ½ inches (6.82 meters), while East Germany's Margitta Gummell heaved the 8-pound (3.63-kilogram) women's shot 64 feet 4 inches (19.61 meters), almost 3 feet beyond her own world record. A Romanian woman won the discus, a Hungarian the javelin, a Czech the high jump, a West German the women's pentathlon.

At the close of track and field on Sunday, October 20, the United States had amassed the greatest trove of medals—37, including 23 golds. Yet a measure of the magnificent competition could be found in the fact that athletes from 39 nations had competed in the final rounds, and the flags of 27 nations had been raised in honor of medals won. As for the record books, they were rewritten in Mexico City, despite the altitude. Either individually or as part of relay teams, the 1968 track and field Olympians had equaled or broken world records no fewer than 14 times and Olympic marks 26 times.

Unless a person happens to be a competition swimmer, all similarly sized, heated, and configured pools seem pretty much alike. But serious swimmers rate pools, just as runners rate tracks, as fast or slow or sometimes even sloppy—and the $3.9-million pool built for the 1968 U.S. Olympic trials by the city of Long Beach, California, was absolute tops. "I've never seen gutters so big," said 18-year-old Mark Spitz, commenting on the pool-edge baffles designed to absorb the splashes and waves

that slow races. Celebrating this fine facility, young Spitz and a couple of dozen other American Olympic hopefuls went out and shattered 14 world records in the qualifying races.

That breathtaking display installed the United States swimmers as favorites at Mexico City. In world rankings, American men headed seven of the 12 individual lists, with three of the four highest seedings in eight events. Bathed in limelight were young Spitz, the California wonder named 1967 Swimmer of the Year by *Swimmers' World* magazine, and Don Schollander, the Yale senior who had won four golds as an 18-year-old at Tokyo 1964. At Long Beach, Spitz had qualified for three individual events—100- and 200-meter butterfly and 200-meter freestyle—along with three relays. He brashly predicted victory for himself in all six contests. Schollander, 22 and fighting both swimmer's old age and an aftertaste of disillusionment after his elevation to stardom in Tokyo, had qualified for the 200-meter freestyle and a relay.

The two swimmers did not get along. Spitz sneered at Schollander as "Joe College," and Schollander shot back: "Mark is not very intelligent. His inane comments used to bother me, but now they make me laugh." Swimming fans could hardly wait for them to meet in the 200 meters.

As for the American women, they were top-rated in 10 of the 12 events and shared an 11th. Experts gave them the potential to win all 14 competitions, including the two relays. In the trials, 16-year-old Debbie Meyer had bettered her existing world marks in the 200-, 400-, and 800-meter freestyle.

But Mexico City imposed its peculiar set of problems. For some reason, swimmers there seemed to be afflicted by intestinal problems to a greater extent than other athletes. And the 7,347-foot elevation exacted its oxygen debt, what swimmers called "the altitude monkey." "You get in that old pool," said 100-meter butterfly ace Douglas Russell, "and suddenly the monkey jumps right in there on top of you."

Moreover, the beautiful new Olympic pool complex, built with such pride and at such expense, proved to be dismally slow. Small but critical flaws in the gutter design permitted waves that bordered on whitecaps during competitions. "It's murder in there," remarked U.S. freestyler Ken Walsh. "You make the turn and suddenly you're going bump, bump, bump, over the waves. Almost enough to make you seasick."

For all of that, the American swimmers lived up to their billing. Even though the pool, the altitude, and the stomach cramps helped protect the record book, in 10 days of competition the U.S. team made off with 58 medals (including 23 golds), leaving just 41 for the rest of the world.

However, the heroics that Mark Spitz predicted for himself never materialized. The overanxious Spitz failed to win an individual event and had to be content with a share of three golds in the relays; his particular Olympics was still four years away. Even Spitz's much-ballyhooed confrontation with Don Schollander in the freestyle 200 fizzled out. Australia's Mike Wenden took care of that.

The 18-year-old Wenden was a dark horse— fast, but erratic and lacking in style. Like some sort of human paddle wheeler, he took 15 more arm-flailing strokes per lap than either Spitz or the classically smooth Schollander. "There's only one way to swim fast," said Wenden, "and that's to swim bloody fast." Practice bloody hard, too: There were stories that Wenden swam as much as 15,000 meters a day preparing for the Olympics.

The Australian teenager met Schollander for the first time on the anchor leg of the 4 x 200-meter relay. The U.S. won, but it wasn't a runaway. Schollander had inherited a body length's lead, but Wenden cut that to half a body length at the finish. "I've worried him," thought Wenden. "He's not going to sleep between now and the individual 200."

When the hour of the eagerly awaited 200 meters finally arrived, Wenden won in an

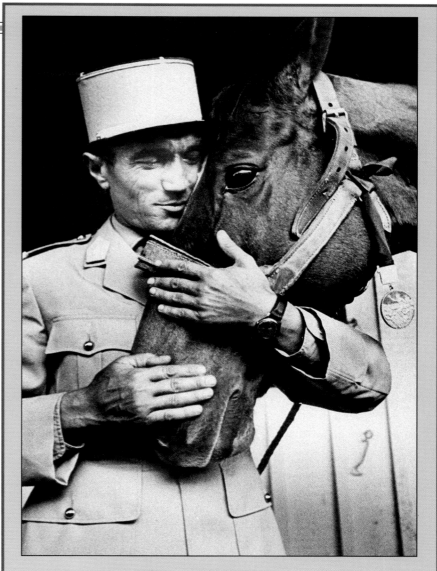

A happy Jean-Jacques Guyon gives a hug to Pitou, his mount for the three-day event of the equestrian competition. Guyon was only the second Frenchman ever to win the event.

ORDEAL IN THE RAIN

Challenges from both man and nature made Mexico City's equestrian competition one of the most difficult in Olympic history. The three-day event was a case in point: Always formidable, the endurance ride became even more treacherous when constant rains created unanticipated hazards. A stream that ran through the course became a howling river; pools became lakes. Horses struggled to keep their footing over swollen, swirling water jumps. Two horses died. Ballerina, a Soviet mount, fell into the stream and was swept away by the current. An Irish horse, Laughlin, broke a leg in a fall and had to be euthanized. In neither incident was the rider seriously hurt.

Despite its hazards, there were few objections to the course itself, though some tactics along its rugged stretches proved controversial. The Soviet team faced disqualification because a Russian official was spotted using a walkie-talkie to communicate with riders—a blatant breach of the rules. None of the Soviet equestrians scored well enough to win a medal, however, so the issue was dropped. France's Jean-Jacques Guyon, riding Pitou, benefited by taking his turn before the rains began. He won the individual title. Great Britain claimed team honors.

Olympic-record 1:55.2. The time was well off Schollander's world mark of 1:54.3, but at Mexico City a slower time was to be expected. The race itself was so agonizing that Wenden virtually blacked out at the end and didn't realize that he had won. Totally spent, hanging on the lane ropes, he slipped off and had to be rescued from the bottom of the pool. Then he had trouble climbing out. When he got to the dressing room, there was Don Schollander on the floor, getting oxygen.

Spitz had finished far out of the running in the 200 meters. Schollander won the silver—and then promptly announced his retirement. (He would soon become a commentator for ABC television.) "I'm finished with water," he said. "In fact, I may not take a bath or a shower for another two years."

BELLO DIBIASI

Italy's Klaus Dibiasi battled tradition to win the first of his three Olympic gold medals in platform diving. Before 1968, Italy had never had an Olympic swimming or diving champion. The dearth may have kept most Italian boys out of the sport—or, conversely, the absence of national enthusiasm for aquatic events may have caused the dearth. In any case, Dibiasi, a physical education student from Bolzano, had a father who was a diving coach and a former national champion diver. At Tokyo 1964, Klaus, then 17, began erasing Italy's aquatic hard times by winning a silver medal in the platform events. His skills grew over the next four years, and he was a solid favorite at Mexico City. He entered the springboard and platform events, not expecting much off the springboard and surprising himself by ending up second after the preliminary rounds. He was consistent in all three of his optional dives the following afternoon, but the day belonged to America's Bernie Wrightson. A 24-year-old naval officer, Wrightson moved from third to first after nailing his final three dives. Even so, Dibiasi held onto second and won the silver.

The platform event developed into a battle against the crowd. A veteran Mexican diver, Alvaro Gaxiola, held the lead after the first day of dives. Not surprisingly, the crowd wildly cheered every effort of their hero and booed loudly if his scores didn't meet their expectations. The lengthy outbursts repeatedly held up the competition and played havoc with the timing of whichever athlete followed Gaxiola. Nevertheless, by the third round of the final, Dibiasi began to show his superiority. He opened a 5-point lead over Gaxiola by his fourth dive and widened the margin after the next

two rounds. The contest was reduced to a match for second place: Gaxiola would hold on for the silver over America's Win Young.

At Munich 1972, Dibiasi was again peerless on the platform. He would win the event a final time at Montreal 1976 to become the first and so far the only diver to win three consecutive Olympic championships.

Laboring under no such phobias, three of Schollander's teammates—Mac Zorn, Ken Walsh, and Mark Spitz—were favorites in the 100 meters. But again, nobody had figured on Mike Wenden. The start was all Zorn's, patently explosive, and for the first 25 meters, said Wenden, "I was looking at the bubbles on his feet. Over the 100, that's the setting for panic." The Aussie was also trailing Walsh and Spitz at that point. But Wenden got a fast turn and caught the fading Zorn at 70 meters, then drove by Walsh and Spitz to slap the wall in a world-record 52.2 seconds.

Another upstart teenager, 17-year-old Roland Matthes of East Germany, won both the 100- and 200-meter backstroke events. The short, slender youngster had been totally unknown two years before, not even ranked among Europe's top 20 backstrokers. But he was so naturally gifted, with high body position and a perfect, bent-arm pull, that he appeared to slip through the water effortlessly. After some quality coaching in 1967, Matthes quickly emerged as a superstar, breaking three world records in the 100 meters and one in the 200 in the space of just seven weeks. He was favored in Mexico City, and he lived up to the billing by beating a pair of American stars at 100

meters in the Olympic-record time of 58.7. A few days later, Matthes again beat two highly regarded U.S. swimmers at 200 meters and set another Olympic record with his time of 2:09.6.

Mexico had its shining moment in the pool when 17-year-old Felipe Muñoz unexpectedly outclassed the field in the men's 200-meter breaststroke; President Díaz Ordaz himself put in a congratulatory phone call to the new national hero. And the crowd went wild again when a diminutive 16-year-old Czechoslovakian, Milena Duckova, overcame a Soviet rival with two flawless final dives in the women's 10-meter tower event. Yet the competitor who captured everyone's attention poolside was Debbie Meyer, a tall, lithe, and tawny blonde, the very stereotype of the California girl.

A fast swimmer since childhood, Meyer began developing her natural talent in 1964 when she came under the wing of Coach Sherman Chavoor at the swim club in Sacramento. "Coaching swimmers is 90 percent conditioning," said Chavoor, and even at Mexico City's daunting altitude, he drove his pupil hard. "Now show some guts," he yelled. "Get moving in that water." The coach gave no quarter, even though Meyer was suffering from tendonitis of the shoulder, a sore ankle, and severe stomach cramps.

Debbie Meyer churns to an easy victory in the 800-meter freestyle. Her achievements at the Olympic trials and the Games won her the 1968 Sullivan Award as America's most outstanding amateur athlete.

Romania's Ivan Patzaichin and Serghei Covaliov maintain a delicate balance as they paddle their canoe toward a gold medal in the 1,000-meter Canadian pairs. Strong headwinds combined with the oxygen-robbing altitude to produce a number of upsets at Xochimilco.

But Chavoor had apparently gauged his protégée correctly. Favored to win the 400-meter freestyle, as well as the newly added 200-meter and 800-meter freestyle events, Meyer churned to victory in all three, thus becoming the first swimmer in Olympic history to earn three individual golds in a single Games. And she knew whom to thank. After the 800 meters, Debbie Meyer ran up and hung her third medal around coach Chavoor's neck.

American athletes had shown themselves preeminent in swimming and diving, but they had no lock whatever on the other water sports at Mexico City. The U.S. water polo team, with five victories, two losses, and a tie, nevertheless wound up fifth to the seven-man powerhouses from Yugoslavia, the USSR, Hungary, and Italy. American sailors won the Star and Dragon classes, but bowed to the Soviets, Swedes, and British in the three other yachting categories. And the rest of the world simply overwhelmed the United States in the canoeing and rowing held at Xochimilco on the man-made course whose ecological travails had been the butt of much humor.

It was at Xochimilco that the effects of Mexico City's elevation proved most severe. Jim Ryun, that student of altitude, noted 80 collapses from oxygen debt in the first two days of rowing, perhaps the most aerobic of all sports. Rescue launches raced out to the drifting or swamped craft, and doctors ashore administered oxygen to the athletes; dangerously low blood pressure was reported in some cases. "At the end of a stroke or a sprint, you take a big breath of air," explained Chet Livingstone of America's eight-oared shell crew. "The insufficient oxygen goes to your brain and you black out."

Kayakers faced similar torture, although Eastern bloc athletes seemed better able to cope with it. In kayaking with double- and single-bladed paddles, at distances of 1,000 meters for men and 500 meters for women, 19 of the 21 medals went to the superbly skilled and conditioned Hungarians, Soviets, Romanians, and West Germans; the Danes and Austrians salvaged a bronze apiece.

Wholly outclassed in the kayaks, Americans hoped for better in the rowing events. For the first time in Olympic history, the U.S. had placed a shell in each of the seven 2,000-meter finals, from single sculls to the heavyweight eight-oared craft. A great start by the eight-man Harvard crew provided an early lead, but at 1,000 meters the oxygen deficit overcame the Americans. Smooth-stroking eights from Austria and West Germany swept by, followed by the Soviets, New Zealanders, and Czechs, leaving the U.S. a gasping sixth. In the pairs, No. 1-ranked American rowers strove gallantly, only to lose out in the last 10 meters to an East German duo with more strength and stamina.

In fact, Germans—both East and West—were the ultimate stars at Xochimilco. Competing separately for the first time, the West Germans

Clubmates in Holzheim, West Germany, create an arch of oars to honor Annemarie Zimmermann *(left)* and Roswitha Esser, the women's 500-meter kayak pairs champions. The Tokyo gold medalists had split up after those Games, only to reunite in 1967 to try for another Olympic title.

went home with two golds and three silvers, while the Easterners collected another two golds and a silver. That put them third and fourth, behind the Hungarians and Soviets. Had they gone to Mexico City as one team, one nation, they would have swamped the world in canoeing and rowing. It seemed that politics, that perpetual enemy of Olympism, had exacted another toll.

When all was said and done, in fact, some dour observers argued that the Games themselves had been victimized in Mexico City—just as prophesied—by political turmoil and unsuitable climate, by air too rich in rhetoric and poor in oxygen. But looking through a rosier lens, others argued that pageantry and prowess had won out over protest in Mexico, and that an abundance of heart proved able to overcome any deficiency of lungs. These optimists pointed to the record books as evidence: 82 world records set, along with 378 Olympic records. Whatever the problems, the Games of the XIX Olympiad had witnessed the most golden harvest of records to date in the first century of modern Olympic history.

Ebullient athletes form a human chain and skip through the infield of the Olympic stadium, despite a new dictum against mass mingling during the closing ceremony. Only seven members of each national team were allowed to take part in the final festivities—a rule inaugurated by the IOC in 1968 with an eye toward controlling the crowded confusion of previous celebrations.

CRUSADES AND COMMERCE

There had not been a great deal of cheer at recent gatherings of the International Olympic Committee, and the mood remained somber when the members reassembled in Amsterdam on May 12, 1970. Opening the 69th Session of the Olympics' governing body, President Avery Brundage told the executives what many of them already acknowledged. "The Olympics," he said, "are in trouble, serious trouble." Brundage went on to deliver a long, scolding lecture about how the Games were growing too big, too expensive, too professional. And, the president added, too political by far. But he didn't dwell on that last, for he knew that all would have their fill of politics before they left Amsterdam.

The consuming question before the IOC was the one that had divided the organization for years: what to do about South Africa. Should that unhappy nation, misruled by a handful of racist whites in a sea of impoverished blacks, be expelled from the Olympic community? The Amsterdam meeting would settle the issue once and for all.

At 83 and in his 18th year as leader and fervent apostle of the Olympics, Brundage had long favored including South Africa. While he might deplore apartheid, he believed in the Olympic movement with a passion that few men could muster for anything; Olympism was his religion—a pure and shining faith in amateur sport for it's sake alone, "free, spontaneous, joyous," as he once put it. And politics, in the aid of any cause whatever, were interlopers at Avery Brundage's Games. The Olympics were above politics and beyond it. But that was not the view of the 32 emerging and aggressively nationalistic states allied in the Supreme Council for Sport in Africa (SCSA). They demanded that South Africa either dismantle its racially segregated sports establishment or depart the Olympic movement.

Each side in the dispute was allowed 30 minutes in Amsterdam to present its case a final time. Representatives of

Signs of apartheid, Cape Town, South Africa

black Africa went first, led by Nigeria's Abraham Ordi, president of the SCSA, and the Congo's Jean-Claude Ganga, another longtime anti-apartheid activist. In a seven-page document, Ordi, Ganga, and their colleagues ignored South Africa's promise of a racially mixed team for the Munich Games in 1972. The real issue, they held, was the climate of sport in South Africa, an atmosphere heavy with segregated facilities and rules prohibiting athletes of different races from competing with one another.

This sort of bigotry ran counter to both the letter and the spirit of the Olympic Charter. Moreover, the South African National Olympic Committee (SANOC) was not an independent entity, as the charter also required, but rather a tool of the government—evidenced by its failure to condemn apartheid among athletes. For these reasons, the black Africans moved to banish South Africa from future Games.

The South African response was as harsh as the charges against it. Frank Braun, president of SANOC, castigated both Brundage and the IOC for even placing the expulsion motion on the agenda; the Olympic Charter protected SANOC from such blatant political attack. The charter, he went on, was meant to bring the nations of the world together. "It was certainly not drawn up as a device for persecution or exclusion." Braun entered a legalistic, item-by-item rebuttal of the charges against SANOC, then got to the meat of his statement: Were any of the accusing Olympic committees innocent of government control and discrimination? He thought not. And he asked if anything could be achieved by South Africa's dismissal other than "personal aggrandizement, chauvinistic aspirations, and satisfactions derived from hatred." Indeed, said Braun, by capitulating to such base emotions, the Olympic movement "carries the seed of its own destruction."

The formal motion took the form of a question: "Do you agree to the withdrawal of recognition of SANOC?" Secretaries circled the room, distributing ballots to the 66 voting members of the IOC present at Amsterdam. The time had come to decide.

Just as Brundage had indicated in his opening remarks, South Africa was only one of several pressing issues on the Olympic agenda. Others included the melancholy fact that numbers of people had come to view the institution itself with distaste. The city of Zurich, biggest and richest in Switzerland, stood as an ominous example. The year before, Zurich's lord mayor had thought to enter a bid for the 1976 Olympic Winter Games; the citizens were asked to decide in a plebiscite. Arguments saturated the media for several weeks, and when the votes were counted, 40,912 Zurichers approved of the idea, but a vastly greater 145,347 did not. Why?

Escalating costs were one reason, said Brundage. The citizens of Grenoble would be a decade absorbing the $240 million spent on the 1968 Winter Games, and the thrifty Swiss wanted no part of such a burden. There was a further reason for rejection, he continued. Zurich had passed moral judgment on the current state of the Olympics and found the Games crassly commercial. He quoted a news story stating that the Swiss "see in the Olympics a symbol of corruption in modern sport and they are reluctant to subsidize it." Other reports deplored a "deterioration of the true sporting spirit" and warned that "the IOC may find it more difficult to place their events as the years pass."

Brundage went beyond that. "The Olympic Games," he intoned, "must be confined to amateurs or they are a commercial enterprise with all idealism lost, and when that day comes, the Olympic Games, mark well my words, are doomed."

The IOC's president was known for hyperbole when he wished to make a point. The Olympics were not exactly tottering on the brink of an abyss. But there was enough truth in what he said

The labels visible in the photograph read: The Lord Killanin, Constantin Andrianov, Avery Brundage, Général Jose de J.Clark, Syed Wajid Ali, Sir Ade Ademola, Le jonkheer Herman A. van Karnebeek

to make the next years difficult, both for the IOC and for Brundage himself. Never at a loss for opinions, Olympism's leader would have something to say about the proper choice of host city for the 1976 Summer Games, thereby provoking charges that he had sabotaged his own country. More corrosive arguments would erupt over the split of television money among the various Olympic partners. There would also be the problem of performance-enhancing drugs, not to mention the gender tests to make sure that only genuine females competed in the women's events.

But the greatest controversy by far would revolve around what was sometimes termed "shamateurism"—professionals or near-professionals posing as Olympic amateurs. The play-for-pay practice incensed Avery Brundage to the point where he urged the elimination of the Winter Games, or at a minimum an end to heavily subsidized Alpine skiing, which he called "a poisonous cancer that must be removed without delay." Both the Winter Games and their Alpine events would remain, however. And so, in fury and frustration, the old warrior would engage the world's best-known skier in a

battle at Sapporo, Japan, that would only add further bitterness to an already rancorous Olympiad. By then, the South African affair would have mercifully passed into history.

The delegates at Amsterdam could reflect on a day of happier sporting relationships among the races inhabiting South Africa. All through the 19th century and into the 20th, blacks, whites, and Asians had enjoyed a considerable level of athletic contact and rapport. Only in June 1956 had the country's National Party, fixated on racial separation, imposed laws forbidding interracial sport: Not only must there be separate facilities and competitions within South Africa, but no mixed teams would be allowed to visit, and none, of course, would be sent abroad.

Apartheid patently violated the Olympic Charter's Rule No. 1: "No discrimination is allowed against any country or person on the grounds of race, religion, or political affiliation." Protests against South Africa poured in. But the mandarins of the IOC—most of them elderly, many wealthy, quite a few titled—tended to conduct Olympic affairs as they would in a private, very

International Olympic Committee president Avery Brundage and members of his Executive Committee listen to arguments to remove South Africa from the Olympic movement at the 1970 IOC Session at Amsterdam. Though South Africa had clearly violated nondiscrimination provisions of the Olympic Charter, the vote to expel the nation was close.

exclusive club. And they were reluctant to take action when their friend Reginald Honey, IOC delegate to South Africa, assured everyone that his country's Olympic committee was on excellent terms with colored sports organizations and treated all athletes as equals.

On the basis of those assurances, South Africa participated at Rome 1960—with an all-white team. Shortly thereafter, Jan de Klerk, South Africa's interior minister, took pains to contradict Honey's earnest declarations by reiterating: "The government policy is that no mixed teams should take part in sports inside or outside the country." Still the IOC temporized. At the 59th Session, held in Moscow in June 1962, Brundage and his colleagues merely threatened SANOC with suspension unless it cleaned up its act by the time of the next assembly, 17 months later.

But nothing had changed when the IOC met at the West German spa of Baden-Baden in October 1963. The South Africans now informed the IOC that apartheid was strictly an internal matter, of no concern to outsiders. They might concede a place for qualified nonwhites on their team, but the trials would have to take place outside the country. At this point, even Brundage grew annoyed. By a vote of 30 to 20, with 3 abstentions, the IOC resolved to suspend SANOC from the Olympics. Then it gave the South Africans three months to reconsider. They refused. The suspension took effect. South Africa was barred from the 1964 Games in Tokyo.

Until then, the impetus to force SANOC into line with Olympic ideals had come from the IOC. But after Tokyo the nations of black Africa took the offensive. Their blunt instrument was the Supreme Council for Sport in Africa, organized in December 1966 by Dennis Brutus, a noted South African poet and leader in the fight against apartheid. At SCSA's founding conference in Bamako, Mali, 32 nations resolved "to use every means to obtain the expulsion of South African sports organizations from the Olympic

movement should South Africa fail to comply fully with the IOC rules." The Supreme Council also invited all members to withdraw from the 1968 Olympic Games if a "racialist team from South Africa takes part." Thus the dread specter of boycott was raised over the Olympics. It would become the ultimate weapon.

Meanwhile, the South Africans were thinking hard. Whatever else they might be, Afrikaners were ardent sports enthusiasts, and they badly wanted to compete. If that had to mean concessions, then they might make a few. At the 1967 Session of the IOC in Teheran, SANOC's president Frank Braun announced that South Africa

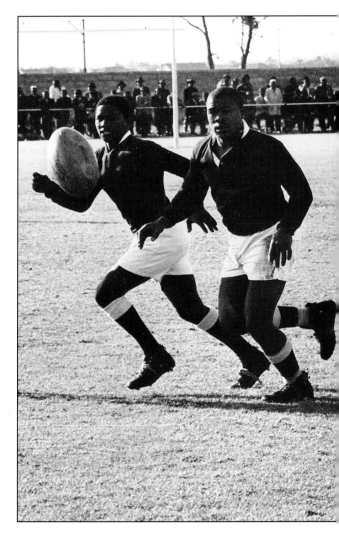

Players on foreign teams competing in South Africa, like Great Britain's Marylebone Cricket Club, had to be white. This discriminatory stance caused the international table tennis federation to expel South Africa in 1956, initiating a process that slowly isolated the white-ruled country from international sport.

South Africa's passion for rugby makes the game the national sport. But black teams could never play white clubs to produce anything like a national championship: Apartheid laws banned all interracial sport.

As the secretary general of the Supreme Council for Sport in Africa, Jean-Claude Ganga was a leading voice in the push to oust South Africa from the Olympic movement. He became the IOC member in the Congo in 1986.

would agree to a mixed team at Mexico City; moreover, the athletes would travel together, live together, wear the same uniform, and compete as one team under one flag. Finally, the team would be chosen by a multiracial committee. Speaking for the government, Prime Minister B. J. Vorster added that mixed teams from abroad could henceforth compete in South Africa—though apartheid would still be enforced internally.

To the IOC—and not a few black South Africans—the new policy represented an enormous step forward. But it failed to satisfy the SCSA. "We do not wish," said Jean-Claude Ganga, "that the blacks of Africa appear like costumed apes presented at a fair and then,

when the fair is over, sent back to their cages." Ethiopia's sports director, Ato Tessewa, called the new policy a farce and threatened to boycott Mexico City if the IOC "dared to allow" South African participation.

Brundage and the IOC decided not to press the question but to wait until the 1968 Session in Grenoble. By then they would have the report of a special investigating commission that the IOC was sending to South Africa. The three-man panel mirrored the IOC's distinction, if not its own racial makeup: Ireland's Lord Killanin, IOC vice president; Kenya's Sir Reginald Alexander, an English-born white; and Nigeria's Sir Adetokunbo Ademola. Ademola, son of a tribal ruler, was Nigeria's first black chief justice and the only nonwhite IOC member from Africa.

In September 1967 the group spent 10 days touring sports facilities and interrogating athletes and officials of all races. Its 114-page report was what most IOC members had hoped for. The investigators found that since 1963, SANOC had been genuinely trying to comply with IOC rules and that its current proposals formed "an acceptable basis for a multiracial team" at Mexico City. They added that "sportsmen of all communities" in South Africa were prepared to accept a team selected by SANOC's promised multiracial committee.

At the IOC's Grenoble Session in early February 1968, Frank Braun again pledged a mixed team chosen on merit, not color. The IOC responded with a resolution that criticized South Africa's internal policies but also stated that SANOC had achieved enough progress on the Olympic level to warrant an invitation to Mexico City. Ordinarily, the IOC would have voted the motion up or down on the spot. But so many members were absent that Brundage put the matter to a vote by cable. All ballots were in by February 15. With obvious pleasure, Brundage announced that "an absolute majority" of the IOC had voted to readmit South Africa. At a press conference he declared that "it was only the power of the Olympic movement that could have secured this change."

The black Africans and their allies were outraged. In the United States, Harry Edwards, the militant California sociologist, announced that African-American athletes would boycott the Olympics "while racism still exists at any level" in South Africa. To show his strength, he sabotaged a track meet celebrating the 100th anniversary of that bastion of white Christianity, the New York Athletic Club. Meanwhile, in Grenoble, the SCSA's Dennis Brutus went privately to Avery Brundage in hopes of changing the IOC president's mind. Brundage was unswayable—and Brutus equally so. "South Africa will not be at Mexico City," he vowed.

One after another, African nations withdrew: Algeria, Ethiopia, Tanzania, Uganda, Mali, Ghana, the United Arab Republic, Kenya, Sudan. The Soviet Union and its satellites accused the IOC of flagrantly violating the Olympic Charter but stopped short of withdrawal. No matter. The boycott was snowballing. From Asia and the Middle East came announcements that Malaysia, India, Iraq, Syria, Saudi Arabia, and Kuwait were pulling out. By the middle of April almost 50 nations had rejected an Olympics that included South Africa. The Games of the XIX Olympiad were falling apart, and the Mexicans, after six years of preparation, were frantic. The same might be said for Avery Brundage, sitting in his Chicago office and counting the defections.

On April 15 the IOC president flew off to South Africa, ostensibly to visit a game park but actually to confer with SANOC's Frank Braun, whom he hoped to persuade to bow out voluntarily. Braun refused and retorted that he "would rather be shot in Mexico City than lynched in Johannesburg." Brundage flew on to IOC headquarters in Lausanne, Switzerland, and an emergency meeting of the Executive Board.

The nine governors conferred on April 21.

Kenya's Sir Reginald Alexander, though his own liberal views often made him unpopular with fellow whites, now urged the IOC to stand firm; SANOC had complied with Olympic rules as best it could. But Brundage was resigned. "We have to face the facts of life," he said. "Political powers have more say than we do."

As a face-saving device, the Executive Board announced that a review of all information had shown the world to be buffeted by such dispute and violence "that it would be most unwise for a South African team to participate in the Games of the XIX Olympiad." In other words, the South Africans might face physical danger at Mexico City. A poll went out to all IOC members unanimously recommending withdrawal of the invitation to SANOC. The vote came back 47-16, with 8 abstentions.

The Games had been saved, but at tremendous cost. The IOC had lost its grip on the administration of Olympic sport. In that place of primacy now would stand any political organization with the clout to enforce its agenda.

At Mexico City that October, Avery Brundage won election to a fifth and final four-year term

South African National Olympic Committee president Frank Braun *(center)* and IOC member Reginald Honey *(right)* meet Avery Brundage on the tarmac of the Johannesburg airport in April 1968. South African officials had invited Brundage to see firsthand the reforms they'd made in racially integrating their athletic clubs. Brundage, impressed, gave a favorable report to the IOC.

as president of the IOC. But the years until his retirement were destined to be unhappy for the man who, more than anyone save possibly Pierre de Coubertin, symbolized the modern Olympics. The never-ending South African nightmare only grew worse as black Africa now mounted a campaign to oust SANOC from the Olympic movement altogether. On the other side, the Afrikaners added fuel to the fire in 1969 by staging an all-white South African games, which they advertised with prominent displays of the Olympic rings.

By the time of Amsterdam, the whole sporting world, it seemed, was lining up against the South Africans. The international federations governing judo and weight lifting had excluded them. They were barred from an international gymnastics competition in Yugoslavia, banned from

the Davis Cup tennis tournament, and advised to cancel a cricket tour of Britain and Northern Ireland when riots and demonstrations erupted in the cities on their route.

Stubborn to the end, Avery Brundage still favored retaining South Africa and working to change its racial policies. But after listening to Frank Braun's inflammatory speech, Brundage turned to a colleague and remarked that the South Africans had "certainly dug their own grave." The vote, however, was surprisingly close, reflecting the members' continuing regard for Brundage and his credo. Of the 66 members present, 35 voted "Aye" on the question of whether to dismiss South Africa, 28 said "Nay," and 3 abstained.

Black Africa had achieved its goal. For the first time in history, a nation had been ejected from

THE TWO GERMANYS

A divided Germany posed a dilemma for the Olympic movement for 30 years. After World War II, Germany metamorphosed into a democratic nation in the west, a communist one in the east, and the International Olympic Committee had to decide what the split meant in terms of German representation at the Games. A national Olympic committee for Germany—the Federal Republic of Germany (F.R.G.)—was recognized in 1951 with the mandate to create a unified team for all Germany for the Summer and Winter Games in 1952. East Germany—the German Democratic Republic (G.D.R.)—refused to accept a marginalized role, and the German teams for Oslo and Helsinki were unified in name only: Both were made up entirely of West Germans.

In 1955, the IOC tried to effect some equity by voting to provisionally recognize an East German NOC. This wasn't enough for the East Germans, who immediately pushed for an independent team. The IOC balked at that and once again asked the two Germanys to field a single team, this time for the 1956 Games. Both sides agreed, then cooperated with each other as little as possible. West Germans

made up the majority of the German teams for Melbourne and Cortina d'Ampezzo, but a few G.D.R. athletes found places on both summer and winter squads. This shaky arrangement persisted through 1960 and 1964.

Irreconcilable differences between the two Germanys finally forced the IOC to face reality in 1965. It voted to allow the East German NOC to send its own team to both 1968 Games, though not without a nod to the fiction of unity: Both German squads would march under a single banner—a neutral flag with the Olympic rings—and use Beethoven's "Ode to Joy" as a national anthem. In 1969 the IOC granted full recognition to the G.D.R., and at Sapporo 1972 an independent East German team appeared under its own flag for the first time.

West Germans precede East Germans into the Estadio Olimpico for the opening ceremony at Mexico City 1968. A unified German team would not march at a Games until Barcelona 1992.

the Olympic movement. It would be 21 years, an entire generation of athletes, before South Africa could return. Yet Nigeria's Abraham Ordi, president of the SCSA, did not bask in his triumph. "It's like having a poisonous leg," he said bleakly. "You have to save the patient by cutting it off."

In time, there would be another amputation. Like South Africa, the neighboring state of Rhodesia was politically poisonous to the nations of the SCSA. But unlike South Africans, Rhodesians did not practice discrimination in sport: Facilities were open, competitions mixed, and Olympic teams multiracial. Where they had run afoul of the new African order was by unilaterally declaring independence from Great Britain to establish minority white rule. Rhodesia had been rejected on a technicality at Mexico City. Munich

1972 was coming up, and black Africa meant to keep the Rhodesians out of those Games as well.

Aside from the South Africa dispute, other major items on the IOC's Amsterdam agenda included the choice of host cities for 1976. For all of Brundage's dark talk about waning interest in the Olympics, eight cities had entered bids for the Games. Denver and Vancouver, along with Sion in the Swiss Alps, and Tampere, Finland's second-biggest city, coveted the 12th Olympic Winter Games; Los Angeles, Montreal, Moscow, and Florence hoped to land the 1976 Summer Games.

The United States, which would celebrate its bicentennial in 1976, was pushing hard for Los Angeles and Denver. The Angelenos had been at

The 1976 Olympic Winter Games were to have been held at Denver Organizers got as far as creating this official logo, but environmental and funding problems forced the Colorado city to return the bid.

work for almost four years, starting at Mexico City, with a high-rolling, hoopla campaign that included junkets to Acapulco and Hollywood for IOC officials, a promotional movie and glossy brochures, even a personal letter from President Richard M. Nixon to every IOC member guaranteeing that Los Angeles had the full support of the U.S. government. The Southern California Committee for the Olympic Games (SCCOG) talked up the TV coverage and how the revenues would come rolling in. What was more, the Games would be relatively inexpensive to stage, since most of the venues already existed. The organizers even predicted a profit in excess of a million dollars.

True, the U.S. political climate was tricky, with dissension over the Vietnam War and the shooting of antiwar student protesters at Kent State University. But the SCCOG figured that it could field questions on such problems, and it had hopes of a majority on the first ballot.

But the Los Angeles effort all came to naught—and because of Avery Brundage. That, anyway, is what the organizers charged. True to form, the IOC president banned the SCCOG from addressing political concerns in its presentation or in the subsequent question-and-answer period. "There will be no politics in this!" Brundage was quoted as insisting. Ironically, in his own speech Brundage chided the United States for its failures abroad and anarchic conditions at home. He opined that the Games should be played elsewhere, and he denounced the Olympics' increasing domination by the world's great powers.

Montreal won on the second ballot, with 41 of the 70 votes cast. The city's mayor, Jean Drapeau, wept for joy at the result.

Denver salvaged something for the U.S. That city's organizers explained that 80 percent of the necessary facilities already existed in their winter sports capital—with 100,000 beds available for visitors—and told how the University of Denver could easily serve as an Olympic Village for 2,500 athletes. The city would, to be sure, build a 5,000-seat speed-skating rink and a 20,000-seat ice hockey and figure-skating coliseum. The Denverites foresaw no crippling expenditure and believed that financing would come easily, since the Olympics would help commemorate both the U.S. bicentennial and Colorado's 100 years of statehood. The IOC awarded Denver the 12th Olympic Winter Games on the third ballot by a vote of 38-30 over Sion.

Both Montreal and Denver would have a tremendous stake in what kind of deal they could cut with the TV networks. No one misunderstood that: The broadcasting rights to the Summer and Winter Games were coming to be the life's blood of the Olympics. Even Avery Brundage acknowledged the fact, though he lamented it. "One

should be suspicious of any amateur organization that has money," he had warned some years before. "The minute this occurs its complexion changes, and not for the better."

Television had been a factor at the Games since the birth of the industry immediately after World War II. But TV did not become big Olympic business until the mid-1960s, when the advent of satellite transmission made it possible to beam live broadcasts from anywhere on earth to anywhere else on earth. The networks and their advertisers were quick to understand the potential of the new technology—as were the organizers of the Games. In 1960 a payment of $50,000 was enough to win CBS rights to the 8th Winter Games, held at Squaw Valley; a dozen years later, those same rights went for $7,401,000 for the 11th Winter Games at Sapporo. The 1960 Rome Summer Games cost CBS $394,000—Munich 1972 set ABC back $13,500,000. In another

dozen years the dollar amounts would climb into the hundreds of millions.

No wonder everybody wanted a slice of this fabulous pie. No wonder the IOC found itself increasingly involved in the negotiations and acting ever more like a corporate parent. Under a complicated formula worked out in 1966, the IOC expected the city organizing committee to retain about 60 percent of the revenue, sharing the remaining 40 percent with the national Olympic committees, or NOCs, and the international federations (IFs) responsible for regulating the various sports.

The ink was not yet dry on the agreement before the shouting and shoving began. Because they governed all the sports that made up the Olympics, the IFs demanded one-third of all TV monies, and they kept pressing their claim without cease. The NOCs, meanwhile, argued that the IFs, precisely because they were technical overseers, had no direct claim to Olympic TV

ABC technicians make the Games a global television venture at Mexico City 1968. Fees for television rights would become the prime subsidy for the Olympic movement for years to come.

funds at all; rather, the NOCs, the IOC, and the city organizing committees should have the whole bundle to themselves. As for the IOC, its leaders soon realized what a cash infusion could do for their small, unsophisticated headquarters operation in Lausanne. More than a few members agreed with West Germany's Georg von Opel when he suggested that "one person at the Lausanne office should do nothing but secure money for the IOC."

That would be some years away. However, in 1967 the IOC established a Finance Commission to oversee the Lausanne office and to work with the organizing committees of Olympic host cities in maximizing TV income. As it happened, both the Munich and Sapporo committees had their own ideas about making the most of TV, and those ideas stunned their partners. The 1966 revenue-sharing agreement allocated shares on the basis of "broadcast rights"—which the IOC, NOCs, and IFs assumed would be the sum total of TV money. Not at all, said the Munich and Sapporo organizers. When the Munich negotiators signed their $13.5-million deal with ABC, they allocated only $7.5 million as money to be shared for broadcast rights; the remaining $6 million belonged to Munich alone as payment for facilities provided to the network. As for the Japanese, they allocated $5 million of their $7.4 million for rights and planned to keep the rest.

The aggrieved IOC put such pressure on the Sapporo organizers that they eventually consented to share the whole $7.4 million. But Munich held its ground, even when Lord Luke, chairman of the IOC Finance Commission, sternly advised the Germans that "this attitude is not conducive to the best of goodwill between us." In the end, the IOC capitulated—thereby setting a damaging precedent for future negotiations with organizing committees.

Observing all this, a distressed and disillusioned Avery Brundage had by the end of the XIX Olympiad fallen back to his original position.

"The IOC should have nothing to do with money," he told the Executive Board just before his retirement in 1972. Nor was the IOC, said Brundage, in the least way obligated to support either the NOCs or the IFs; let them fend for themselves. And let the host cities have all the TV revenues. Then let them take on the responsibility of funding the IOC's budget during the four years of each Olympiad.

The idea was wholly unrealistic, and the IOC plunged deeper into commerce—until by 1974 it was deriving more than 98 percent of its income from television.

Citius, altius, fortius—"swifter, higher, stronger." Brundage would have rejected as unthinkable any suggestion that the Olympics' Latin credo itself had contributed to another of the IOC's difficulties. Yet that exhortation, coupled with the visceral human need to excel, encouraged certain athletes to grasp whatever it took for victory. And among the means to an end were performance-enhancing substances. In a word, drugs. Dope.

The problem had been around since the beginning of the Games. The ancient Greek physicians Galen and Phylostratus reported that Olympians in the third century BC commonly used certain herbs and mushrooms to improve their capabilities. In the modern era, nitroglycerine, sugar cubes dipped in ether, and brandy laced with strychnine compounds were the stimulants of choice among early swimmers, boxers, cyclists, and track and field competitors. At St. Louis 1904, America's Thomas Hicks so souped up his central nervous system with strychnine that he won the marathon by 6 minutes—then fell into a life-threatening stupor that required the urgent attention of four doctors. Half a century later, at Oslo, officials were alarmed to find a litter of broken amphetamine ampules and syringes in the dressing rooms of the speed skaters.

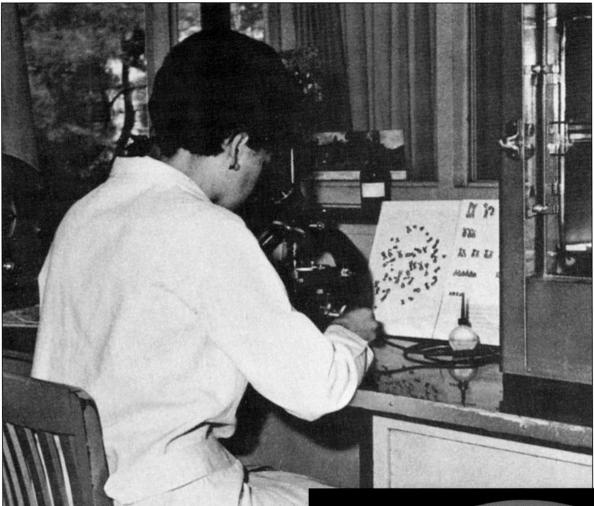

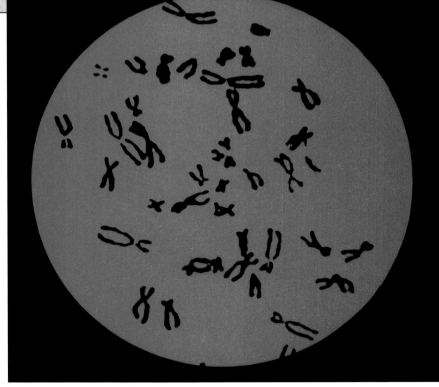

A lab technician checks an athlete's buccal sample for signs of gender anomaly. In years to come, mannishness in female athletes would invariably prove to result from the use of anabolic steroids, not from chromosomal peculiarities.

A microphoto of a female buccal smear shows normal chromosome configuration. To date, no female athlete has ever failed the Olympic gender tests.

But neither the IOC, nor the NOCs, nor the regulatory international federations did much about drugs until after the 1960 Olympics in Rome. There, in a senseless tragedy, Danish cyclist Kurt Enemark Jensen collapsed and died after his trainer dosed him with amphetamines and nicotinic acid. That brought action, of a sort: In 1961, the IOC established a Medical Commission to study the drug problem; the next year it passed a resolution condemning doping; and in 1963 it published a list of proscribed drugs. These included fatigue-blocking, euphoria-inducing amphetamines, stimulants such as strychnine and various analeptic substances, along with pain-killing narcotics such as morphine and methadone. Alcohol also was banned for what appeared to be obvious reasons.

Yet it was not until 1968, at Grenoble and then a few months later at Mexico City, that officials actually started testing. The delay stemmed partly

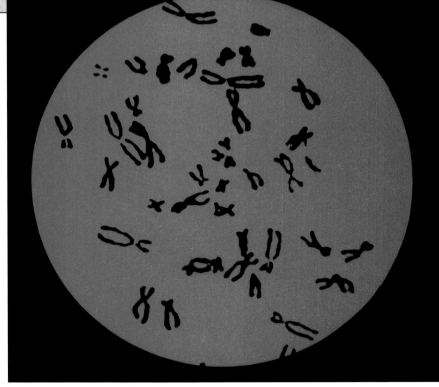

Jim Thorpe keeps his eye on the ball during spring training for the New York Giants in 1916. A contract with a minor league club several years earlier caused Thorpe to lose the decathlon and pentathlon gold medals he'd won at Stockholm 1912. The great Native American athlete was one of the earliest Olympians to run afoul of IOC amateurism regulations.

from the IOC's determination to act only in a supervisory capacity. It wanted none of the expense and responsibility for drug testing and enforcement; these must remain with the IFs and the host-city organizing committees. "It was never, never, never intended that the IOC itself should take the responsibility for testing seven or eight thousand competitors," insisted Avery Brundage. "We are not equipped for that sort of an operation, ignoring the expense involved."

To assert control meant devising test procedures, discovering which would work for which drugs, and making judgments about exceptions. Marksmen had long used minute quantities of alcohol to steady their aim; were they to be disqualified for that? The answer was yes. Jim Ryun, the world's premier miler, suffered from hay fever and mild asthma, for which his doctor occasionally prescribed antihistamines. Was he to be barred? That answer was no, although he would have to take a substitute medication.

Then there was what the IOC's Medical Commission quaintly termed "femininity control." The commissioners rejected the idea of putting hundreds of young women through an embarrassing anatomical exam—which would have been inconclusive anyway. Because of the caprice of nature, certain individuals might appear to be female but because of chromosomal abnormalities have a more masculine muscle development and thus a competitive advantage. To be absolutely fair, the Medical Commission decided to test for chromosomal imbalance—just once per athlete—and award certificates to everyone verified female positive. Women who had given birth were exempt.

At Grenoble 50 young women were selected at random. They all tested female. The number of tests reached 803 at Mexico City, with the same result. The drug testing, which involved urinalysis along with blood work in some cases, produced equally heartening results. Of 86 samples tested in a prototype program at Grenoble, none showed evidence of prohibited drugs. Testing on a wide scale began at Mexico City, with checks on the top six finishers plus four others chosen at random in selected events. Only one of the 995 samples tested positive for drugs, and at Sapporo 1972 there was but one positive test among 192 samples. Indeed, only one athlete at either Games was disqualified: a Swedish pentathlete whose blood showed traces of alcohol. The Swedes protested vigorously, but to no avail.

The outcome led some officials to suggest that the mere threat of getting caught had dramatically reduced drug use. That conclusion was as naive as it was optimistic. A lot of athletes simply had not been caught. Sometime later, a U.S. weight lifter who had been at Mexico City admitted that he and most of his friends popped amphetamines for that extra competitive punch. "What ban?" he asked coolly. "Everyone used a new one from West Germany. They couldn't pick it up on the test they were using. When they get a test for that one, we'll find something else. It's like cops and robbers."

Insidious as they were, drugs weren't the matter uppermost in Avery Brundage's mind. Olympism was. For Brundage, every subject, every problem, must sooner or later be weighed on the scales of the sacred Olympic ideal as he interpreted it. He liked to proclaim that "the amateur code, coming to us from antiquity, embraces the highest moral laws. No philosophy, no religion, preaches loftier sentiments." The amateur competing "for the love of game" was a person of freedom and dignity, whereas professionals were nothing more than "trained seals" in "a branch of the entertainment business."

Brundage's reference to antiquity held a truth he might not have cared to examine too closely. For the term "amateur" was unknown to the ancient Greeks. The code of the earliest Games was that of the aristocracy; only the high-born had the leisure for sport, and if they eschewed material gain, it was because they could afford to. But that singular state of affairs soon passed. With the growing influence of the Greek merchant class the Games opened up, until by 600 BC the pursuit of Olympic excellence was a major civic endeavor. The victorious athlete might come away from Olympia with nothing more than an olive wreath caressing his brow. But back home he was deluged with honors and monetary rewards. One scholar calculated that a victory at Olympia was worth the equivalent of $330,000 cash to an Athenian athlete, and other Greek cities undoubtedly followed suit.

Brundage ignored not only ancient truths but more recent ones as well: Baron Pierre de Coubertin—founder of the modern Games and a great believer that sport should be for everyone, not just the wealthy—had never been a hard-liner on the question of amateurism. Coubertin's interest in having an Olympic amateur rule lay mainly with his desire to keep the Games free of the brutality and corruption that were rife in the professional sports of his time and to distance the Olympics from the shady practice, common in his day, of hiring ringers to compete on teams that were supposed to be amateur.

But blind to both historic circumstance and fiscal reality, Brundage—the self-made millionaire—gave his whole heart to the credo that professionalism in any form would never sully his Olympic temple. "Sport is recreation," he said. "It is a pastime or a diversion, it is play, it is action for amusement—it is the opposite of work." If his version of amateurism meant that only the wealthy could afford the time and training necessary to play on an Olympic level, then so be it.

The list of Olympians who came to grief on the rocks of such Olympic rectitude was a distinguished one. At Stockholm 1912, the great Jim Thorpe, to some minds the finest all-around athlete ever to represent the U.S., won both the pentathlon and decathlon—only to have to relinquish his medals because in 1909 and 1910 he had played minor league pro baseball for a few dollars a game in North Carolina. Many observers felt that Thorpe's gravest error was playing under his own name. Paavo Nurmi at least knew what he was doing. The legendary Finnish distance runner, holder of nine Olympic golds, had a reputation for milking expense money from sponsors of track meets. The practice caught up with him when he was barred from the Los Angeles 1932 Games. Those Games saw the debut of 18-year-old Babe Didriksen, a sort of Thorpe among women, the first of America's great female track and field stars. A few weeks after her three-medal Olympic performance, she lost her amateur standing when she turned up with a shiny red Dodge coupe after burbling about the car in an ad. Officialdom harrumphed and relented when she swore that she had bought the coupe and had never agreed to the plug; the ad men were charlatans, everybody concurred. Didriksen said she was delighted at the reinstatement—and went pro a day or two later.

One of the curiosities of the crusade for Olympic purity was that the battles all seemed to be fought in the capitalist West. When the Soviet Union joined the Olympic movement in 1952, it brought with it an avowed philosophy of state-subsidized athletics, while blandly insisting that there were no professionals in the USSR. Looking at things through a different lens, Westerners might conclude that there were no amateurs.

The preparation for Olympic championships began with coordination tests for Soviet tykes in the first grade. Likely candidates went to one of 17 "youth sports schools," where, like Roman gladiators of yore, the children were raised to do one thing only—compete. They ate special diets, soaked up what the coaches told them, and practiced endlessly with the finest equipment. That went on for 10 years before the kids entered college, usually as physical education majors programmed for more of the same. Those who made it to the top enjoyed rare privileges: well-paying dummy jobs, nice apartments and exclusive places to shop, fashionable vacations on the Black Sea, a chance to travel abroad, and even personal cars.

In 1960 a Soviet hockey star whose touring team was trouncing U.S. collegians explained that he was a lieutenant in the Red Army—but he reported to the Defense Ministry for only a couple of hours two or three times a week. The rest of the time he was free to practice—or loaf. Had he been an enlisted man, he added, he

The elaborate sports systems of Eastern bloc countries prompted the IOC to reexamine its amateurism code. Socialist regimes often provided gymnasts such as Natalya Kuchinskaya with nonexistent jobs, leaving them free to train full time.

would not have needed to report at all. More-over, victory—Communist style—had its capital-ist rewards: The Soviets made no secret of the fact that members of Moscow's Dynamos soccer team got 10,000 rubles after a successful tour of the British Isles.

All evidence pointed to much the same thing throughout the Communist bloc. But Avery Brundage turned a blind eye to it. He returned from a 1954 tour of the USSR exulting that the Soviets were creating "the greatest mass army of athletes the world has ever known." There were four million specialists in track and field alone, he enthused. And all of them amateurs? a reporter asked. Brundage replied that the Sovi-ets had assured him of their belief in and re-spect for Olympic rules; they had denied all al-legations of phony jobs, year-round training, cash prizes, or other inducements. "In my long trip," he said, "I saw nothing that would make me question those statements."

The disciple of Olympism was no fool. In his defense, Brundage's allies explained that the universality of the Games was the higher issue; just as the IOC president championed South Africa as a member of the family, so he wrapped his arms around Communist Eastern Europe. If creating a truly catholic Olympism meant that Brundage saw only what he wanted to see, it was hardly the first time.

The cost of this willful blindness would eventu-ally include a Canadian boycott of Olympic ice hockey. The rugged northerners had invented the modern game in the 1850s and supplied just about every player in the North American pro-fessional leagues. Therein lay the problem. While Canadian pros were the class of the world, they could not compete under the Olympic rules governing amateur status. Canada could be rep-resented only by squads of college and club play-ers. In Europe, however, the line between profes-sional and amateur was fuzzy at best, and it disappeared altogether behind the Iron Curtain.

That rankled the Canadians—particularly since they had not won an Olympic gold medal in hockey since Helsinki 1952—to the point where they decided to sit out the Sapporo Games in 1972.

Meanwhile, Brundage continued his quixotic struggle against shamateurism on the Western side of the world. For years, ever-increasing numbers of top-flight Western athletes, nominal amateurs, had demanded compensation either in cash or in kind. Wes Santee, the world's fastest miler in the mid-1950s, got between $250 and $800 in "expenses" per track meet, plus posh ho-tel accommodations, rental cars, and free meals in fancy restaurants. The AAU, which at the time allowed $15 in expense money per day, revoked Santee's amateur standing when officials learned that he had collected $10,000 in 1955 alone. The unrepentant Santee said that, given the chance, he would do it all over again.

By Rome 1960 the shamateurism situation had reached the stage where André Chassaignon, a French sports magazine editor, penned a stinging column aimed at Brundage. Under the title "The Olympic Flag Is the Symbol of a Lie," Chas-saignon wrote: "The man who delivers the Olympic oath in Rome will lie in the name of every athlete in the world. Nearly all of the so-called Olympic 'amateurs' in the world today are not amateurs at all, but hypocritical profession-als!" Chassaignon went on to relate the Alexan-dre Dumas parable of one Gorneflot, who during Lent had a rabbit baptized as a carp in order not to break the rules of abstinence. "Monsieur Brundage plays the role of Gorneflot," jibed Chassaignon. "He sits down at his table before a rabbit stew and says, 'My, what a delicious carp.'"

Brundage sued for defamation of character. A French court awarded him damages of $200.

The same year, Olympism took another body blow when a pair of feuding Bavarian shoemak-ers launched what came to be celebrated as "The Shoe Wars." The Dassler brothers, Adolf and

Rudolf, had once been partners. But they had learned to detest each other, Adolf splitting off to found Adidas, Rudolf to start up Puma. Both were successful and both promoted their lines by dispensing free shoes to athletes. Then Rudolf fancied up his footwork at the Rome Games by offering cash and a piece of the action to Germany's Armin Hary, world-record holder in the 100 meters. Being a sensible young man, Hary stepped out of his Adidas and streaked to victory in a pair of Pumas.

Adolf had to retaliate. By Tokyo 1964, the bidding sounded like a tobacco auction—and the current fastest human, America's Bob Hayes, got a laugh out of shopping back and forth until Adidas agreed to a cash payment of $7,800, plus $1,100 for a wardrobe of silk suits that Hayes had his eye on. "All that," chuckled the sprinter, "for wearing the shoes I had been planning to run in all along."

Four years later, at Mexico City, a gag going around the Olympic Village defined an inferiority complex as the athlete who had not been offered money by either Adidas or Puma. One opportunistic star bargained his way to $10,000; another got $6,000; payments of $500 and $1,000 were routine. Overall, something like 200 track and field athletes collected an estimated $100,000 from Adidas and Puma, not to mention $350,000 worth of free shoes and other gear passed out during the Olympic year.

Adidas wound up shoeing 85 percent of the Olympic track and field medalists, but at such cost that the company fell into the red. Thus after the Games, Horst Dassler, Adolf's son and top lieutenant, went to see Avery Brundage. Horst told all and asked what to do. The IOC president said that yes, he had heard about the payoffs, but all would soon be put right: The International Amateur Athletic Federation, governing body of track and field, was about to approve a plan whereby only unrecognizable all-white or neutral shoes would be permitted

A CHÂTEAU TO CALL HOME

Baron Pierre de Coubertin, founder of the modern Olympic movement, had always loved Lausanne. Well-ordered and serene, the lovely Swiss city reminded him in some ways of Olympia, Greece. Moreover, neutral Switzerland was home to the international peace movement and the International Red Cross, whose pacifist aims he so admired. There were also more personal reasons for his attachment: His mentally troubled daughter needed the care of medical specialists in Switzerland.

So it was that in 1915, when Lausanne offered a home for the Coubertins and office space for his Olympic endeavors, he was quick to accept. The family moved into the villa of Mon Repos, which, by virtue of Coubertin's presence, also became the headquarters of the International Olympic Committee.

The IOC was a tiny entity in Coubertin's day, but by the 1960s its growing bureaucracy required more space than Mon Repos could provide. In 1966 the mayor of St. Gallen, Switzerland, offered to provide a larger space. Lausanne, wanting to keep its prestigious tenant, countered by offering the Château de Vidy (*above*), an 18th-century mansion on the shores of Lake Leman, as a new headquarters. The IOC accepted and operated out of the mansion until 1993, when there was renewed pressure to expand. A modern office annex was built on the grounds next to the château, but the gracious old home continues to house the president's office.

for important competitions. Brundage had indeed proposed the plan, but it would die in committee. The Shoe Wars would escalate for another decade.

Shoes were one thing, but skis were something else altogether. Among Olympic sports, Alpine skiing enjoyed by far the greatest international cachet and commercial potential. People went skiing wherever there were hills and a little snow. It was a thrilling pastime, and its stars were demigods. Could there be any doubt that the purveyors of equipment, the national ministries of tourism—the whole multibillion-dollar enterprise—would see a gold mine in the Olympics? Inevitably the industry winked amorously at the athletes. Inevitably the athletes winked back.

Before the Winter Games at Grenoble in 1968, Avery Brundage buttonholed Colonel Marceau Crespin, France's minister of sports. "I hear that half the skiers on the French team don't live up to our definition of amateurism," Brundage accused. "Is that true?" "You have been misinformed, Monsieur," Crespin haughtily replied. "No one on the French ski team lives up to your definition."

If Brundage thought the colonel was kidding, he soon knew different. The hero of Grenoble was France's Jean-Claude Killy, a 24-year-old "customs inspector" who swept all three men's Alpine events—downhill, slalom, giant slalom. After each victory, Killy shamelessly shilled for the skis that carried him to victory. Brundage was deeply offended, and more so when the press reported that Killy had received $7,000 from *Paris Match* magazine for an exclusive picture story, that another deal got him a snappy orange Porsche, and that overall, Jean-Claude knocked down $75,000 a year from endorsements, personal appearances, and the like. (Irony of ironies, the IOC would in 1995 elect Killy an IOC member.)

For a week or so, the Fédération Internationale de Ski (FIS) mumbled unhappily about looking into Killy's amateur standing. But nobody was going to dethrone France's Olympic champion—not when he swore that there was no truth in the *Paris Match* story and when his grandparents insisted that they had given him the Porsche. All parties said what rules forced them to say. And the appalling hypocrisy of it all led *Le Monde*, France's most influential newspaper, to suggest that the FIS take another look at its regulations—"otherwise it isn't one skier who should be disqualified but all the actors in the white circus."

Avery Brundage had precisely that in mind when he arrived at Sapporo four years later. By then the commercialization of the Alpine events so infuriated the 84-year-old IOC chief that he meant to cap his tenure as president by cleansing the sport of its shamateurs. Rumor had it that he carried evidence condemning 48 skiers for being on manufacturers' payrolls. He announced at a news conference that he would not tolerate brazen violations of the Olympic code. But he named no names, and it became apparent that whatever he knew to be true, he was having a hard time proving it.

It might have ended there had not Karl Schranz handed Brundage a bullet for the pistol he was brandishing. At 33, Schranz was the quintessential poor-boy-made-good, an Austrian peasant's son whose brilliance on skis had won him three World Cup championships—plus a resort hotel, plus $50,000 a year in cash subsidies. All he needed to complete his success was an Olympic gold medal at Sapporo.

But Schranz had strong thoughts about Avery Brundage's passion for Olympic probity, and he made the mistake of sharing them with a reporter. "If Mr. Brundage had been as poor as I was and as poor as many other athletes, I wonder if he wouldn't have had a different attitude," mused Schranz. "If we followed Mr. Brundage's recommendations to their true end, then the

Officials tell Austria's Karl Schranz that he's been barred from competing at Sapporo 1972. Sacrificing Schranz as a highly visible scapegoat of money-soaked Alpine skiing didn't fully satisfy Avery Brundage, who was so disgusted by the sport's commercialism that he threatened to abolish the Olympic Winter Games.

Olympics would be a competition only for the very rich." Schranz went on to heap scorn on amateur purity as "something that dates back to the 19th century when amateur sportsmen were regarded as gentlemen and everyone else was an outcast. The Olympics should be a competition of skill and strength and speed and no more."

Splashed across the papers, those sentiments were construed as a direct challenge not only to Brundage but to the IOC itself. Schranz, in Brundage's words, had confessed himself to be a "blatant and verbose offender," and worse, a man "disrespectful of the Olympic movement." A bare quorum of the IOC was present in Sapporo for the Session just prior to the Games. And while Avery Brundage might not be able to do anything about the scores of athletes accepting money under the table, he certainly could slap down the contemptuous Mr. Schranz. Three days before the opening ceremonies of the 11th Olympic Winter Games, the IOC voted 28 to 14 to disqualify Karl Schranz from competition.

The decision would cast a pall over Sapporo and solve nothing. Shamateurism would continue to plague the Olympic movement until the IOC under new leadership at last faced up to reality some years later.

SPLENDOR IN SAPPORO

The exuberance of youth and the majesty of tradition were the twin themes of the opening ceremony of Asia's first Olympic Winter Games. Festivities began when Japan's emperor Hirohito, heir to 14 centuries of monarchy, entered Sapporo's Makomanai Speed-Skating Rink with his empress, to be greeted by a 21-gun salute. As Hirohito settled into his box, national flags of countries taking part in the Games were raised around the stadium. The Parade of Nations followed, with more than 1,000 competitors from 35 countries marching onto the infield. IOC president Avery Brundage and Kogoro Uemura, president of the Sapporo organizing committee, welcomed visitors, and the emperor declared the Games open. A blast from trumpets announced the raising of the Olympic flag. A second fanfare signaled the entrance of children from Grenoble, France—host city for the previous Winter Games—who exchanged greetings with a delegation of boys and girls from Sapporo. As the children exited the infield, the Olympic torch reached the stadium. Izumi Tsujimara, a Sapporo schoolgirl dressed in white and wearing ice skates (left), glided with the fire three-quarters of a lap around the rink, then handed it off to Hideki Takada, a 16-year-old Sapporo student. Silence enveloped the stadium as Takada bounded up a flight of 103 stairs. Cheers shattered the quiet as Takada ignited a blaze in the Olympic cauldron. Hundreds of elementary-school children holding balloons skated into the stadium, slowly inscribing three circles on the ice around the national delegations. After Keiichi Suzuki, a speed skater, took the athlete's oath and Fumino Aaki the oath for judges, the children released their balloons. The tiny spheres lofted lazily upward, and fireworks blazed across the blue sky as the athletes filed out of the stadium.

THROUGH THE LOOKING GLASS

Every enterprise worth pursuing has its risks—the nightmares that haunt sleep and jolt the waking hours. For the organizers of the Olympic Winter Games, the perpetual torment is snow. What if the weather gods somehow fail to decree enough snow? What if they exhale a succession of warm zephyrs? The runs are patchy, the officials distraught, the athletes and fans morose.

But dreams were sweet at Sapporo in January of 1972. A satisfying succession of storm fronts swept across Hokkaido, the northernmost of the Japanese islands, garbing its capital city in sparkling white and making a delight of the ski jumps, the Nordic courses, the downhill and slalom runs. The snows continued into the contests themselves.

Thick flakes fell during the morning of February 3 when the hour arrived for the first speed-skating event, the 5,000 meters. But here the snow brought no smiles to the faces of Holland's Ard Schenk and his fellow competitors. Unlike other winter athletes, speed skaters abhorred snow; clear ice was essential to their sport. The 400-meter oval at the Makomanai Speed-Skating Rink was open to the elements, and snow meant a slow rink.

Schenk was particularly concerned. Massive and handsome, with a shock of blond hair and cobalt blue eyes, the 27-year-old Dutch racer lived in his compatriots' hearts as a sort of modern-day Hans Brinker, he of the fabled silver skates. Schenk had glided on stage as a strapping 19-year-old in 1964 when he won the overall national speed-skating title. Two years later, the Flying Dutchman, as he naturally was called, won the European championships in Deventer, Holland, to such wild enthusiasm that the town's cafés remained open to celebrants throughout the night. That same year Schenk set world records at 1,500 meters and 3,000 meters. He had to settle for a second-place silver in the 1,500 meters at the Grenoble Olympic Winter Games in 1968. But he had reigned supreme as world champion since

Ard Schenk, Olympic Gold Medalist, Sapporo 1972

1970 and presently held six records for distances from 1,000 to 10,000 meters. At Sapporo, Schenk had entered four events: the 500, 1,500, 5,000, and 10,000 meters. Everybody looked forward to a virtuoso performance in both the sprints and the endurance races.

Yet the snow and the luck of the draw worked against Holland's hero: The flake-filmed ice was certain to cut Schenk's speed. Equally bad, the pairings for the 5,000 had him and another skater racing first; there would be nothing, no earlier times, to pace themselves against. And if the weather improved and the ice could be kept clear, Schenk would be at a grave disadvantage as later skaters on a cleaner course assaulted his time.

The snow was coming down in curtains as Schenk drove off the mark, mighty thighs thrusting, a veiled figure easily outdistancing his competitor around the oval. He had no choice but to skate as fast as he could without fading at the finish. The one favorable factor, the experts noted, was a virtual absence of wind. Even so, the slow ice had its effect. A groan went up when the electronic timers caught Schenk's time and flashed it to the scoreboard: 7 minutes 23.61 seconds, almost 12 miserable seconds off his world mark.

That did not look at all good when the snow ended and mechanical sweepers managed at last to polish the ice to a mirror finish. But then the weather demons called down another hex: The

Lanterns illuminate the shops of Sapporo's Tanuki Koji, or Raccoon-Dog Alley. In Japanese folklore, the Tanuki is an impish little character with a fondness for sake. His name supplied an ironic touch to a new shopping district, replete with bars, built with Olympic tourists in mind.

Japanese artists Kazumi Yagi and Ikko Tanaka created the design for the square Sapporo winners' medals. The yin-yang curve down the front represents the flux of ice and snow that make winter sport possible. The medal's reverse uses the official emblems of the Sapporo Games: a rising sun, a snowflake, and the Olympic rings.

wind came up, and the times climbed with it as bedeviled skaters fought through the blasts.

Racing in the final pair was Kees Verkerk, Schenk's teammate, good friend, and archrival. As Verkerk set out, the wind reached such force that it snuffed out any contest. The best Verkerk could manage for 5,000 meters was 7:39.17—and the laurels belonged to Ard Schenk. After accepting his first Olympic gold, the victor faced the usual crush of reporters, one of whom could scarcely wait to ask about his slow time and how he felt about not breaking the Olympic record. "I don't even know what the Olympic record is," smiled the Dutch giant. "All that is important is this gold medal."

There might easily have been three more of those prized medallions, save for a mishap in the 500-meter sprint. Powering off the line after a false gun had aborted the initial start, Schenk had taken only four strides when his skate blade caught on the ice, sending him sprawling on his stomach. He was up in a flash. Yet in a burst-to-the-wire race like the 500, he had no chance and finished 34th among 38 competitors. But Holland's champion made up for it handsomely in the next few days. With cool mastery, he captured the 1,500 meters in an Olympic-record 2:02.96 and then set his sights on the 10,000 meters.

Unlike the 5,000, where he had to sweat it out while everybody took a shot at his time, Schenk now skated last. When his turn came, he knew that the man to beat was Kees Verkerk. His old friend had posted an Olympic-record 15:04.70 for the 10,000. But on this day, Ard Schenk had it all, long legs gracefully stroking down the straights, a picture of precision through the turns, pacing himself through the 25 circuits. At the finish the timers caught him in 15:01.35, nearly 4 seconds ahead of Verkerk—and 22.35 seconds better than the Olympic record.

The little band of Netherlanders at Makomanai joyfully turned their orange woolen hats and scarves into fluttering victory banners. They took off their traditional wooden shoes and clacked them together in noisy unison. To the cacophony of his compatriots and 50,000 others jamming the stadium, young Ard Schenk entered the pantheon of Olympic gods, one of only six men ever to claim three gold medals in a single Winter Games.

The men's speed-skating competition had run true to expectations, and the women's would, too. But so much else would go awry at Sapporo that *Newsweek* would term the 11th Olympic Winter Games an "Alice-in-Wonderland" spectacle, all topsy-turvy "as though viewed through a shifting, distorting looking glass." Through this glass would be seen the superb Austrians languishing without a

A snow sculpture of Jonathan Swift's Gulliver, as gigantic to tourists as he must have been to the Lilliputians, welcomes spectators to Sapporo.

ART IN SNOW AND ICE

Ordinarily, winter in Sapporo means short days, long, cold nights—and little or no activity until springtime. But the last part of that pattern began changing in 1950 when a group of students, bored by enforced hibernation, began making extravagant snow sculptures as a diversion. The snow art was such a hit with townspeople that the city began sponsoring an annual event in February called the Sapporo Snow Festival. The Japanese debated its value as high culture, but Olympic organizers nevertheless saw it as a perfect element to incorporate into the Sapporo Arts Festival that was held in conjunction with the Games. Running from January 25 to February 13, the cultural program was a colorful blend of old and new Japan. Ten snow sculptures were featured, the most impressive of them a giant rendering of Lemuel Gulliver, the peripatetic hero of Jonathan Swift's 18th-century satire. The gelid Gulliver, situated in Sapporo's Odori Park, was surrounded by scale models of each Olympic venue. Smaller snow figures focused attention on the Ainu, the aboriginal people of Sapporo's island of Hokkaido. Ainu groups also gave song and dance recitals, allowing audiences a rare view of life in Japan's northernmost reaches. More classically, Kabuki and Noh performances represented ancient, traditional Japanese theater. An exhibition of ukiyo-e prints, works that champion common folk, offered a unique genre of Japanese painting seldom seen by international audiences.

Like the ice sculpture that relieved the tedium of restless students some 20 years before, the cultural program armed visitors against the cold and dark and helped them enjoy wintertime in Sapporo.

Noh plays were a classical element in the Sapporo Arts Festival. Noh drama began in the 14th century. Characteristically, it features a sparse stage set, peopled by actors whose songs and dances tell a story of salvation through Buddhism.

single gold in Alpine skiing. There grieved the French, yearning to repeat the 1968 triumphs of Grenoble triple-medalist Jean-Claude Killy. They, like the Austrians, would mine no gold on the Alpine slopes this year. Instead, the Swiss would dominate those slopes, along with the Italians and a gritty young American. The Spaniards would have their day as well, when a 21-year-old from Seville would ski out of nowhere to win his country's first gold medal in any Winter Olympics.

Surprise would follow surprise. No Asian had ever won a medal in the winter events—until Japan's ski jumpers took wing like Hokkaido's famed sea eagles. Scandinavians had long dominated the punishing cross-country Nordic events, but now a band of tireless Soviet men and women would challenge for world primacy. As usual, the precision-made USSR ice hockey team would skate off with the gold; but at Sapporo, for the first time in several Winter Games, the Soviets would have to fight and even spill a little blood to do it. As for figure skating, the losers would be such winners for their freestyle artistry, as opposed to the dreary compulsory figures, that officials would at last be encouraged to amend their method of scoring. Sapporo 1972 would even offer a tangled love story to heighten the drama.

Then there was the city itself. Compared with many previous sites of the Winter Games, Sapporo seemed an unlikely Olympic host. The place was no charming Chamonix or Lake Placid nestled among the peaks, but a sprawling industrial metropolis of more than a million people, neon-lit by night and gray by day from the grit of factory stacks. Yet to the Japanese, the chance to play host represented a rebirth of faith. In 1940 Sapporo was to host the Winter Games, but Japan was then on the point of joining the Axis powers in World War II, and the peaceful festival of sport was a casualty of war. Now, 32 years later, all Sapporo was determined to make a triumph of this second chance.

The city had spent six years and an astronomical $688 million in preparation. If the organizers had not quite moved mountains, they certainly had carved a few into shape. On 4,327-foot Mt. Eniwa, 15 miles south of the city, an army of 15,000 men with 800 bulldozers and six tons of explosives invaded a nature preserve to hew a pair of downhill runs out of the forest; once the Olympics were over, that same army would return to tear down the stands and ski lifts and replant the runs with their former cloak of beech, birch, and evergreen. A set of spectacular runs for the slalom races was scooped out of 3,356-foot Mt. Teine, seven miles west of Sapporo. The men's giant slalom alone required the removal of more than 425,000 cubic feet of rock, most of it carried out on human backs. As on Mt. Eniwa, the facilities were scheduled to be dismantled and the land restored to nature after the Games.

For the jumping events, Sapporo's organizers built a 70-meter hill with stands for 24,000 spectators in a forest a few miles outside town. Next they went to work on an existing 90-meter jump that had never been exactly right: Winds blowing upslope produced performance-robbing eddies of air along the jumpers' flight path. No problem. Engineers merely moved the whole jump 30 feet forward, dug it down 21 feet into the mountainside, and shifted its axis 3 degrees 35 minutes to the north. That, plus excavating an area for 50,000 fans, required the manipulation of 8.5 million cubic feet of earth. But the results were magnificent.

Made of bronze, the Sapporo commemorative medals were designed by Japanese artist Shigeo Fukuda. A meandering arrow represents the human body in motion. The reverse of the medal displays the Sapporo Games icons.

THE GAMES AT A GLANCE

	FEBRUARY 3	FEBRUARY 4	FEBRUARY 5	FEBRUARY 6	FEBRUARY 7	FEBRUARY 8	FEBRUARY 9	FEBRUARY 10	FEBRUARY 11	FEBRUARY 12	FEBRUARY 13
OPENING CEREMONY	■										
ALPINE SKIING			■		■	■		■	■	■	■
BIATHLON								■		■	
BOBSLED		■	■						■	■	
FIGURE SKATING		■	■	■	■	■	■		■		
HOCKEY	■	■	■	■	■	■	■			■	■
LUGE		■	■		■		■				
NORDIC SKIING		■	■	■	■		■	■		■	■
SKI JUMPING				■					■		
SPEED SKATING		■	■	■	■		■	■	■	■	
CLOSING CEREMONY											■

In Sapporo itself, a complex of 28 new facilities took form, including ultramodern arenas, press centers, living quarters, and other Olympic structures, all connected by a new rapid transit system whispering along on rubber wheels. Across the Makomanai River from the giant speed-skating oval stood the indoor rink, a vast mushroom-shaped building where 12,000 spectators could enjoy ice hockey and figure skating. In the Olympic Village the athletes could refresh themselves by burrowing into an enzyme ion bath of fermenting cedar sawdust—and choose from menus offering everything from milk shakes and burgers to such local delicacies as fried squid and hairy crab.

The only gripes were about the cramped rooms built to Japanese, not Western, dimensions. Nor did anybody have nice things to say about a sense of decorum so powerful that the men's dorms were separated from the women's by barbed wire and patrolling guards. But the Sapporo organizers were determined to avoid the slightest problem—to the point of backing up their $12-million computer system with a team of six abacus champions. And all in all, they had gotten it splendidly right.

As the February 3 opening day approached, the city and its environs fairly twanged with enthusiasm and energy. Fresh snow was heaved off Sapporo's streets almost as soon as it fell, while on Olympic slopes and jumps a battalion of 3,500 soldiers tamped down the new fall with their combat boots. The 700 cleaning women responsible for the various Olympic buildings took a solemn oath to "carry out our internationally important duty," and taxi company officials visited Shinto shrines to beseech the deities to keep Sapporo's kamikaze-style drivers out of accidents. At City Hall a corps of interpreters manned a switchboard 12 hours a day to assist visitors in English, German, French, Russian, and Spanish. YOKOSO—"Welcome!"—proclaimed the huge banners festooning the city. No one could doubt that Sapporo meant it from the heart.

With Avery Brundage at their side, Emperor Hirohito and Empress Nagako presided over the opening ceremony—1,355 athletes from 35 nations marching in a kaleidoscope of color around the infield of Makomanai Stadium, where the Olympic flame burned brightly in its cauldron. The only departure from custom was a decision to forgo the usual mass release of pigeons: The Japanese organizers, thoughtful as always, feared that the birds might mar the glassy surface of the ice. Then it was on with the Winter Games.

They may as well carve Annie's name on the gold medal right now," advised U.S. speed-skating coach Ed Rudolph. "Unless she breaks a leg or gets the measles, she simply cannot lose the 500." As far as her mentor was concerned, 16-year-old Anne Henning had a lock on the 500-meter sprint.

The curly-haired blonde teenager from Northbrook, Illinois, never traveled anywhere without her bedraggled Snoopy doll and figured that God's gift to degustation was peanut butter. "Everything I am today I owe to Snoopy and peanut butter," she giggled to a reporter just before the Games. But, young as Anne Henning was, no woman in the world could muster the intense speed that she delivered in the 500. At a pre-Olympic warm-up meet in Switzerland, Henning had bettered her own world record with a clocking of 42.5. The next day she clipped 0.4 of a second off the 1:26.9 world record for 1,000 meters.

Olympic decorations dot the streets of downtown Sapporo. The city adopted the slogan *Yokoso,* Japanese for "Welcome," as part of its campaign to make Sapporo a congenial Winter Games host. The word was ubiquitous along the city's avenues and at Olympic venues.

WHERE THE GAMES WERE PLAYED

Makomanai Indoor Skating Rink

Makomanai Speed-Skating Rink

Mt. Teine Luge Course

Hideki Takada, a figure skater, raises his torch in a salute after igniting the fire in the Olympic cauldron. Torches lit from the fire kindled at Olympia were relayed along three different routes through Japan, then unified in a rite at Odori Park a day before the opening ceremony. The Japanese relay runners carried torches that were 25-inch-long stainless steel shafts in holders designed as miniatures of the cauldron.

All of this made Coach Rudolph extremely proud, for he had been training Henning since she was 10. A landscape contractor who coached as a hobby, Rudolph recalled thinking that Henning had a genius for competition the first time he spied her on skates. "I saw nothing but gold medals dancing before my eyes," he said. "She was born for it."

Nor was Henning Coach Rudolph's only discovery. No fewer than five members of the U.S. Olympic speed-skating team in 1972 were from little Northbrook (population 27,000), and the three women among them were veterans of Rudolph's program. One of the three was 20-year-old Dianne Holum, who had made her auspicious debut at 16 at Grenoble, tying for second in the 500 and taking the bronze at 1,000 meters. As intense as Henning was sunny, Holum had subsequently fallen out with Rudolph and spent most of the year training with the Dutch in Holland. At Sapporo she had entered the 1,000, 1,500, and 3,000 meters, while Henning concentrated on the 500 and 1,000.

Holum's turn came first, in the 1,500 meters on Wednesday, February 9. Of all the women's distances, the metric mile was regarded as the most demanding, both because it was just long enough to be exhausting and because European skaters so thoroughly dominated it. As the pairings would have it, Holum was matched against the Soviet Union's Nina Statkevitch, the current world champion. But Holum jumped away to a split-second start that gave her a stride before Statkevitch even got off the line. "Come on, baby. Come on, baby," bellowed Dianne's father from the stands each time his daughter swept past. And come on she did, in a flawlessly paced race that put her ahead at the finish by 2.34 seconds in an Olympic-record 2:20.85. No one could beat that time, though Holland's Christina Baas-Kaiser, an ageless 33-year-old, came within 0.2 of a second. Northbrook, and the United States, had their first gold of the Winter Games.

More came the next day, when Anne Henning made a prophet of her coach in the 500 meters. Yet it was one of those desperate occasions when only a true champion's strength and poise forestalls calamity. Henning was paired with an 18-year-old Canadian named Sylvia Burka, who was blind in her left eye and thus lacked normal peripheral vision. In time, Burka would win stardom for herself, but at Sapporo she was notable

Crouched for a finishing kick, the Netherlands' Christina Baas-Kaiser sprints for the wire in the 3,000-meter race. Baas-Kaiser led the powerful Dutch women's team that won five of the 12 medals on offer.

Exhausted from a winning effort, America's Anne Henning coasts after crossing the finish line. Henning's time in the 500-meter race was more than half a second faster than that of the second-place finisher, yet well short of her own world record.

for almost scuttling Henning's chances. Starting in the outside lane, Henning was overtaking Burka and was about to reach the crossover point where she could take the inner lane. The right-of-way was hers. But the Canadian didn't see her and didn't yield.

Henning straightened up from her racing crouch and dragged a skate to avoid collision, losing at least a second. Many competitors would have given up, but Henning settled back down, raced past Burka, powered around the final turn, and flashed across the finish line to a thunderclap of applause. Time: 43.73, a little more than a second off her world record but still better than the Olympic standard by 1.27 seconds. It was a stunning performance by any measure. But because she had been fouled, Henning was given another chance to race. Thinking of what might have been, Coach Rudolph urged her to take it—a mistake that likely cost his star a

second gold. While Henning shaved 0.4 of a second from her Olympic mark in the 500, she so spent herself that the best she could manage, on pure heart, was a bronze in the 1,000 meters the next day.

As for Dianne Holum, she finished a disappointed sixth in the 1,000. But two days later she came back to earn a silver in the grueling 3,000 meters, second only to Holland's venerable Christina Baas-Kaiser, who took the gold with an Olympic-record 4:52.14. The two Americans went home from Sapporo with four medals between them—exactly half the total won by the entire 131-member U.S. team. In Northbrook, the Chamber of Commerce ordered new stationery engraved "Speed-skating Capital of the World."

If the weather wasn't always kind to the speed skaters, it was the Alpine skiers at Sapporo who suffered the real storms—none meteorological, and most swirling around Karl Schranz. The great skier's ejection from the Olympics had turned him into a martyr—for his fans, if not especially for his colleagues. Austria's minister of education called for the country's entire Olympic team to return home in protest. When it declined, enraged Schranz partisans threatened to burn the home and kill the children of Karl Heinz Klee, president of the Austrian ski federation. But if Schranz's admirers were furious, his teammates were not. Longtime hero Toni Sailer put the issue in perspective. "The public does not think clearly," observed Austria's triple-winner at Cortina 1956. "Our skiers have trained for years to win a medal. They're not going to give up the chance now."

Particularly not for Karl Schranz, Sailer might have added. The world champion came across as aloof and disdainful of lesser mortals. Besides, he was a schussing advertisement for Kneissl skis, while most of his erstwhile teammates peddled Atomic and other brands. One morning after the storm hit, Annemarie Pröll, the 18-year-old prodigy favored to win at least two of the three women's Alpine events, encountered Schranz at breakfast. "It's your affair, not mine," she informed him. "I have to think of myself." Later, Pröll told newsmen: "How can they

speak of solidarity when Schranz has never contributed any solidarity to the Austrian team."

For window dressing, the man in the eye of the storm held a press conference at which he earnestly pleaded for the team to remain in Sapporo and carry on. The exhortation was laughably superfluous, since his teammates had left two hours earlier for Mt. Eniwa, there to polish their form for the downhill races. After meeting the press, Schranz himself emplaned for Vienna, where he was welcomed by the greatest demonstration to rock the city since the end of World War II—200,000 Viennese chanting their devotion. Hawkers worked the crowd doing a tidy business in Schranz autographs at 25 schillings (about $1) apiece—every one of them a fake.

Schranz's disqualification crushed Austrian hopes in the men's Alpine events, but everybody still looked for Annemarie Pröll to win the women's downhill and giant slalom, and maybe

Thousands of Austrians cheer Karl Schranz *(waving from car)* **as police escort him through the streets of Vienna. Schranz's endorsement of Kneissl ski products got him expelled from Sapporo 1972 for professionalism.**

BIATHLON BRILLIANCE

Fog descended on the Makomanai biathlon course the morning of the 20-kilometer individual race, temporarily scuttling a competition in which visibility is all-important: Biathletes must stop four times at a firing range during their long trek and take five shots at targets 150 meters away. The shooting is done twice from a standing position and twice while prone. Each miss adds a minute's penalty to a shooter's skiing time. In thick fog, obviously, accurate marksmanship is almost impossible, so at Sapporo the event had to be postponed for a day.

But the weather was perfect on February 8, and 54 competitors from 14 nations slogged through the staggered starts that began at 8:30 a.m. The Soviet Union's favored Aleksandr Tikhonov was foiled by poor shooting: He was the second-fastest skier, but four missed targets pushed him into fourth place. The gold went to Norway's Magnar Solberg (above), a Trondheim policeman, who won the individual title for the second consecutive Winter Games. Solberg had only the fourth-fastest time, but his marksmanship gave him the winning edge.

even the slalom. One of seven children in a farm family living at the head of an Alpine valley, she had grown up skiing down the mountain to school, then climbing back up after classes. In summer she tended the fields and animals, cranking the heavy reel used to haul hay bales up the steep slopes. She grew into a very strong 150-pounder, 5 feet 6 inches tall, and as aggressive as she was muscular: In competition she attacked the course with an élan that bordered on ferocity.

Going into Sapporo, Pröll had won four of the five major downhill races thus far in the season and had seen the three Frenchwomen who were her toughest competitors fall victim to injuries. Moreover, the relatively short, steep Mt. Eniwa course so ideally suited her blitzing style that ski fans took to calling it Pröll Boulevard. Still, there were reports that the Schranz affair had undercut her concentration; a rumor even had her confiding to a friend, "Maybe once, I will not win."

There was a further complication over coaching. Pröll's old tutor and confidant, Karl Kahr, had been sacked as the Austrian women's coach for spending too much time with his star at the expense of the other team members. Kahr now worked for the British. But at Sapporo, Pröll was with him constantly. She even had him apply the critical coat of speed-enhancing wax to her skis just before the downhill. Skiers wax differently for different conditions, and Kahr was uncomfortable. "Every day it is snowing," he said. "The downhill is slow. The snow temperature is cold but the humidity is high, so it will be very difficult to wax."

On Mt. Eniwa that afternoon, Pröll looked unbeatable as she blazed down the course, her body tucked into its powerful crouch, her instincts picking the perfect line. Finishing in a spray of snow, she looked up at the scoreboard—and her eyes widened in horror. The lights flashed 1:37.0, impressive for the conditions. But Pröll was .032 of a second slower than Switzerland's Marie-Theres Nadig, a chunky, happy-go-lucky

A tight turn on the giant slalom course helps Austria's Annemarie Pröll to another impressive run. Pröll's two Olympic campaigns were disappointing compared to the rest of her career. She would win 17 World Cup titles before retiring in 1980, but would win only one gold medal in two Olympic Winter Games.

17-year-old who had never before won a major race. The impossible had happened. Pröll had lost, and Austrians immediately started howling for Kahr's scalp. Obviously, criminally, he had chosen the wrong wax. Pröll herself was so overwhelmed that she refused to attend the usual postrace press conference. "You must forgive her," said a sympathetic fan. "She has learned how to win, and now she must learn how to lose. And remember, she is only a child."

Three days later, in the giant slalom on Mt. Teine, the child goddess absorbed another lesson in humility. Again she raced flawlessly, conquering wind-driven snow and poor visibility to twist through the 51 gates along the 1,240-meter course in a fine 1:30.75. And again Marie-Theres Nadig negotiated the same conditions a little faster—by almost a full second this time, in 1:29.90. Another gold for Switzerland, another silver for Austria.

The remarkable Nadig might have made it three for three had she not fallen in the slalom when the skiers returned to Mt. Teine. But that did Annemarie Pröll little good. By now the Austrian was so demoralized that the best she could manage was a distant fifth. The theatrics focused on France and the United States, on

17-year-old Danièlle Debernard and 21-year-old Barbara Cochran.

Cochran belonged to a family that was, by American standards, a skiing dynasty. Under the tutelage of father Mickey, a high-school coach in Vermont, the three oldest Cochran children—Marilyn, 22, Barbara, 21, and Bobby, 20—had developed into world-class competitors and strong members of the U.S. ski team. (A younger sister, Linda, would compete at Lake

Celebratory Swiss carry on their shoulders a new national heroine, young Marie-Theres Nadig. Lightly regarded before Sapporo, Nadig surprised the field in two of the Alpine specialties.

Skiers speeding down Mt. Eniwa could catch a glimpse of Lake Shikotsu. Mt. Eniwa, site for the downhill races, is an active volcano located in Shikotsu-Toya National Park, 22 miles north of Sapporo. After the Games, the course was dismantled and the mountain restored to its natural state.

Placid 1980.) Marilyn had a tough run in the downhill, finishing 28th, and Bobby, suffering from a bad ankle, hit a gate and went down in the slalom. That left it up to Barbara, a shy, diminutive blonde whose technical proficiency needed only a bit more "punch or pizzazz," as her coach, Hank Tauber, put it.

Evidently finding the pizzazz, Barbara Cochran got off an excellent first run of 46.05 seconds, weaving down the 52-gate, 450-meter course with verve and precision. But so did Danièlle Debernard, who was scarcely .03 of a second slower. On the second run, Cochran clocked an even better 45:19. Then came Debernard, slashing through the gates, the flagsticks plucking at her arms and hips, attacking furiously. Up on the scoreboard went her time: 45:18—great, but not quite great enough.

With whoops, screams, and tears of joy, family and friends leaped the barrier to hoist Barbara Cochran onto their shoulders. The first ski-racing gold for an American in 20 years was hers by the margin of .02 of a second, closest in Olympic history.

French hopes rose again in the men's downhill. With the departure of Karl Schranz, the experts were divided between two favorites, Henri Duvillard of France and Switzerland's Bernhard Russi. The Alpine events were becoming a matter of national honor for France, and now the French, being French, decided to gamble, while the Swiss, being Swiss, did not. The oddsmaker was the weather: Ordinarily, racers like to ski early in the competition when the course is still fresh, but new snow was forecast for race day. French strategists thought the advantage would go to those who raced later, after the new snow had been packed down a bit. Thus they placed Duvillard among their lower-seed racers, to whom race officials accord later starts. Duvillard ended up skiing 27th among the 55 competitors.

The Swiss shrugged off the reports of snow and went about their methodical preparations, studying the slopes, testing for humidity, checking air and snow temperatures, and mixing their wax accordingly. Bernhard Russi, listed among the top Swiss seeds, drew the No. 4 starting position.

It didn't snow. Russi attacked the steep hill, encountering near the top a sharp, precipitous turn, the sort of place the Japanese called "a steep where even the bears fall down." But Russi had been brought up tending goats in rugged Alpine pastures. He zipped through the perilous turn and shot on down the mountain, controlling the rolls and gullies, leaping the bumps, his speed approaching 80 miles per hour on some of the 40-degree gradients. His time of 1:51.43

Switzerland's Bernhard Russi is airborne and in control on the Mt. Eniwa downhill course. Swiss skiing officials made an in-depth study of Sapporo's mountains and snowfall patterns to make their skiers the best prepared at the Winter Games.

Leaning into a turn, Spain's Francisco Ochoa works the slalom course on Mt. Teine. Spain, hardly a winter playground, ended a lengthy Winter Olympic medal drought at Sapporo.

easily won him the gold over teammate Roland Collombin and Austria's Heinrich Messner. For Duvillard there was only disaster. Fighting the chopped-up course, he finished 19th, nearly 4 seconds behind the champion.

The French met further disappointment in both the slaloms—not that they were favored to win. The world's top-ranked slalomist was Italy's 20-year-old Gustavo Thöni, a small, wiry Tyrolean customs guard with remarkable neuromuscular coordination. Toni Sailer called him "the greatest natural skier today, one of the greatest of all time." In 1971 Thöni had won the first of four consecutive World Cups, yet there were those who regarded France's Jean-Noël Augert as nearly his equal. The experts picked Augert for silvers in both the giant slalom and slalom. With a little luck, he might do better.

But in the giant slalom, Thöni proved invincible. Zigzagging down Mt. Teine, he mastered the two steepest courses in Olympic history, each 1,100 meters long with vertical drops of 400 meters. There were 63 gates on the first run, 66 on the second. Thöni breezed through them with a combined time of 3:09.62, his closest competitor 1.13 seconds behind. That was Switzerland's Edmund Bruggmann, followed by Werner Mattle of Sweden. The shining French hope, Jean-Noël Augert, had to fight for fifth, more than 2 seconds back.

Nor was that the end of the hard times for France. Practicing the slalom, Augert jabbed a ski pole into his ribs with such force that he had to be taped and injected with novocaine for the final. Skiing with brilliance and courage, he posted the second-best time for the 530-meter, 71-gate course on his first run, but then faded to an exhausted and pain-racked fifth on his second try. Gustavo Thöni and his cousin Roland Thöni took second and third. And the winner? That was probably the single greatest surprise of these topsy-turvy Games.

Francisco Fernandez Ochoa had never finished higher than sixth in an international meet. But the 21-year-old Spaniard, whose father ran a skiing school north of Madrid, had been training with the French and gradually climbing in the rankings. He was gaining confidence as well, and had written his mother from Sapporo: "Mama, pray not for me but for you. I will win and for you it is very emotional. So pray for your own strength."

On his first run, Ochoa angled through the gates in 55.36 seconds, half a second better than Augert. Then the Spaniard added a run of 53.91 on the second course, only .32 of a second slower than the hard-charging Gustavo Thöni. Together, Ochoa's times were good enough to defeat Thöni by better than a second. Emotional

reactions of the winner's mother are not recorded, but the winner himself was nearly delirious. "I can't believe it," he kept saying, as he capered madly in the snow. "It can't be true."

After Ochoa, still other untouted athletes erected monuments to themselves at Sapporo, this time in the ski jumps. Scandinavians had virtually owned ski jumping since the first Winter Games at Chamonix in 1924. The Norwegians alone had won 17 of 30 medals in the 90-meter large hill jump, and the Swedes and Finns had sailed off with almost all the rest. Austrians and Czechs became factors at Innsbruck 1964 with the inauguration of a 70-meter small hill event. But no one had ever regarded the Japanese as world-class jumpers—until Sapporo 1972.

As in so much else, the hosts of the 11th Winter Games had prepared with care. Japanese athletes had soaked up every European technique and worked industriously to put the pieces together. Their ace jumper, 28-year-old Yukio Kasaya, had practiced the 70-meter jump countless times in the winter of 1971-72 before going off to win three European meets in a row one month before Sapporo.

At the hour of the 70 meters on the fourth day of competition, city streets throughout the home islands emptied of traffic; all Japan, it seemed, found TV sets to watch as one Japanese jumper after another came speeding down the approach slope to soar above the gasping spectators. Here and there cries of "Banzai!" went up when the distances were announced: 82.5 meters (270 feet 6 inches) for Akitsugu Konno, 83.5 meters (274 feet) for Seiji Aochi—then 84 meters (275 feet 6 inches) for Yukio Kasaya. With outstanding second jumps, stylish as well as long, Japan's athletes swept all three medals: Kasaya, Konno, Aochi. The closest European was Norway's Ingolf Monk, after a pair of 78-meter (256-foot) efforts—and he found a sportsmanlike way to celebrate Japan's first Winter Olympics victory. With a wide grin, the big Norwegian reached down and hoisted

Yukio Kasaya up onto his shoulder to the roaring approval of 40,000 fans.

A number of experts had seen the Japanese triumph coming. But no one had the least inkling that five days later a callow 19-year-old Polish youth named Wojciech Fortuna would trounce all comers on the 90-meter large hill.

This was one of those wonderful moments in sport, as with Bob Beamon's miracle jump at Mexico City 1968, when everything goes just right. Thrusting off into the approach, racing down the slope to loft up and away, Fortuna jumped 111 meters (364 feet 2 ½ inches), 4 meters (13 feet 2 inches) better than his closest rival, farther than any Olympian had ever jumped, farther than anyone would jump until Lake Placid 1980.

The remainder of the 11th Olympic Winter Games—the Nordic cross-country skiing, the sled races, ice hockey, and figure skating—might best be characterized as demonstrations of Soviet and East German prowess.

That had not always been so in the Nordic events. Since the first steel-limbed athletes poled silently into the forests surrounding Chamonix 48 years before, Scandinavian men had captured 82 of 93 cross-country medals, including 29 of

Stretching beyond the tips of his skis, Poland's Wojciech Fortuna soars off the 90-meter hill. An exceptional first jump made him a gold medalist in spite of a mediocre second try.

Czechoslovakian team badges *(left and center)* and souvenir pins were among the collectibles bought and traded at Sapporo 1972.

the 31 golds. Their only real rivals, the Soviets, had won only eight medals, one gold. The women's competition, dating from 1952, was less lopsided: 17 medals, six of them gold, going to the Scandinavians, and 16, including five golds, for the Soviets. But then a massive Soviet training program paid off. Soviet skiers carried off the 1970 Nordic world championships, and at Sapporo they cemented their hold on the sport.

Their first victor was Vyacheslav Vedinine, 31, a tenacious little man whose difficult life had equipped him for the trials of long-distance skiing. Born in a tiny Russian village and orphaned by World War II, Vedinine had done heavy farm work as a youngster to keep himself alive. Only about 5 feet 4 inches tall, he was as tough as he was small, and by 1970 he had become the world champion of Nordic skiing. Rival Swedish skiers sniffed that his sole profession was "ski-runner." But, professional or not, on the opening day of competition in Sapporo, Vedinine glided across 30 kilometers of hills and valleys in little more than an hour and a half to defeat a pair of towering Norwegians by almost a minute. A few days later, one of those Norwegians, Pål Tyldum, came back to take Vedinine's measure at 50 kilometers, and there were further cheers in Scandinavia when Sweden's Sven-Ake Lundbäck won the 15 kilometers, practically sprinting the distance in 45:28.24.

But then came the 4 x 10-kilometer relay and another Soviet triumph. Racing the final leg, Vedinine started out 61.5 seconds behind Norway's anchorman. The situation seemed all but hopeless—like being behind 10-0 in the third period of a hockey match. Nevertheless, the Soviet ace caught his opponent a kilometer from the finish and surged ahead to win by 9.12 seconds.

Socialist skiers had still more to cheer about in the classic Nordic combined—a 15-kilometer cross-country followed by a jump from the 70-meter hill. The gold medalist there was an unheralded 19-year-old East German named Ulhrich Wehling, who outclassed 40 of his elders by placing third in the cross-country and fourth in the jump. Some observers were inclined to shrug off the outcome as a fluke, but no one at Sapporo had worked harder for his championship: Training for the event, young Wehling had skied something like 2,500 miles and sailed off 850 jumps. A classic product of the G.D.R. sport system, reared from childhood to excel in his sport, Wehling would take part in two more Olympics and win two more golds, one in 1976 and the other in 1980.

In the women's competition, the only question was the order in which Soviet skiers would collect their medals. As it turned out, Galina Kulakova, a 29-year-old physical education teacher, carried off all the gold by winning both the 5- and 10-kilometer races, then anchoring the victorious 3 x 5-kilometer relay team. That gave the Communist bloc six of the eight Nordic championships and bragging rights in the most arduous of winter sports.

Things briefly brightened for the West in the bobsled competition. Bobs had been on the Olympic program almost from the beginning, first with five-man teams, then with two- and four-man squads rocketing down a twisting, icy chute on sleds that had brakes—but only for stopping at the end of a run. Braking during the run itself meant immediate disqualification. In the years since World War II, the class of the

The massed start of the women's 3 x 5-kilometer relay marked the last chance to break the Soviet march to the victory podium. Soviet women claimed top honors in all three women's Nordic events.

The Soviet Union's Galina Kulakova cuts through a fresh layer of snow on the 10-kilometer course en route to the most impressive of her three championships at Sapporo. Kulakova beat the second-place finisher by 36 seconds.

Powerful strides propel the
diminutive Vyacheslav
Vedinine along Sapporo's
30-kilometer cross-country
course. Vedinine was the
first Soviet man to win an
individual Nordic skiing
gold medal.

breakneck field had been the Swiss and the Italians. Teams from those countries would indeed finish one-two in the four-man bobs at Sapporo, while West Germans would take the bronze and then race away from the field with both the gold and silver in the two-man sleds.

But the Eastern bloc would hurtle to the fore again in the luge contests. These events—considered insane by sensible people—featured toboggan-like steel frames on which the contestants—"sliders" in popular parlance—careened down the course feet first, steering with their feet and shoulders. Luge had been on the Olympic program since 1964, and since then all but two of the 18 medals had gone to German-speaking athletes. Sapporo was no different. East Germany's men swept the singles competition, then followed with the gold

The four-man Switzerland I team gets off to a good start on its way to winning the bobsled competition. Switzerland II had the best times in the final two runs, but a disastrous first run kept it out of medal contention.

138

Wolfgang Scheidel holds a perfect line as he streaks down the Mt. Teine luge course. Scheidel's consistency made him a champion of the dominant East German luge team. He finished first in three out of four runs.

(in a tie with the Italians) and the bronze in the two-man event. The East German women, however, needed to redeem themselves—not for any lack of skill, but for cheating: They had been disqualified at Grenoble 1968 for heating the runners of their single luges to make them go faster. No blowtorches were needed at Sapporo. In perfect control of their odd contraptions, Anna-Maria Müller and her East German teammates wiped out the competition one-two-three,

with only .36 of a second separating the gold from the bronze.

Sapporo's ice hockey round-robin could not be quite the same without the usual hard-skating sextet from Canada. Yet there was still more than enough action to satisfy the Japanese who jammed the Makomanai and Tsukisamu indoor arenas for 45 matches among eight finalists. Hockey, in fact, had to rate as Sapporo's

America and the Soviet Union face off in an early-round ice hockey match. Canada boycotted the Sapporo ice hockey tournament to protest the inclusion of what it regarded as a professional Soviet team.

American stamps promote U.S. participation at Sapporo 1972. The 11¢ issue at left is the first Olympic-related airmail postage ever created by the United States.

favorite Olympic sport. The crowds started lining up hours in advance and shook the walls with cries of *"Hayaku! Pasu! Izo nanniyattenno!"*— "Quick! Pass! What are you doing, stupid!"

What they were doing mainly was trying to beat up on the Soviets, winners of nine straight world championships and the last two Olympic titles. Ordinarily, Olympic hockey—all amateur hockey—is a more gentlemanly affair than the brawling professional game, with greater emphasis on smooth passing than on cross-checking an opponent into next week. But the Soviets were so experienced, so superior, that the Swedish, Czech, Finnish, Polish, German, Norwegian, and U.S. coaches decided to try a little muscle in hopes of slowing down the champions. The Japanese looked on in delight. "The players start beating and biting one another," observed one matron, "but when the game is over, they shake hands. It is exhilarating."

Actually, the well-disciplined Soviets skated away from most of the fisticuffs. Only the Swedes managed to provoke coach Anatoli Tarasov's men into a bloody fracas—and only the Swedes emerged with a 3-3 tie. "I don't know why the journalists are all excited," said Tarasov, wryly. "The Russian team did not lose." Indeed, the Soviets swept their remaining four games, concluding with a 5-2 victory over Czechoslovakia to wrap up the third Olympic gold in a row.

The silver went to the Americans, a Cinderella squad made up mostly of college boys, few of whom had played together before the Olympic training camp. No one expected such a ragtag team to finish better than fourth, and even that seemed optimistic after the Swedes shellacked the U.S. squad 5-1 in the opening match. But the Americans had going for them

youthful enthusiasm, top conditioning, and an acrobatic goalie named Mike Curran, who stopped 51 shots in an extraordinary 5-1 upset of the second-seeded Czechs. As expected, the Soviets gave the American youngsters a 7-2 hockey lesson, but there was solace enough in a 4-2 record and the best U.S. showing since a surprise gold medal at Squaw Valley 1960.

The underdog Americans won shouts of approval from the hockey-mad Japanese, but the fans at Makomanai were less enthusiastic over the outcome of the women's figure skating. The scoring system was a bafflement to most Japanese—and a sore point among many skaters and fans. It seemed nonsensical to weight equally the compulsory school figures—the tedious tracing on the ice of figure-eight variations—with the artistry and agility of the free-skating program. Initiative and daring were, after all, the soul of the sport.

Yet 50-50 was the rule at Sapporo, and it made a prohibitive favorite of 20-year-old Beatrix Schuba, a 5-foot-10-inch Austrian who could doodle near-perfect patterns with her skates, even though her free skating was so unexceptional that audiences had booed her on occasion. In the 1971 world championships, Schuba had placed next to last among 22 contestants in free skating; but by then she had such a commanding lead in the figures that she won anyway. Sapporo looked to be the same story: She emerged from the compulsories with her usual huge lead and was annoyed when a nervy newsman asked if she were worried about her free-skating deficiencies. "Never," she replied coldly. "I win the gold, I think."

The hopes of free-skating enthusiasts rested with Canada's Karen Magnussen, also 20, and America's Janet Lynn, an 18-year-old blonde

Elegant form displayed by Canada's Karen Magnussen pleased the Sapporo crowd. Magnussen's exceptional free-skate routine placed her second in the women's competition. Rule changes that reduced the impact of figures on overall scores would help her win a world championship in 1973.

pixie who, like Magnussen, had started winning national championships in her early teens. As expected, both women enchanted the fans with their sparkle and style. Despite a stumble at the start, Lynn whirled through her four-minute program with such buoyant grace that she won the free skate. Magnussen was close behind, yet neither of them had the compulsory points to overtake Schuba. The champion's

Austria's Beatrix Schuba keeps a close eye on the ice as she traces her figures. Effortless balance and a great feel for her edges contributed to Schuba's near-perfect compulsory exercises. Her expertise in the figures compensated for her uninspired free skating.

place on the podium belonged to her, with Magnussen second and Lynn third.

Something similar happened in the men's singles event. The greatest freestyle skaters in the world were two Americans, Ken Shelley and John Petkevich. But like the North American women, they couldn't match the more disciplined Europeans in the compulsories and often lagged far behind when they got to their specialty. At Sapporo, the king of the figures was Czechoslovakia's Ondrej Nepela, the reigning world champion, who had competed in his first Olympics as a 13-year-old at Innsbruck 1964. He finished 22nd out of 24 entrants then, improved to eighth at Grenoble four years later, and was now rated a cinch for the gold.

Predictably, no one could touch Nepela for precision. But both Shelley and Petkevich outclassed him in the freestyle, and the young Czech even fell during his performance. Yet he took his tumble in the noble cause of attempting a difficult jump, the triple toe loop. That sort of effort counted for a lot, and the judges awarded him a fourth in the freestyle and the gold overall. No one begrudged the decision, though many felt that Shelley and Petkevich deserved better than finishing out of the medals—fourth and fifth respectively.

But change was coming. Starting in the 1972-73 championship season, the number of compulsory figures was reduced from six to three, and the point value lowered to 40 percent. That year, Magnussen and Lynn placed one-two in the world championships; Schuba decided to retire. Nepela, who was a solid if uninspired free skater, retained his title. In time, the compulsories would be dropped altogether.

The pairs competition had never suffered the banality of routine figures, but fans were still

unhappy with the scoring. The judges seemed excessively conservative, and the Japanese often reacted with anger when the nine-person panel appeared to favor the polished East Europeans over the showier and more acrobatic Americans. "If we had skated 10 times better we still wouldn't have won a medal," complained Jojo Starbuck, who with partner Ken Shelley wowed the crowd but placed only fourth. Yet it was hard to fault the brilliant Soviet pairs: Irina Rodnina and Aleksei Ulanov won the gold, followed closely for the silver by Lyudmila Smirnova and Andrei Suraikin.

Rodnina and Ulanov had arrived at the European championships at Garmisch-Partenkirchen in 1969 when she was 19 and he 21. At the time, pairs skating had been dominated by Oleg Protopopov and his wife, Lyudmila Belousova, whose exquisite grace was reminiscent of the Bolshoi ballet. Rodnina and Ulanov could not match their elegance, so they didn't try. Instead, under

the tutelage of their famed coach, Stanislav Zhuk, the younger pair countered at Garmisch-Partenkirchen with five uninterrupted minutes of leaps, spins, lifts, and other stunts, each more complicated than the one before. This more muscular approach to pairs skating added a new dimension to the event. Judges, spectators, and the press were overwhelmed. "An inexhaustible fountain of energy"; "super-complex, cosmically ultramodern skating," said the rave reviews.

Rodnina was on her way, with Ulanov and other partners, to a nine-year rule as world and Olympic champion, a record unsurpassed in pairs skating. But she was not a kindly queen, particularly since she didn't much care for her prince consort. Poor Ulanov. He had fallen in love with his pretty, hazel-eyed partner as soon as Coach Zhuk brought them together. Irina wasn't interested. At times, early on, she skated as if Ulanov were a mere robot, a sort of mechanical appendage. Zhuk

Czechoslovakia's Ondrej Nepela attains good altitude on this camel jump. After winning the world championship in 1973, Nepela would win a rare concession for a socialist athlete: the opportunity to perform in Holiday on Ice, a professional skating revue.

Lyudmila Smirnova and
Andrei Suraikin shadow one
another perfectly during their
routine. In real life, though,
Smirnova was involved with
another partner, pairs champion Aleksei Ulanov.

quickly cured her of that. But when they were not on the ice together, Rodnina remained openly contemptuous and mocked her love-smitten partner in front of her friends at the practice rink.

Ulanov suffered through it for years. But at last, in 1972, he started dating Rodnina's rival, Lyudmila Smirnova, who, with her partner, Suraikin, stood second in the world rankings. At first the warmhearted Lyudmila went out with Aleksei just to be polite. But then love took root. Now it was Irina's turn to be upset—possibly worried about losing her partner, perhaps a little jealous, certainly quite angry.

The triangle was the chatter of Sapporo. There were the lovers, snuggling and nuzzling in public. There was Rodnina, glaring daggers at Ulanov and warming up separately on the far side of the rink. But once the music started, the pair managed to convey pure passion—a mystery and triumph of the Winter Games. They were magnificent, gaining six of the nine first-place votes. On the podium, though, they accepted victory with stone-faced stares; when Rodnina stepped down she was in tears. Time, as always, would resolve the matter. Aleksei Ulanov and Lyudmila Smirnova would get married and skate together, mainly for silver, while Rodnina and Coach Zhuk would interview literally hundreds of applicants before selecting a new foil for the frosty diva.

The 11th Olympic Winter Games came to an end on the evening of Sunday, February 13. Before an overflow crowd at Makomanai indoor rink, the 12 medal-winning figure skaters put on a final performance—after which delegations of athletes from the competing nations, this time all mixed together in a spirit of Olympic friendship, paraded into the arena amid singing, dancing, and music specially composed for the occasion. From the royal box, where he presided with Japan's crown prince and princess, Avery Brundage made a brief speech declaring the Winter Games closed. The Olympic flame that had burned for 11 days grew smaller and gradually died—"returned to the sun," as the Japanese so nicely put it. Finally, to a chorus of voices rendering the "Olympic Hymn," the five-ring banner fluttered down from its flagstaff. The hour-long ceremony was at an end. As the athletes started marching out to the strains of "Auld Lang Syne," the electronic scoreboard flashed: SAYONARA. WE MEET AGAIN IN DENVER '76.

But they would not meet again in Denver. The mile-high Colorado city would succumb to overwhelming problems and drop out as host of the 1976 Winter Games. That would be the least of the woes to come. The same bitter disputes over race, amateurism, and other divisive issues that had afflicted the XIX Olympiad would continue into the XX. And there would be worse—much worse. Within a few months the 1972 Summer Games would commence in Munich, Germany, and the festival of peace would know, for the first time, true terror.

Caught in a death spiral, Irina Rodnina swoons in the grasp of partner Aleksei Ulanov. The grace the Soviet pair displayed on the ice was a far cry from their behavior off it. Ulanov's romantic pursuit of Rodnina's skating rival, pairs silver medalist Lyudmila Smirnova, left him and Rodnina barely on speaking terms.

Australia's flagbearer marches past waving Japanese students at the closing ceremony at Sapporo. The indoor ceremony featured a TV screen so that spectators could watch the Olympic fire, still burning in its cauldron at the neighboring Makomanai Speed-Skating Rink, go out.

$\mathcal{O} \hspace{-0.5em} \mathcal{O} \hspace{-0.5em} \mathcal{O}$ APPENDIX

CALENDAR OF THE XIX OLYMPIAD

1968

SEPTEMBER 30, OCTOBER 6, 10, 15, 17, & 22	80th IOC Executive Board meeting at Mexico City
OCTOBER 3-5	13th IOC Executive Board with NOCs at Mexico City
OCTOBER 7-11	**68th Session of the IOC at Mexico City**
OCTOBER 12-27	**MEXICO CITY 1968 16th Olympic Games**

1969

FEBRUARY 1-2	81st IOC Executive Board meeting at Lausanne
MARCH 22-23	82nd IOC Executive Board meeting at Lausanne
APRIL 19	13th USOC Quadrennial meeting at the Denver Hilton Hotel, Denver, Colorado
JUNE 2-3	83rd IOC Executive Board meeting at Lausanne
JUNE 3	21st IOC Executive Board with IFs at Lausanne
JUNE 5-9	84th IOC Executive Board meeting at Warsaw
JUNE 7-9	**69th Session of the IOC at Warsaw**
AUGUST 9-16	11th World Summer Games for the Deaf at Belgrade
AUGUST 13-23	3rd South Pacific Games at Port Moresby
OCTOBER 23-27	85th IOC Executive Board meeting at Dubrovnik
OCTOBER 25-26	14th IOC Executive Board with NOCs at Dubrovnik

DECEMBER 6-13	5th South East Asian Games at Rangoon

1970

FEBRUARY 21-23	86th IOC Executive Board meeting at Lausanne
FEBRUARY 27-MARCH 14	11th Central American and Caribbean Games at Panama
APRIL 3-9	6th Winter University Games at Rovaniemi
MAY 8-10, 12-16	87th IOC Executive Board meeting at Amsterdam
MAY 9	22nd IOC Executive Board with IFs at Amsterdam
MAY 13-15	**70th Session of the IOC at Amsterdam**
JULY 16-25	9th Commonwealth Games at Edinburgh
AUGUST 13-15	2nd International Special Olympics at Chicago
AUGUST 28-SEPTEMBER 6	6th University Games at Turin
OCTOBER 3-4	88th IOC Executive Board meeting at Lausanne
DECEMBER 9-22	6th Asian Games at Bangkok

1971

JANUARY 25-29	7th World Winter Games for the Deaf at Abelboden
MARCH 13-15	89th IOC Executive Board meeting at Lausanne
JULY 16-17, 19	90th IOC Executive Board meeting at Moscow
JULY 25-AUGUST 8	6th Pan-American Games at Cali

SEPTEMBER 8-19	4th South Pacific Games at Papeete
SEPTEMBER 9	91st IOC Executive Board meeting at Munich
SEPTEMBER 10-11	15th IOC Executive Board with NOCs at Munich
SEPTEMBER 12-13, 16-17	92nd IOC Executive Board meeting at Luxemburg
SEPTEMBER 15-17	**71st Session of the IOC at Luxembourg**
OCTOBER 6-17	4th Mediterranean Games at Izimir
DECEMBER 11-18	6th South East Asian Games at Kuala-Lampur

1972

JANUARY 28	93rd IOC Executive Board meeting at Tokyo
JANUARY 28, FEBRUARY 1, & 7	94th IOC Executive Board meeting at Sapporo
JANUARY 31-FEBRUARY 1	**72nd Session of the IOC at Sapporo**
FEBRUARY 3-13	**SAPPORO 1972 11th Olympic Winter Games**
FEBRUARY 26-MARCH 5	7th Winter University Games at Lake Placid
APRIL 2-3	1st CARIFTA Games at Barbados
MAY 27-30	95th IOC Executive Board meeting at Lausanne
MAY 29	23rd IOC Executive Board with IFs at Lausanne
AUGUST 13-18	3rd International Special Olympics at Los Angeles

149

Saturday, OCTOBER 12

PM	EVENT	VENUE
1:45	**OPENING CEREMONY**	Olympic Stadium

Sunday, OCTOBER 13

AM	EVENT	VENUE
9:00	**BASKETBALL**	Sports Palace
	1st round (4 games)	
	ROWING	Rowing and Canoeing Course
	heats (all races)	
10:00	**ATHLETICS**	Olympic Stadium
	• 100 meters, heats	
	• shot put, qualifications	
	MODERN PENTATHLON	Campo Militar No. 1
	riding	
	TENNIS	Guadalajara
	preliminaries (demonstration sport)	
	VOLLEYBALL	Olympic Gymnasium
	women's (2 games)	
	WEIGHT LIFTING	Insurgentes Theater
	bantamweight	
10:30	**ATHLETICS**	Olympic Stadium
	women's javelin, qualifications	
	FIELD HOCKEY	Municipal Stadium
	preliminaries (3 games)	

PM	EVENT	VENUE
12:00	**SOCCER**	Aztec, Cuauhtémoc, Jalisco, León Stadiums
	preliminaries (4 games)	
	FIELD HOCKEY	Municipal Stadium
	preliminaries (3 games)	
2:30	**BOXING**	Arena México
	preliminary bouts	
3:00	**ATHLETICS**	Olympic Stadium
	• 400-meter hurdles, heats	
	• women's long jump, qualifications	
3:50	**ATHLETICS**	Olympic Stadium
	800 meters, heats	
4:00	**FIELD HOCKEY**	Municipal Stadium
	preliminaries (2 games)	
	WEIGHT LIFTING	Insurgentes Theater
	bantamweight	
4:30	**ATHLETICS**	Olympic Stadium
	100 meters, 2nd round	
5:00	**ATHLETICS**	Olympic Stadium
	10,000 meters, final	
	BASKETBALL	Sports Palace
	1st round (4 games)	
	VOLLEYBALL	Olympic Gymnasium
	women's (2 games)	
7:00	**BOXING**	Arena México
	preliminary bouts	

Monday, OCTOBER 14

AM	EVENT	VENUE
8:00	**MODERN PENTATHLON**	Fencing Hall
	fencing	
9:00	**BASKETBALL**	Sports Palace
	1st round (4 games)	
10:00	**ATHLETICS**	Olympic Stadium
	• women's 100 meters, heats	
	• pole vault, qualifications	
	• discus, qualifications	

	FRONTON	Chapultepec Sports Center, Lebanese Sports Center
	frontennis and paleta with rubber ball (demonstration sport)	
	TENNIS	Guadalajara
	preliminaries	
	VOLLEYBALL	Olympic Gymnasium
	women's (2 games)	
	WATER POLO	Olympic Pool
	(3 games)	
	WEIGHT LIFTING	Insurgentes Theater
	featherweight	
10:30	**FIELD HOCKEY**	Municipal Stadium
	preliminaries (3 games)	
10:40	**ATHLETICS**	Olympic Stadium
	women's 400 meters, 1st round	
11:00	**FRONTON**	Deportivo Asturiano
	handball	

PM	EVENT	VENUE
12:00	**FIELD HOCKEY**	Municipal Stadium
	preliminaries (3 games)	
1:00	**YACHTING**	Acapulco Bay
	1st race	
2:30	**BOXING**	Arena México
	preliminary bouts	
3:00	**ATHLETICS**	Olympic Stadium
	• 400-meter hurdles, semifinals	
	WATER POLO	Olympic Pool
	(3 games)	
3:30	**ATHLETICS**	Olympic Stadium
	• women's 100 meters, 2nd round	
	• shot put, final	
	• women's javelin, final	
	SOCCER	Aztec, Cuauhtémoc, Jalisco, León Stadiums
	preliminaries (4 games)	
4:00	**ATHLETICS**	Olympic Stadium
	• 100 meters, semifinals	
	• women's long jump, final	
	FIELD HOCKEY	Municipal Stadium
	preliminaries (2 games)	
	WEIGHT LIFTING	Insurgentes Theater
	featherweight	
4:20	**ATHLETICS**	Olympic Stadium
	800 meters, semifinals	
4:50	**ATHLETICS**	Olympic Stadium
	20-kilometer walk	
5:00	**ATHLETICS**	Olympic Stadium
	3,000-meter steeplechase, heats	
	BASKETBALL	Sports Palace
	1st round (4 games)	
	VOLLEYBALL	Olympic Gymnasium
	women's (2 games)	
6:00	**ATHLETICS**	Olympic Stadium
	100 meters, final	
7:00	**BOXING**	Arena México
	preliminary bouts	
	FRONTON	Frontón Metropolitano
	paleta with leather ball	

Tuesday, OCTOBER 15

AM	EVENT	VENUE
8:30	**FENCING**	Fencing Hall
	individual foil, eliminations	
9:00	**BASKETBALL**	Sports Palace
	1st round (4 games)	
	ROWING	Rowing and Canoeing Course
	repechages	

10:00	**ATHLETICS**	Olympic Stadium
	javelin, qualifications	
10:30	**ATHLETICS**	Olympic Stadium
	• women's pentathlon (80-meter hurdles; shot put)	
	• 200 meters, heats	
	CYCLING	Olympic Velodrome
	100-kilometer team time trial	
	FRONTON	Chapultepec Sports Center, Lebanese Sports Center
	frontennis and paleta with rubber ball	
	MODERN PENTATHLON	Shooting Range
	shooting	
	TENNIS	Guadalajara
	preliminaries	
	VOLLEYBALL	Olympic Gymnasium, Revolution Ice Rink
	(2 games)	
	WATER POLO	Olympic Pool
	(3 games)	
	WEIGHT LIFTING	Insurgentes Theater
	lightweight	
11:00	**FIELD HOCKEY**	Municipal Stadium
	preliminaries (2 games)	

PM	EVENT	VENUE
12:00	**VOLLEYBALL**	Olympic Gymnasium, Revolution Ice Rink
	women's (2 games)	
12:30	**FIELD HOCKEY**	Municipal Stadium
	preliminaries (2 games)	
1:00	**YACHTING**	Acapulco Bay
	2nd race	
2:30	**BOXING**	Arena México
	preliminary bouts	
3:00	**ATHLETICS**	Olympic Stadium
	• women's 100 meters, semifinals	
	• discus, final	
	WATER POLO	Olympic Pool
	(3 games)	
3:20	**ATHLETICS**	Olympic Stadium
	women's 400 meters, semifinals	
3:30	**SOCCER**	Aztec, Cuauhtémoc, Jalisco, León Stadiums
	preliminaries (4 games)	
3:40	**ATHLETICS**	Olympic Stadium
	200 meters, 2nd round	
4:00	**ATHLETICS**	Olympic Stadium
	women's pentathlon (high jump)	
	WEIGHT LIFTING	Insurgentes Theater
	lightweight	
4:10	**ATHLETICS**	Olympic Stadium
	5,000 meters, heats	
5:00	**BASKETBALL**	Sports Palace
	1st round (4 games)	
	FENCING	Fencing Hall
	individual foil, eliminations	
	VOLLEYBALL	Olympic Gymnasium, Revolution Ice Rink
	(2 games)	
5:35	**ATHLETICS**	Olympic Stadium
	400-meter hurdles, final	
5:50	**ATHLETICS**	Olympic Stadium
	women's 100 meters, final	
6:10	**ATHLETICS**	Olympic Stadium
	800 meters, final	
7:00	**BOXING**	Arena México
	preliminary bouts	
	FRONTON	Frontón Metropolitano
	paleta with leather ball	
	VOLLEYBALL	Olympic Gymnasium
	(1 game)	

Wednesday, OCTOBER 16

AM	EVENT	VENUE
8:30	**FENCING**	Fencing Hall
	individual saber, eliminations	
9:00	**BASKETBALL**	Sports Palace
	1st round (4 games)	
	FENCING	Fencing Hall
	individual foil, repechage	
10:00	**ATHLETICS**	Olympic Stadium
	• 110-meter hurdles, heats	
	• triple jump, qualifications	
	• hammer throw, qualifications	
	• women's high jump, qualifications	
	FRONTON	Deportivo Asturiano
	TENNIS	Guadalajara
	preliminaries	
	VOLLEYBALL	Olympic Gymnasium, Revolution Ice Rink
	• men's (1 game)	
	• women's (1 game)	
	WATER POLO	Olympic Pool
	(3 games)	
	WEIGHT LIFTING	Insurgentes Theater
	middleweight	
11:00	**FIELD HOCKEY**	Municipal Stadium
	preliminaries (2 games)	
	MODERN PENTATHLON	Olympic Pool
	swimming	
11:30	**ATHLETICS**	Olympic Stadium
	women's pentathlon (long jump)	

PM	EVENT	VENUE
12:00	**VOLLEYBALL**	Olympic Gymnasium, Revolution Ice Rink
	• men's (1 game)	
	• women's (1 game)	
12:30	**ATHLETICS**	Olympic Stadium
	pole vault, final	
	FIELD HOCKEY	Municipal Stadium
	preliminaries (2 games)	
1:00	**YACHTING**	Acapulco Bay
	3rd race	
2:30	**BOXING**	Arena México
	preliminary bouts	
3:00	**ATHLETICS**	Olympic Stadium
	• 110-meter hurdles, 2nd round	
	• javelin, final	
	WATER POLO	Olympic Pool
	(3 games)	
3:20	**ATHLETICS**	Olympic Stadium
	200 meters, semifinals	
3:30	**SOCCER**	Aztec, Cuauhtémoc, Jalisco, León Stadiums
	preliminaries (4 games)	
3:40	**ATHLETICS**	Olympic Stadium
	400 meters, heats	
4:00	**FENCING**	Fencing Hall
	individual saber, eliminations	
	WEIGHT LIFTING	Insurgentes Theater
	middleweight	
4:30	**ATHLETICS**	Olympic Stadium
	women's pentathlon (200 meters)	
5:00	**ATHLETICS**	Olympic Stadium
	women's 400 meters, final	
	BASKETBALL	Sports Palace
	1st round (4 games)	
	VOLLEYBALL	Olympic Gymnasium, Revolution Ice Rink
	(2 games)	
5:20	**ATHLETICS**	Olympic Stadium
	3,000-meter steeplechase, final	
5:50	**ATHLETICS**	Olympic Stadium
	200 meters, final	

7:00 **BOXING** ....Arena México
preliminary bouts
FENCING ....Fencing Hall
individual foil, final
VOLLEYBALL ....Olympic Gymnasium
(1 game)

Thursday, OCTOBER 17

AM	EVENT	VENUE

9:00 **FENCING** ....Fencing Hall
individual saber, eliminations
10:00 **ATHLETICS**.............Olympic Stadium
• women's 200 meters, heats
• women's discus,
qualifications
10:30 **ATHLETICS**.............Olympic Stadium
long jump, qualifications
FIELD HOCKEY ....Municipal Stadium
preliminaries (3 games)
11:00 **ATHLETICS**.............Olympic Stadium
women's 800 meters, heats
CYCLING ....Olympic Velodrome
4,000-meter individual pursuit,
qualifications
DIVING ....Olympic Pool
women's 3-meter springboard,
preliminaries
FRONTON ....Chapultepec Sports
Center, Lebanese Sports Center
frontennis and paleta with
rubber ball
MODERN PENTATHLON ....Campo
Militar No. 1
cross-country race
ROWING ....Rowing and
Canoeing Course
semifinals
SWIMMING ....Olympic Pool
• women's 4 x 100-meter
medley, eliminations
• 4 x 100-meter freestyle,
eliminations
TENNIS ....Guadalajara
preliminaries
VOLLEYBALL ...Olympic Gymnasium,
Revolution Ice Rink
(2 games)
WATER POLO..............Olympic Pool
(2 games)
WEIGHT LIFTING ....Insurgentes
Theater
light heavyweight
WRESTLING.......Insurgentes Ice Rink
freestyle, eliminations

PM	EVENT	VENUE

12:00 **FIELD HOCKEY** ....Municipal Stadium
preliminaries (3 games)
VOLLEYBALL ...Olympic Gymnasium,
Revolution Ice Rink
• men's (1 game)
• women's (1 game)
1:00 **YACHTING** ....Acapulco Bay
4th race
2:00 **CYCLING** ....Olympic Velodrome
• 1,000-meter individual time
trial, final
• 4,000-meter individual
pursuit, quarterfinal
2:20 **ATHLETICS**.............Olympic Stadium
50-kilometer walk
2:30 **BOXING** ....Arena México
preliminary bouts
3:00 **ATHLETICS**.............Olympic Stadium
• 110-meter hurdles, semifinals
• triple jump, final
• women's high jump, final
• hammer throw, final
3:20 **ATHLETICS**.............Olympic Stadium
400 meters, 2nd round

3:30 **SOCCER**............Aztec, Cuauhtémoc,
Jalisco, León Stadiums
preliminaries (4 matches)
WATER POLO..............Olympic Pool
(2 games)
4:00 **ATHLETICS**.............Olympic Stadium
women's 200 meters, semifinals
FIELD HOCKEY ....Municipal Stadium
preliminaries (2 games)
WEIGHT LIFTING ....Insurgentes
Theater
light heavyweight
4:20 **ATHLETICS**.............Olympic Stadium
women's 80-meter hurdles,
heats
5:00 **ATHLETICS**.............Olympic Stadium
110-meter hurdles, final
DIVING ....Olympic Pool
women's 3-meter springboard,
preliminaries
SWIMMING ....Olympic Pool
• women's 4 x 100-meter
medley, final
• women's 4 x 100-meter
freestyle, final
VOLLEYBALL ...Olympic Gymnasium,
Revolution Ice Rink
• men's (1 game)
• women's (1 game)
WRESTLING.......Insurgentes Ice Rink
freestyle, eliminations
5:20 **ATHLETICS**.............Olympic Stadium
5,000 meters, final
6:00 **ATHLETICS**.............Olympic Stadium
400 meters, semifinals
7:00 **BOXING** ....Arena México
preliminary bouts
FENCING ....Fencing Hall
individual saber, final
FRONTON .....Frontón Metropolitano
paleta with leather ball
VOLLEYBALL ....Olympic Gymnasium
(1 game)

Friday, OCTOBER 18

AM	EVENT	VENUE

8:00 **FENCING** ....Fencing Hall
team foil, eliminations
8:30 **SHOOTING**................Shooting Range
Olympic trap
9:00 **BASKETBALL**..................Sports Palace
1st round (4 games)
SHOOTING...............Shooting Range
free pistol
9:30 **EQUESTRIAN**......Avándaro Golf Club
three-day event (dressage)
10:00 **ATHLETICS**.............Olympic Stadium
1,500 meters, heats
CYCLING ....Olympic Velodrome
• sprints, heats and repechages
• 4,000-meter individual
pursuit, semifinal
SWIMMING ....Olympic Pool
• women's 100-meter freestyle,
preliminaries
• 100-meter freestyle,
preliminaries
• women's 100-meter breaststroke, preliminaries
• 100-meter breaststroke,
preliminaries
TENNIS ....Guadalajara
quarterfinals
WEIGHT LIFTING ....Insurgentes
Theater
middle heavyweight
WRESTLING.......Insurgentes Ice Rink
freestyle, eliminations
10:40 **ATHLETICS**.............Olympic Stadium
decathlon (100 meters; long
jump)

11:00 **FIELD HOCKEY** ....Municipal Stadium
preliminaries (2 games)
FRONTON ....Deportivo Asturiano
fronton handball
ROWING ....Rowing and
Canoeing Course
consolation final (7-12 places)

PM	EVENT	VENUE

12:30 **FIELD HOCKEY** ....Municipal Stadium
preliminaries (2 games)
2:00 **CYCLING** ....Olympic Velodrome
• sprints, round of 16 and
repechages
• 4,000-meter individual
pursuit, final (1-4 places)
2:30 **BOXING** ....Arena México
preliminary bouts
3:00 **ATHLETICS**.............Olympic Stadium
women's 80-meter hurdles,
semifinals
3:30 **ATHLETICS**.............Olympic Stadium
• women's 200 meters, final
• long jump, final
• women's discus, final
SOCCER............Aztec, Cuauhtémoc,
Jalisco, León Stadiums
preliminaries (4 games)
3:50 **ATHLETICS**.............Olympic Stadium
400 meters, final
4:00 **WEIGHT LIFTING** ....Insurgentes
Theater
middle heavyweight
4:20 **ATHLETICS**.............Olympic Stadium
• decathlon (shot put, high
jump)
• women's 80-meter hurdles,
final
4:40 **ATHLETICS**.............Olympic Stadium
women's 800 meters, semifinals
5:00 **BASKETBALL**..................Sports Palace
1st round (4 games)
DIVING ....Olympic Pool
women's 3-meter springboard,
final
SWIMMING ....Olympic Pool
• women's 100-meter freestyle,
semifinals
• 100-meter freestyle,
semifinals
• women's 100-meter
breaststroke, semifinals
• 100-meter breaststroke,
semifinals
WRESTLING.......Insurgentes Ice Rink
freestyle, eliminations
5:30 **FENCING** ....Fencing Hall
team foil, eliminations
6:10 **ATHLETICS**.............Olympic Stadium
decathlon (400 meters)
7:00 **BOXING** ....Arena México
preliminary bouts

Saturday, OCTOBER 19

AM	EVENT	VENUE

8:30 **FENCING** ....Fencing Hall
women's individual foil,
eliminations
SHOOTING...............Shooting Range
Olympic trap
9:00 **BASKETBALL**..................Sports Palace
1st round (4 games)
FENCING ....Fencing Hall
team foil, semifinals
SHOOTING...............Shooting Range
small-bore rifle (prone)
9:30 **EQUESTRIAN**......Avándaro Golf Club
three-day event (dressage)
10:00 **ATHLETICS**.............Olympic Stadium
women's shot put, qualifications

CYCLING ....Olympic Velodrome
• sprints, quarterfinals (1st and
2nd series); eventual belle
• 4,000-meter team pursuit,
qualification
FRONTON ....Chapultepec Sports
Center and Lebanese
Sports Center
frontennis and paleta with
rubber ball
SWIMMING ....Olympic Pool
• 200-meter individual medley,
preliminaries
• women's 400-meter freestyle,
preliminaries
TENNIS ....Guadalajara
semifinals
VOLLEYBALL ...Olympic Gymnasium,
Revolution Ice Rink
(2 games)
WATER POLO..............Olympic Pool
• (2 games)
• (3 games)
WEIGHT LIFTING ....Insurgentes
Theater
heavyweight
WRESTLING.......Insurgentes Ice Rink
freestyle, eliminations
10:40 **ATHLETICS**.............Olympic Stadium
decathlon (110-meter hurdles;
discus)
11:00 **ATHLETICS**.............Olympic Stadium
4 x 100-meter relay, heats
FIELD HOCKEY ....Municipal Stadium
preliminaries (2 games)
ROWING ....Rowing and
Canoeing Course
four-oared shell with coxswain,
finals
11:30 **ROWING** ....Rowing and
Canoeing Course
pair-oared shell without
coxswain, finals

PM	EVENT	VENUE

12:00 **ROWING** ....Rowing and
Canoeing Course
single skulls, finals
VOLLEYBALL ...Olympic Gymnasium,
Revolution Ice Rink
• men's (1 game)
• women's (1 game)
12:30 **ATHLETICS**.............Olympic Stadium
• pole vault
• high jump, qualifications
FIELD HOCKEY ....Municipal Stadium
preliminaries (2 games)
ROWING ....Rowing and
Canoeing Course
pair-oared shell with coxswain,
finals
1:00 **ROWING** ....Rowing and
Canoeing Course
four-oared shell without
coxswain, finals
YACHTING ....Acapulco Bay
5th race
1:30 **ROWING** ....Rowing and
Canoeing Course
double sculls, finals
2:00 **CYCLING** ....Olympic Velodrome
• sprints, semifinals and final
• 4,000-meter team pursuit,
quarterfinals
ROWING ....Rowing and
Canoeing Course
eight-oared shell with
coxswain, finals
2:30 **BOXING** ....Arena México
preliminary bouts
3:30 **ATHLETICS**.............Olympic Stadium
women's 4 x 100-meter relay,
heats

151

WATER POLO.............*Olympic Pool*
(2 games)

4:00 ATHLETICS.............*Olympic Stadium*
• 4 x 100-meter relay, semifinals
• decathlon (javelin)
FENCING ....*Fencing Hall*
team foil, (3-6 places)
WEIGHT LIFTING ....*Insurgentes Theater*
heavyweight

4:30 FENCING ....*Fencing Hall*
women's individual foil, eliminations

4:40 ATHLETICS.............*Olympic Stadium*
4 x 400-meter relay, heats

5:00 BASKETBALL..................*Sports Palace*
1st round (4 games)
DIVING ....*Olympic Pool*
3-meter springboard, preliminaries
SWIMMING ....*Olympic Pool*
• women's 100-meter breast-stroke, final
• 100-meter breaststroke, final
• women's 100-meter freestyle, final
• 100-meter freestyle, final
WATER POLO.............*Olympic Pool*
(2 games)
VOLLEYBALL ...*Olympic Gymnasium, Revolution Ice Rink*
• men's (1 game)
• women's (1 game)
WRESTLING.......*Insurgentes Ice Rink*
freestyle, eliminations

5:20 ATHLETICS.............*Olympic Stadium*
1,500 meters, semifinals

5:50 ATHLETICS.............*Olympic Stadium*
women's 800 meters, final

6:10 ATHLETICS.............*Olympic Stadium*
1,500 meters

7:00 BOXING ....*Arena México*
preliminary bouts
FENCING ....*Fencing Hall*
team foil, final
FRONTON .....*Frontón Metropolitano*
paleta with leather ball
VOLLEYBALL ....*Olympic Gymnasium*
(1 game)

Sunday, OCTOBER 20

AM	EVENT	VENUE

8:30 FENCING ....*Fencing Hall*
team saber, eliminations
SHOOTING...............*Shooting Range*
Olympic trap (reserve day)

9:00 BASKETBALL..................*Sports Palace*
1st round (4 games)
WATER POLO.............*Olympic Pool*
(4 games)

9:30 EQUESTRIAN......*Avándaro Golf Club*
three-day event (endurance test)

10:00 CYCLING ....*Olympic Velodrome*
• tandem, heats, repechages, quarterfinals (1st and 2nd series)
• 4,000-meter team pursuit, semifinals
DIVING ....*Olympic Pool*
3-meter springboard, preliminaries
FENCING ....*Fencing Hall*
women's individual foil, eliminations and repechage
FRONTON ....*Chapultepec Sports Center, Lebanese Sports Center*
frontennis and paleta with rubber ball

SWIMMING ....*Olympic Pool*
• women's 100-meter butterfly, preliminaries
• 100-meter butterfly, preliminaries
• women's 200-meter medley, preliminaries
TENNIS ....*Guadalajara*
final
VOLLEYBALL ...*Olympic Gymnasium, Revolution Ice Rink*
women's (2 games)
WATER POLO.............*Olympic Pool*
(1 game)
WRESTLING.......*Insurgentes Ice Rink*
freestyle, semifinals

10:30 FIELD HOCKEY ...*Municipal Stadium*
preliminaries (3 games)

11:00 FRONTON ....*Deportivo Asturiano*
fronton handball

PM	EVENT	VENUE

12:00 FIELD HOCKEY ....*Municipal Stadium*
preliminaries (3 games)
SOCCER............*Aztec, Cuauhtémoc, Jalisco, León Stadiums*
quarterfinals (4 games)
VOLLEYBALL ...*Olympic Gymnasium, Revolution Ice Rink*
(2 games)

1:00 YACHTING ....*Acapulco Bay*
6th race

2:30 ATHLETICS.............*Olympic Stadium*
high jump, final

3:00 ATHLETICS.............*Olympic Stadium*
• marathon
• women's shot put, final

3:30 ATHLETICS.............*Olympic Stadium*
1,500 meters, final
BOXING ....*Arena México*
preliminary bouts
FENCING ....*Fencing Hall*
team saber, eliminations
WATER POLO.............*Olympic Pool*
(2 games)

4:00 ATHLETICS.............*Olympic Stadium*
4 x 100-meter relay, final
FIELD HOCKEY ....*Municipal Stadium*
preliminaries (3 games)

4:30 ATHLETICS.............*Olympic Stadium*
women's 4 x 100-meter relay, final

4:50 ATHLETICS.............*Olympic Stadium*
4 x 400-meter relay, final

5:00 BASKETBALL..................*Sports Palace*
1st round (4 games)
DIVING ....*Olympic Pool*
3-meter springboard, final
SWIMMING ....*Olympic Pool*
• women's 100-meter butterfly, semifinals
• 100-meter butterfly, semifinals
• women's 200-meter medley, final
• 200-meter individual medley, final
• women's 400-meter freestyle, final
VOLLEYBALL ...*Olympic Gymnasium, Revolution Ice Rink*
(2 games)
WATER POLO.............*Olympic Pool*
(1 game)
WRESTLING.......*Insurgentes Ice Rink*
freestyle, final

7:00 BOXING ....*Arena México*
preliminary bouts
FENCING ....*Fencing Hall*
women's individual foil, final
FRONTON .....*Frontón Metropolitano*
paleta with leather ball
VOLLEYBALL ....*Olympic Gymnasium*
(1 game)

Monday, OCTOBER 21

AM	EVENT	VENUE

8:00 FENCING ....*Fencing Hall*
individual épée, eliminations

8:30 GYMNASTICS ....*National Auditorium*
women's compulsories, individual and team
SHOOTING...............*Shooting Range*
skeet (small-bore rifle, 3 positions)

10:00 CYCLING ....*Olympic Velodrome*
• tandem, semifinals and final
• 4,000-meter team pursuit, final (1-4 places)
FRONTON ....*Deportivo Asturiano*
fronton handball
SWIMMING ....*Olympic Pool*
• 4 x 200-meter freestyle relay, preliminaries
• women's 200-meter freestyle, preliminaries
• 200-meter breaststroke, preliminaries
• 100-meter backstroke, preliminaries
VOLLEYBALL ...*Olympic Gymnasium, Revolution Ice Rink*
• men's (1 game)
• women's (1 game)
WATER POLO.............*Olympic Pool*
• (1 game)
• (3 games)

10:30 FIELD HOCKEY ....*Municipal Stadium*
preliminaries (3 games)

11:00 FENCING ....*Fencing Hall*
team saber, semifinals

PM	EVENT	VENUE

12:00 FIELD HOCKEY ....*Municipal Stadium*
preliminaries (3 games)
VOLLEYBALL ...*Olympic Gymnasium, Revolution Ice Rink*
(2 games)

1:00 EQUESTRIAN......*Avándaro Golf Club*
jumping test
YACHTING ....*Acapulco Bay*
7th race

2:30 BOXING ....*Arena México*
preliminary bouts

3:30 WATER POLO.............*Olympic Pool*
(2 games)

4:00 FENCING ....*Fencing Hall*
• individual épée, eliminations and repechage
• team saber, 3-6 places
FIELD HOCKEY ....*Municipal Stadium*
preliminaries (2 games)

5:00 GYMNASTICS ....*National Auditorium*
women's compulsories, individual and team
SWIMMING ....*Olympic Pool*
• 100-meter backstroke, semifinals
• 100-meter butterfly, final
• women's 100-meter butterfly, final
• 4 x 200-meter freestyle relay, final
VOLLEYBALL ...*Olympic Gymnasium, Revolution Ice Rink*
• men's (1 game)
• women's (1 game)
WATER POLO.............*Olympic Pool*
(2 games)

7:00 BOXING ....*Arena México*
preliminary bouts
FENCING ....*Fencing Hall*
team saber, final
VOLLEYBALL ....*Olympic Gymnasium*
(1 game)

8:30 FRONTON ....*Frontón México*
jai alai

Tuesday, OCTOBER 22

AM	EVENT	VENUE

8:30 GYMNASTICS ....*National Auditorium*
compulsories, individual and team
SHOOTING...............*Shooting Range*
• rapid-fire pistol, 1st round
• skeet

9:00 BASKETBALL..................*Sports Palace*
semifinals (4 games, 9-16 places)
CANOEING ....*Rowing and Canoeing Course*
heats (all 7 events)
WATER POLO.............*Olympic Pool*
(4 games)

10:00 FENCING ....*Fencing Hall*
individual épée, eliminations and repechage
FRONTON ....*Chapultepec Sports Center, Lebanese Sports Center*
frontennis and paleta with rubber ball
SWIMMING ....*Olympic Pool*
• women's 100-meter back-stroke, preliminaries
• 400-meter medley, preliminaries
• women's 200-meter breaststroke, preliminaries
• women's 800-meter freestyle, preliminaries
• 400-meter freestyle, preliminaries

PM	EVENT	VENUE

2:30 BOXING ....*Arena México*
quarterfinals

3:30 SOCCER ....*Aztec, Jalisco Stadiums*
semifinals (2 games)
WATER POLO.............*Olympic Pool*
(2 games)

5:00 BASKETBALL..................*Sports Palace*
semifinals (4 games, 1-8 places)
DIVING ....*Olympic Pool*
women's high dive, preliminaries
SWIMMING ....*Olympic Pool*
• women's 100-meter backstroke, semifinals
• 100-meter backstroke, final
• women's 200-meter freestyle, final
• 200-meter breaststroke, final
FENCING ....*Fencing Hall*
women's foil, team, direct eliminatories of quarterfinals
GYMNASTICS ....*National Auditorium*
compulsories, individual and team

7:00 BOXING ....*Arena México*
quarterfinals
FENCING ....*Fencing Hall*
individual épée, final
FRONTON .....*Frontón Metropolitano*
paleta with leather ball

Wednesday, OCTOBER 23

AM	EVENT	VENUE

8:30 FENCING ....*Fencing Hall*
women's team foil, eliminations
GYMNASTICS ....*National Auditorium*
women's optional exercises, individual and team
SHOOTING...............*Shooting Range*
• free rifle, 3 positions
• rapid-fire pistol, 2nd round
• skeet (reserve day)

9:00 CYCLING ....*Olympic Velodrome*
individual road race

Time	Event	Venue
10:00	**Canoeing** ....*Rowing and Canoeing Course* repechages	
	Equestrian ....*Campo Marte* grand prix jumping, individual (1st and 2nd rounds)	
	Fronton ....*Chapultepec Sports Center* frontennis	
	Volleyball ...*Olympic Gymnasium, Revolution Ice Rink* (4 games)	
	Water Polo ....*Olympic Pool* (2 games)	
	Wrestling ....*Insurgentes Ice Rink* Greco-Roman, eliminations	
11:00	**Field Hockey** ....*Municipal Stadium* quarterfinals (3 games)	

PM	EVENT	VENUE
12:00	**Fronton** ....*Deportivo Asturiano* fronton handball	
12:30	**Field Hockey** ....*Municipal Stadium* quarterfinals (3 games)	
2:30	**Boxing** ....*Arena México* quarterfinals	
4:00	**Fronton** .....*Frontón Metropolitano* paleta with leather ball	
5:00	**Basketball** ....*Sports Palace* final (4 games, 9-16 places)	
	Diving ....*Olympic Pool* women's high dive, final	
	Fencing ....*Fencing Hall* women's team foil, quarterfinals	
	Gymnastics ....*National Auditorium* women's optional exercise, individual and team	
	Swimming ....*Olympic Pool*	
	• 400-meter freestyle, final	
	• women's 200-meter breaststroke, final	
	• 400-meter individual medley, final	
	• women's 100-meter backstroke, final	
	Volleyball ...*Olympic Gymnasium, Revolution Ice Rink* women's (2 games)	
	Wrestling ....*Insurgentes Ice Rink* Greco-Roman, eliminations	
7:00	**Boxing** ....*Arena México* quarterfinals	
	Volleyball ....*Olympic Gymnasium* (1 game)	
8:30	**Fronton** ....*Frontón México* jai alai	

Thursday, OCTOBER 24

AM	EVENT	VENUE
8:00	**Fencing** ....*Fencing Hall* team épée, eliminations	
8:30	**Gymnastics** ....*National Auditorium* optional exercises, individual and team	

Time	Event	Venue
9:00	**Canoeing** ....*Rowing and Canoeing Course* semifinals (7 events)	
	Fencing ....*Fencing Hall* women's team foil, semifinals	
	Water Polo ....*Olympic Pool* (4 games)	
10:00	**Equestrian** ....*Campo Marte* Olympic dressage, grand prix	
	Fronton ....*Chapultepec Sports Center, Lebanese Sports Center* frontennis and paleta with rubber ball	
	Swimming ....*Olympic Pool*	
	• 200-meter butterfly, preliminaries	
	• women's 200-meter butterfly, preliminaries	
	• 200-meter freestyle, preliminaries	
	• women's 400-meter medley, preliminaries	
	Volleyball ...*Olympic Gymnasium, Revolution Ice Rink* (2 games)	
	Wrestling ....*Insurgentes Ice Rink* Greco-Roman, eliminations	
11:00	**Field Hockey** ....*Municipal Stadium* quarterfinals (1 game)	

PM	EVENT	VENUE
12:00	**Volleyball** ...*Olympic Gymnasium, Revolution Ice Rink*	
	• men's (1 game)	
	• women's (1 game)	
12:45	**Field Hockey** ....*Municipal Stadium* quarterfinals (1 game)	
2:30	**Boxing** ....*Arena México* semifinals	
3:00	**Water Polo** ....*Olympic Pool* (3 games)	
3:30	**Soccer** ....*Aztec Stadium* 3rd place	
4:00	**Fencing** ....*Fencing Hall* team épée, eliminations	
4:30	**Fencing** ....*Fencing Hall* women's team foil, 3-6 places	
5:00	**Diving** ....*Olympic Pool* high dive, preliminaries	
	Gymnastics ....*National Auditorium* optional exercises, individual and team	
	Swimming ....*Olympic Pool*	
	• women's 800-meter freestyle, final	
	• 200-meter butterfly, final	
	• women's 200-meter butterfly, final	
	• 200-meter freestyle, final	
	Volleyball ...*Olympic Gymnasium, Revolution Ice Rink*	
	• men's (1 game)	
	• women's (1 game)	
	Water Polo ....*Olympic Pool* (1 game)	
	Wrestling ....*Insurgentes Ice Rink* Greco-Roman, eliminations	

Time	Event	Venue
7:00	**Boxing** ....*Arena México* semifinals	
	Fencing ....*Fencing Hall* women's team foil, final	
	Fronton .....*Frontón Metropolitano* paleta with leather ball	
	Volleyball ....*Olympic Gymnasium* (1 game)	

Friday, OCTOBER 25

AM	EVENT	VENUE
8:00	**Fencing** ....*Fencing Hall* team épée, eliminations	
10:00	**Canoeing** ....*Rowing and Canoeing Course* final	
	Swimming ....*Olympic Pool*	
	• 200-meter backstroke, preliminaries	
	• women's 200-meter back-stroke, preliminaries	
	• 1,500-meter freestyle, preliminaries	
	Volleyball ...*Olympic Gymnasium, Revolution Ice Rink*	
	• men's (1 game)	
	• women's (1 game)	
	Water Polo ....*Olympic Pool* (3 games)	
	Wrestling ....*Insurgentes Ice Rink* Greco-Roman, eliminations	
11:00	**Field Hockey** ....*Municipal Stadium* semifinal (consolation)	

PM	EVENT	VENUE
12:00	**Fronton** ....*Deportivo Asturiano* fronton handball, final	
	Volleyball ...*Olympic Gymnasium, Revolution Ice Rink*	
	• men's (1 game)	
	• women's (1 game)	
12:45	**Field Hockey** ....*Municipal Stadium* semifinals	
2:00	**Equestrian** ....*Campo Marte*	
	• Olympic dressage, grand prix	
	• ride-off test (rappel)	
3:30	**Fencing** ....*Fencing Hall* team épée, 3-6 places	
	Water Polo ....*Olympic Pool* (2 games)	
5:00	**Basketball** ....*Sports Palace* final (4 games, 1-8 places)	
	Diving ....*Olympic Pool* high dive, preliminaries	
	Swimming ....*Olympic Pool*	
	• women's 200-meter back-stroke, final	
	• 200-meter backstroke, final	
	• women's 400-meter medley, final	
	Volleyball ....*Olympic Gymnasium* (2 games)	
	Water Polo ....*Olympic Pool* (1 game)	

Time	Event	Venue
	Wrestling ....*Insurgentes Ice Rink* Greco-Roman, eliminations	
7:00	**Fencing** ....*Fencing Hall* team épée, final	
	Gymnastics ....*National Auditorium* women's individual finals (vault, bars, beam, floor)	
9:00	**Fronton** ....*Frontón México* jai alai, final	

Saturday, OCTOBER 26

AM	EVENT	VENUE
10:00	**Swimming** ....*Olympic Pool*	
	• 4 x 100-meter medley relay, preliminaries	
	• women's 4 x 100-meter freestyle relay, preliminaries	
	Water Polo ....*Olympic Pool* 3rd place	
	Wrestling ....*Insurgentes Ice Rink* Greco-Roman, semifinals	
11:00	**Field Hockey** ....*Municipal Stadium* final (consolation)	

PM	EVENT	VENUE
12:45	**Field Hockey** ....*Municipal Stadium* final	
3:30	**Soccer** ....*Aztec Stadium* final	
4:00	**Volleyball** ....*Olympic Gymnasium* women's (2 games)	
5:00	**Diving** ....*Olympic Pool* high dive, final	
	Swimming ....*Olympic Pool*	
	• 1,500-meter freestyle, final	
	• women's 4 x 100-meter freestyle relay, final	
	• 4 x 100-meter medley relay, final	
	Water Polo ....*Olympic Pool* final	
	Wrestling ....*Insurgentes Ice Rink* Greco-Roman, final	
7:00	**Gymnastics** ....*National Auditorium* individual final (horse, rings, vault, parallel bars, horizonal bars)	
8:00	**Boxing** ....*Arena México* final	
	Volleyball ....*Olympic Gymnasium* championship round	

Sunday, OCTOBER 27

AM	EVENT	VENUE
8:00	**Equestrian** ....*Campo Marte*	
	• Olympic grand prix jumping, team (1st round)	
	• (demonstration)	

PM	EVENT	VENUE
12:30	**Equestrian** ....*Olympic Stadium* Olympic grand prix jumping, team (2nd round)	
	Closing Ceremony............*Olympic Stadium*	

153

MEXICO CITY 1968
16TH OLYMPIC GAMES

ATHLETICS (TRACK & FIELD)

Event	Gold	Silver	Bronze	Place	Country	Name	Mark
100 METERS	USA 9.95 — James Hines	JAM 10.04 — Lennox Miller	USA 10.07 — Charles Greene	4. / 5. / 6.	CUB / FRA / USA	Pablo Montes / Roger Bambuck / Melvin Pender	10.14 / 10.15 / 10.17
200 METERS	USA 19.83 — Tommie Smith	AUS 20.06 — Peter Norman	USA 20.10 — John Carlos	4. / 5. / 6.	TRI / FRA / USA	Edwin Roberts / Roger Bambuck / Larry Questad	20.34 / 20.51 / 20.62
400 METERS	USA 43.86 — Lee Evans	USA 43.97 — Larry James	USA 44.41 — Ronald Freeman	4. / 5. / 6.	SEN / FRG / ETH	Amadou Gakou / Martin Jellinghaus / Tegegne Bezabeh	45.01 / 45.32 / 45.42
800 METERS	AUS 1:44.40 — Ralph Doubell	KEN 1:44.57 — W. Kiprugut Chuma	USA 1:45.46 — Thomas Farrell	4. / 5. / 6.	FRG / CHE / GDR	Walter Adams / Josef Plachy / Dieter Fromm	1:45.83 / 1:45.99 / 1:46.30
1,500 METERS	KEN 3:34.91 — H. Kipchoge Keino	USA 3:37.89 — James Ryun	FRG 3:39.08 — Bodo Tümmler	4. / 5. / 6.	FRG / GBR / FRA	Harald Norpoth / John Whetton / Jacques Boxberger	3:42.57 / 3:43.90 / 3:46.65
5,000 METERS	TUN 14:05.01 — Mohamed Gammoudi	KEN 14:05.16 — H. Kipchoge Keino	KEN 14:06.41 — Naftali Temu	4. / 5. / 6.	MEX / AUS / ETH	Juan Martinez / Ronald Clarke / Wohib Masresha	14:10.76 / 14:12.45 / 14:17.70
10,000 METERS	KEN 29:27.40 — Naftali Temu	ETH 29:27.75 — Mamo Wolde	TUN 29:34.20 — Mohamed Gammoudi	4. / 5. / 6.	MEX / URS / AUS	Juan Martinez / Nikolai Sviridov / Ronald Clarke	29:35.00 / 29:43.20 / 29:44.80
MARATHON	ETH 2:20:26.4 — Mamo Wolde	JPN 2:23:31.0 — Kenji Kimihara	NZL 2:23:45.0 — Michael Ryan	4. / 5. / 6.	TUR / GBR / ETH	Ismail Akcay / William Adcocks / Merawi Gebru	2:25:18.8 / 2:25:33.0 / 2:27:16.8
110-METER HURDLES	USA 13.3 — Willie Davenport	USA 13.4 — Ervin Hall	ITA 13.4 — Eddy Ottoz	4. / 5. / 6.	USA / FRG / SWE	Leon Coleman / Werner Trzmiel / Bo Forssander	13.6 / 13.6 / 13.7
400-METER HURDLES	GBR 48.12 — David Hemery	FRG 49.0 — Gerhard Hennige	GBR 49.0 — John Sherwood	4. / 5. / 6.	USA / URS / USA	Geoffry Vanderstock / Vyacheslav Skomorokhov / Ronald Whitney	49.0 / 49.1 / 49.2
3,000-METER STEEPLECHASE	KEN 8:51.0 — Amos Biwott	KEN 8:51.6 — Benjamin Kogo	USA 8:51.8 — George Young	4. / 5. / 6.	AUS / URS / BUL	Kerry O'Brien / Aleksandr Morozov / Mikhail Chelev	8:52.0 / 8:55.8 / 8:58.4
4 x 100-METER RELAY	USA 38.24 — Charles Greene, Ronnie Ray Smith, Melvin Pender, James Hines	CUB 38.40 — Hermes Ramirez, Juan Morales, Pablo Montes, Enrique Figuerola Camue	FRA 38.43 — Gérard Fénouil, Jocelyn Delecour, Claude Piquemal, Roger Bambuck	4. / 5. / 6.	JAM / GDR / FRG	Stewart/Fray/Forbes/Miller / Erbstösser/Eggers/Haase/Schelter / Schmidtke/Metz/Wucherer/Eigenherr	38.47 / 38.66 / 38.76
4 x 400-METER RELAY	USA 2:56.16 — Vincent Matthews, Ronald Freeman, Larry James, Lee Evans	KEN 2:59.64 — Charles Asati, Matesi Munyoro Nyamau, Naftali Bon, Daniel Rudisha	FRG 3:00.57 — Helmar Müller, Gerhard Hennige, Manfred Kinder, Martin Jellinghaus	4. / 5. / 6.	POL / GBR / TRI	Werner/Badeński/Balachowski/Grędziński / Campbell/Hemery/Sherwood/Winbolt-Lewis / Simon/Bobb/Cayenne/Roberts	3:00.58 / 3:01.21 / 3:04.54
20,000-METER WALK	URS 1:33:58.4 — Vladimir Golubnichiy	MEX 1:34:00.0 — José Pedraza Zuniga	URS 1:34:03.4 — Nikolai Smaga	4. / 5. / 6.	USA / GDR / URS	Rudolph Haluza / Gerhard Sperling / Otto Bartsch	1:35:00.2 / 1:35:27.2 / 1:36:16.8
50,000-METER WALK	GDR 4:20:13.6 — Christoph Höhne	HUN 4:30:17.0 — Antal Kiss	USA 4:31:55.4 — Larry Young	4. / 5. / 6.	GDR / SWE / ITA	Peter Selzer / Stig-Erik Lindberg / Vittorio Visini	4:33:09.8 / 4:34:05.0 / 4:36:33.2
HIGH JUMP	USA 2.24 — Richard Fosbury	USA 2.22 — Edward Caruthers	URS 2.20 — Valentin Gavrilov	4. / 5. / 6.	URS / USA / ITA	Valery Skvortsov / Reynaldo Brown / Giacomo Crosa	2.16 / 2.14 / 2.14
POLE VAULT	USA 5.40 — Robert Seagren	FRG 5.40 — Claus Schiprowski	GDR 5.40 — Wolfgang Nordwig	4. / 5. / 6.	GRE / USA / URS	Christos Papanicolaou / John Pennel / Gennady Bliznyetsov	5.35 / 5.35 / 5.30

Event	1st	2nd	3rd	4th–6th
LONG JUMP	USA 8.90 ROBERT BEAMON	GDR 8.19 KLAUS BEER	USA 8.16 RALPH BOSTON	4. URS Igor Ter-Ovanesyan 8.12 5. URS Tonu Lepik 8.09 6. AUS Allen Crawley 8.02
TRIPLE JUMP	URS 17.39 VIKTOR SANEYEV	BRA 17.27 NELSON PRUDENCIO	ITA 17.22 GIUSEPPE GENTILE	4. USA Arthur Walker 17.12 5. URS Nikolai Dudkin 17.09 6. AUS Philip May 17.02
SHOT PUT	USA 20.54 JAMES RANDEL MATSON	USA 20.12 GEORGE WOODS	URS 20.09 EDUARD GUSHCHIN	4. GDR Dieter Hoffmann 20.00 5. USA David Maggard 19.43 6. POL Wladyslaw Komar 19.28
DISCUS THROW	USA 64.78 ALFRED OERTER	GDR 63.08 LOTHAR MILDE	CHE 62.92 LUDVIK DANĚK	4. GDR Hartmut Losch 62.12 5. USA L. Jay Silvester 61.78 6. USA Gary Carlsen 59.46
JAVELIN THROW	URS 90.10 JĀNIS LŪSIS	FIN 88.58 JORMA KINNUNEN	HUN 87.06 GERGELY KULCSÁR	4. POL Wladislaw Nikiciuk 85.70 5. GDR Manfred Stolle 84.42 6. SWE Åke Nilsson 83.48
HAMMER THROW	HUN 73.36 GYULA ZSIVÓTZKY	URS 73.28 ROMUALD KLIM	HUN 69.78 LÁZÁR LOVÁSZ	4. JPN Takeo Sugawara 69.78 5. HUN Sándor Eckschmidt 69.46 6. URS Gennady Kondrashov 69.08
DECATHLON	USA 8,193 WILLIAM TOOMEY	FRG 8,111 HANS-JOACHIM WALDE	FRG 8,064 KURT BENDLIN	4. URS Nikolai Avilov 7,909 5. GDR Joachim Kirst 7,861 6. USA Thomas Wadell 7,719
100 METERS	USA 11.08 WYOMIA TYUS	USA 11.15 BARBARA FERRELL	POL 11.19 I. SZEWIŃSKA-KIRSZENSTEIN	4. AUS Raelene Boyle 11.20 5. USA Margaret Bailes 11.37 6. AUS Dianne Burge 11.44
200 METERS	POL 22.58 I. SZEWIŃSKA-KIRSZENSTEIN	AUS 22.74 RAELENE BOYLE	AUS 22.88 JENNIFER LAMY	4. USA Barbara Ferrell 22.93 5. FRA Nicole Montandon 23.08 6. USA Wyomia Tyus 23.08
400 METERS	FRA 52.03 COLETTE BESSON	GBR 52.12 LILLIAN BOARD	URS 52.25 NATALYA PECHENKINA	4. GBR Janet Simpson 52.57 5. CUB Aurelia Penton 52.75 6. USA Jarvis Scott 52.79
800 METERS	USA 2:00.92 MADELINE MANNING	ROM 2:02.58 ILEANA SILAI	NED 2:02.63 MARIA GOMMERS	4. GBR Sheila Taylor 2:03.81 5. USA Doris Brown 2:03.98 6. GBR Patricia Lowe 2:04.25
80-METER HURDLES	AUS 10.39 MAUREEN CAIRD	AUS 10.46 PAMELA KILBORN	TPE 10.51 CHI CHENG	4. USA Patricia Van Wolvelaere 10.60 5. GDR Karin Balzer 10.61 6. POL Danuta Straszyńska 10.66
4 x 100-METER RELAY	USA 42.87 BARBARA FERRELL MARGARET BAILES MILDRETTE NETTER WYOMIA TYUS	CUB 43.36 MARLENE ELEJARDE FULGENCIA ROMAY VIOLETTA QUESADA MIGUELINA COBIÁN	URS 43.41 LYUDMILA ZHARKOVA GALINA BUKHARINA VYERA POPKOVA LYUDMILA SAMOTYSOVA	4. NED Hennipman/Sterk/Bakker/van den Berg 43.44 5. AUS Lamy/Bennett/Boyle/Burge 43.50 6. FRG Meyer/Stöck/Jahn/Becker 43.70
HIGH JUMP	CHE 1.82 MILOSLAVA REŽKOVÁ	URS 1.80 ANTONINA OKOROKOVA	URS 1.80 VALENTINA KOZYR	4. CHE Jaroslava Valentová 1.78 5. GDR Rita Schmidt 1.78 6. CHE Maria Faithová 1.78
LONG JUMP	ROM 6.82 VIORICA VISCOPOLEANU	GBR 6.68 SHEILA SHERWOOD	URS 6.66 TATYANA TALISHEVA	4. GDR Burghild Wieczorek 6.48 5. POL Miroslawa Sarna 6.47 6. FRG Ingrid Becker 6.43
SHOT PUT	GDR 19.61 M. GUMMEL-HELMBOLDT	GDR 18.78 MARITA LANGE	URS 18.19 NADEZHDA CHIZHOVA	4. HUN Judit Bognar 17.78 5. GDR Renate Garisch-Boy 17.72 6. BUL Ivanka Hristova 17.25
DISCUS THROW	ROM 58.28 LIA MANOLIU	FRG 57.76 LIESEL WESTERMANN	HUN 54.90 JOLÁN KLEIBER	4. GDR Anita Otto 54.40 5. URS Antonina Popova 53.42 6. USA Olga Fikatová-Connolly 52.96
JAVELIN THROW	HUN 60.36 ANGÉLA NÉMETH	ROM 59.92 MIHAELA PENEŞ	AUT 58.04 EVA JANKO	4. HUN Márta Rudas 56.38 5. POL Daniela Jaworska 56.06 6. YUG Nataša Urbančič 55.42
PENTATHLON	FRG 5,098 INGRID BECKER	AUT 4,966 ELISABETH PROKOP	HUN 4,959 ANNAMÁRIA TÓTH	4. URS Valentina Tichomirova 4,927 5. FRG Manon Bornholdt 4,890 6. USA Patricia Winslow 4,877

BASKETBALL

Event	1st	2nd	3rd	4th–6th
FINAL STANDINGS	USA	YUG	URS	4. BRA 5. MEX 6. POL

BOXING

| LIGHT FLYWEIGHT
106 lbs. (48 kg) | VEN
Francisco Rodriguez | KOR
Yong-ju Jee | USA
Harlan Marbley
POL
Hubert Skrzypczak | 5. four-way tie |
| MIDDLE | | | | |

| FLYWEIGHT
112.5 lbs. (51 kg) | MEX
Ricardo Delgado | POL
Artur Olech | BRA
Servilio Oliveira
UGA
Leo Rwabwogo | 5. four-way tie |

| BANTAMWEIGHT
119.5 lbs. (54 kg) | URS
Valery Sokolov | UGA
Eridari Mukwanga | JPN
Eiji Morioka
KOR
Kyou-Chull Chang | 5. four-way tie |

| FEATHERWEIGHT
126 lbs. (57 kg) | MEX
Antonio Roldan | USA
Albert Robinson | KEN
Philipp Waruinge
BUL
Ivan Mihailov | 5. four-way tie |

| LIGHTWEIGHT
132 lbs. (60 kg) | USA
Ronald Harris | POL
Józef Grudzień | ROM
Calistrat Cuţov
YUG
Zvonimir Vujin | 5. four-way tie |

| LIGHT WELTERWEIGHT
140 lbs. (63.5 kg) | POL
Jerzy Kulej | CUB
Enrique Regueiferos | FIN
Arto Nilsson
USA
James Wallington | 5. four-way tie |

| WELTERWEIGHT
148 lbs. (67 kg) | GDR
Manfred Wolke | CMR
Joseph Bessala | URS
Vladimir Mussalimov
ARG
Mario Guilloti | 5. four-way tie |

| LIGHT MIDDLEWEIGHT
156 lbs. (71 kg) | URS
Boris Lagutin | CUB
Rolando Garbey | USA
John Baldwin
FRG
Günther Meier | 5. four-way tie |

| MIDDLEWEIGHT
165.5 lbs. (75 kg) | GBR
Christopher Finnegan | URS
Aleksei Kisselyov | MEX
Agustin Zaragoza
USA
Alfred Jones | 5. four-way tie |

| LIGHT HEAVYWEIGHT
179 lbs. (81 kg) | URS
Dan Poznyak | ROM
Ion Monea | BUL
Georgi Stankov
POL
Stanislaw Dragan | 5. four-way tie |

| SUPER HEAVYWEIGHT
unlimited weight | USA
George Foreman | URS
Ionas Chepulis | ITA
Giorgio Bambini
MEX
Joaquin Rocha | 5. four-way tie |

CANOEING

| KAYAK SINGLES
1,000 METERS | HUN 4:02.63
Mihály Hesz | URS 4:03.58
Aleksandr Shaparenko | DEN 4:04.39
Erik Hansen | 4. POL W. Szuszkiewicz 4:06.36
5. SWE Rolf Peterson 4:07.86
6. CHE Václav Mára 4:09.35 |

| KAYAK DOUBLES
1,000 METERS | URS 3:37.54
Aleksandr Shaparenko
Vladimir Morozov | HUN 3:38.44
Csaba Giczi
István Timár | AUT 3:40.71
Gerhard Seibold
Günther Pfaff | 4. NED Hoekstra/Geurts 3:41.36
5. SWE Andersson/Utterberg 3:41.99
6. ROM Sciotnic/Vernescu 3:45.18 |

KAYAK FOURS — 1,000 METERS

	Gold	Silver	Bronze
	NOR 3:14.38	**ROM** 3:14.81	**HUN** 3:15.10
	Steinar Amundsen	Anton Calenic	Csaba Giczi
	Egil Söby	Dimitrie Ivanov	Istvan Timár
	Tore Berger	Haralambie Ivanov	Imre Szöllösi
	Jan Johansen	Mihai Turcaş	István Csizmadia

4. SWE Larsson/Nilsson/Sahlén/Sandin 3:16.68
5. FIN von Alfthan/Mäkelä/Lehtosalo/Nummisto 3:17.28
6. GDR Wenzke/Will/Riedrich/Ebeling 3:18.03

CANADIAN SINGLES — 1,000 METERS

	Gold	Silver	Bronze
	HUN 4:36.14	**FRG** 4:38.31	**URS** 4:40.42
	Tibor Tatai	Detlef Lewe	Vitaly Galkov

4. CHE Jiří Čtvrtečka 4:40.74
5. BUL Boris Lyubenov 4:43.43
6. SWE Ove Emanuelsson 4:45.80

CANADIAN PAIRS — 1,000 METERS

	Gold	Silver	Bronze
	ROM 4:07.18	**HUN** 4:08.77	**URS** 4:11.30
	Ivan Patzaichin	Tamás Wichmann	Naum Prokupets
	Serghei Covaliov	Gyula Petrikovics	Mikhail Zamotin

4. MEX Martinez/Altamirano 4:15.24
5. SWE Lindelöf/Zeidlitz 4:16.60
6. GDR Harpke/Wagner 4:22.53

KAYAK SINGLES — 500 METERS

	Gold	Silver	Bronze
	URS 2:11.09	**FRG** 2:12.71	**ROM** 2:13.22
	L. Pinayeva-Khvedosyuk	Renate Breuer	Victoria Dumitru

4. USA Marcia Smoke-Jones 2:14.68
5. CHE Ivona Vávrová 2:14.78
6. GDR Anita Nüssner 2:16.02

KAYAK DOUBLES — 500 METERS

	Gold	Silver	Bronze
	FRG 1:56.44	**HUN** 1:58.60	**URS** 1:58.61
	Roswitha Esser	Anna Pfeffer	L. Pinayeva-Khvedosyuk
	Annemarie Zimmermann	Katalin Rozsnyói	Antonina Seredina

4. ROM Serghei/Dumitru 1:59.17
5. GDR Kobuss/Haftenberger 2:00.18
6. NED Jaapies/Bergers-Duif 2:02.02

CYCLING

1,000-METER SPRINT

	Gold	Silver	Bronze
	FRA 2-0	**ITA**	**FRA**
	Daniel Morelon	Giordano Turrini	Pierre Trentin

4. URS Omari Phakadze
5. four-way tie

2,000-METER TANDEM SPRINT

	Gold	Silver	Bronze
	FRA 2-0	**NED**	**BEL**
	Daniel Morelon	Johannes Jansen	Daniel Goens
	Pierre Trentin	Leijn Loevesijn	Robert van Lancker

4. ITA Gorini/Borghetti
5. four-way tie

1,000-METER TIME TRIAL

	Gold	Silver	Bronze
	FRA 1:03.91	**DEN** 1:04.61	**POL** 1:04.63
	Pierre Trentin	Niels Fredborg	Janusz Kierzkowski

4. ITA Gianni Sartori 1:04.65
5. TRI Roger Gibbon 1:04.66
6. NED Leijn Loevesijn 1:04.84

4,000-METER INDIVIDUAL PURSUIT

	Gold	Silver	Bronze
	FRA 4:41.71	**DEN** 4:42.43	**SUI** 4:39.42
	Daniel Rebillard	Mogens Frey Jensen	Xaver Kurmann

4. AUS John Bylsma 4:41.60
5. four-way tie

4,000-METER TEAM PURSUIT

	Gold	Silver	Bronze
	DEN 4:22.44	**FRG** 4:18.94	**ITA** 4:18.35
	Gunnar Asmussen	Udo Hempel	Lorenzo Bosisio
	Per Pedersen Lyngemark	Karl Link	Cipriano Chemello
	Reno Olsen	Karlheinz Henrichs	Luigi Roncaglia
	Mogens Frey Jensen	Jürgen Kissner	Giorgio Morbiato

4. URS Latsis/Moskvin/Kuznyetsov/Kolyuschev 4:33.39
5. four-way tie

ROAD RACE, INDIVIDUAL — 196.2 km

	Gold	Silver	Bronze
	ITA 4:41:25.24	**DEN** 4:42:49.71	**SWE** 4:43:15.24
	Pierfranco Vianelli	Leif Mortensen	Gösta Pettersson

4. FRA S. Abrahamian 4:43:36.54
5. NED Marinus Pijnen 4:43:36.81
6. BEL J. Monsère 4:43:51.77

ROAD RACE, TEAM — 104 KILOMETERS

	Gold	Silver	Bronze
	NED 2:07:49.06	**SWE** 2:09:26.60	**ITA** 2:10:18.74
	Fedor den Hertog	Erik Pettersson	Giovanni Bramucci
	Jan Krekels	Gösta Pettersson	Vittorio Marcelli
	Marinus Pijnen	Sture Pettersson	Mauro Simonetti
	Gerardes Zoetemelk	Tomas Pettersson	Pierfranco Vianelli

4. DEN Blaudzun/Hansen/Pedersen/Mortensen 2:12:41.41
5. NOR Andresen/Yli/Andresen/Milsett 2:14:32.85
6. POL Magiera/Kegel/Czechowski/Blawdzin 2:14:40.98

DIVING

PLATFORM

	Gold	Silver	Bronze
	ITA 164.18	**MEX** 154.49	**USA** 153.93
	Klaus Dibiasi	Alvaro Gaxiola	Edwin Young

4. USA Keith Russell 152.30
5. MEX José Robinson 143.62
6. GDR Lothar Matthes 141.75

SPRINGBOARD

	Gold	Silver	Bronze
	USA 170.15	**ITA** 159.74	**USA** 158.09
	Bernard Wrightson	Klaus Dibiasi	James Henry

4. MEX Luis Niño de Rivera 155.71
5. ITA Franco Giorgio Cagnotto 155.70
6. USA Keith Russell 151.75

PLATFORM

	Gold	Silver	Bronze
	CHE 109.59	**URS** 105.14	**USA** 101.11
	Milena Duchková	Natalya Lobanova	Ann Peterson

4. CAN Beverly Boys 97.97
5. POL Boguslawa Pietkiewicz 95.28
6. two-way tie 93.08

SPRINGBOARD

	Gold	Silver	Bronze
	USA 150.77	**URS** 145.30	**USA** 145.23
	Sue Gossick	Tamara Pogoscheva	Keala O'Sullivan

4. USA Maxine King 137.38
5. GDR Ingrid Gulbin 135.82
6. URS Vyera Baklanova 132.31

EQUESTRIAN

THREE-DAY EVENT, INDIVIDUAL	⚪ FRA -38.86 JEAN-JACQUES GUYON	⚪ GBR -41.61 DEREK ALLHUSEN	⚫ USA -52.31 MICHAEL PAGE	4. GBR Richard Meade -64.46 5. GBR Reuben Jones -69.86 6. USA James Wofford -74.06
THREE-DAY EVENT, TEAM	⚪ GBR -175.93 DEREK ALLHUSEN RICHARD MEADE REUBEN JONES	⚪ USA -245.87 MICHAEL PAGE JAMES WOFFORD J. MICHAEL PLUMB	⚫ AUS -331.26 WAYNE ROYCROFT BRIEN COBCROFT WILLIAM ROYCROFT	4. FRA Guyon/Le Goupil/ Sarrazin -505.83 5. FRG Karsten/Mehrdorf/ Wagner -518.22 6. MEX Del Castillo/Mejia/ Avalos -631.56
DRESSAGE, INDIVIDUAL	⚪ URS 1,572 IVAN KIZIMOV	⚪ FRG 1,546 JOSEF NECKERMANN	⚫ FRG 1,537 REINER KLIMKE	4. URS Ivan Kalita 1,519 5. GDR Horst Köhler 1,475 6. URS Yelena Petushkova 1,471
DRESSAGE, TEAM	⚪ FRG 2,699 JOSEF NECKERMANN REINER KLIMKE LISELOTT LINSENHOFF	⚪ URS 2,657 IVAN KIZIMOV IVAN KALITA YELENA PETUSHKOVA	⚫ SUI 2,547 GUSTAV FISCHER HENRI CHAMMARTIN MARIANNE GOSSWEILER	4. GDR Köhler/Brockmüller/ Müller 2,357 5. GBR Lawrence/Johnstone/ Hall 2,332 6. CHI Squella/Piraino/ Escudero 2,015
JUMPING, INDIVIDUAL	⚪ USA 4 WILLIAM STEINKRAUS	⚪ GBR 8 MARION COAKES	⚫ GBR 12 DAVID BROOME	4. USA Frank Chapot 12 5. FRG Hans-Günter Winkler 12 6. CAN James Elder 12
JUMPING, TEAM	⚪ CAN 102.75 JAMES ELDER JAMES DAY THOMAS GAYFORD	⚪ FRA 110.50 JANOU LEFEBVRE MARCEL ROZIER P. JONQUÈRES D'ORIOLA	⚫ FRG 117.25 ALWIN SCHOCKEMÖHLE HANS-GÜNTER WINKLER HERMANN SCHRIDDE	4. USA Chapot/Kusner/ Chapot 117.50 5. ITA D'Inzeo/D'Inzeo/ Mancinelli 129.25 6. SUI Weier/Bachmann/ Blickenstorfer 136.75

FENCING

ÉPÉE, INDIVIDUAL	⚪ HUN GYÖZÖ KULCSÁR	⚪ URS GRIGORY KRISS	⚫ ITA GIANLUIGI SACCARO	4. URS Viktor Modzalevsky 5. AUT Herbert Polzhuber 6. FRA Jean-Pierre Allemand
ÉPÉE, TEAM	⚪ HUN	⚪ URS	⚫ POL	4. FRG 5. GDR 6. ITA
FOIL, INDIVIDUAL	⚪ ROM IONEL DRIMBĂ	⚪ HUN JENÖ KAMUTI	⚫ FRA DANIEL REVENU	4. FRA Christian Noël 5. FRA Jean-Claude Magnan 6. ROM Mihai Tiu
FOIL, TEAM	⚪ FRA	⚪ URS	⚫ POL	4. ROM 5. HUN 6. FRG
SABER, INDIVIDUAL	⚪ POL JERZY PAWLOWSKI	⚪ URS MARK RAKITA	⚫ HUN TIBOR PÉZSA	4. URS Vladimir Nazlymov 5. ITA Rolando Rigoli 6. POL Józef Nowara
SABER, TEAM	⚪ URS	⚪ ITA	⚫ HUN	4. FRA 5. POL 6. USA
FOIL, INDIVIDUAL	⚪ URS YELENA NOVIKOVA	⚪ MEX M. DEL PILAR ROLDAN	⚫ HUN ILDIKÓ UJLAKI-REJTÖ	4. FRA Brigitte Gapais 5. SWE Kerstin Palm 6. URS Galina Gorokhova
FOIL, TEAM	⚪ URS	⚪ HUN	⚫ ROM	4. FRA 5. FRG 6. ITA

FIELD HOCKEY

FINAL STANDINGS	⚪ PAK	⚪ AUS	⚫ IND	4. FRG 5. NED 6. ESP

FOOTBALL (SOCCER)

	①	②	③	
FINAL STANDINGS	HUN	BUL	JPN	4. MEX 5. four-way tie

GYMNASTICS

	①		②		③		
ALL-AROUND, INDIVIDUAL	JPN 115.90 SAWAO KATO		URS 115.85 MIKHAIL VORONIN		JPN 115.65 AKINORI NAKAYAMA		4. JPN Eizo Kenmotsu 114.9 5. JPN Takeshi Kato 114.85 6. URS Sergei Diomidov 114.1
ALL-AROUND, TEAM	JPN 575.90		URS 571.10		GDR 557.15		4. CHE 557.10 5. POL 555.40 6. YUG 550.75
FLOOR EXERCISES	JPN 19.475 SAWAO KATO		JPN 19.400 AKINORI NAKAYAMA		JPN 19.275 TAKESHI KATO		4. JPN Mitsuo Tsukuhara 19.050 5. URS Valery Karassev 18.950 6. JPN Eizo Kenmotsu 18.925
HORIZONTAL BAR	URS 19.550 MIKHAIL VORONIN JPN 19.550 AKINORI NAKAYAMA				JPN 19.375 EIZO KENMOTSU		4. GDR Klaus Köste 19.225 5. URS Sergei Diomidov 19.150 6. JPN Yukio Endo 19.025
HORSE VAULT	URS 19.000 MIKHAIL VORONIN		JPN 18.950 YUKIO ENDO		URS 18.925 SERGEI DIOMIDOV		4. JPN Takeshi Kato 18.775 5. JPN Akinori Nakayama 18.725 6. JPN Eizo Kenmotsu 18.650
PARALLEL BARS	JPN 19.475 AKINORI NAKAYAMA		URS 19.425 MIKHAIL VORONIN		URS 19.225 VLADIMIR KLIMENKO		4. JPN Takeshi Kato 19.200 5. JPN Eizo Kenmotsu 19.175 6. CHE Václav Kubička 18.950
POMMELED HORSE	YUG 19.325 MIROSLAV CERAR		FIN 19.225 OLLI EINO LAIHO		URS 19.200 MIKHAIL VORONIN		4. POL Wilhelm Kubica 19.150 5. JPN Eizo Kenmotsu 19.050 6. URS Viktor Klimenko 18.950
RINGS	JPN 19.450 AKINORI NAKAYAMA		URS 19.325 MIKHAIL VORONIN		JPN 19.225 SAWAO KATO		4. JPN Mitsuo Tsukuhara 19.125 5. JPN Takeshi Kato 19.050 6. URS Sergei Diomidov 18.975
ALL-AROUND, INDIVIDUAL	CHE 78.25 VERA ČÁSLAVSKÁ		URS 76.85 ZINAIDA VORONINA		URS 76.75 NATALYA KUCHINSKAYA		4. URS Larissa Petrik 76.70 4. GDR Erika Zuchold 76.70 6. GDR Karin Janz 76.55
ALL-AROUND, TEAM	URS 382.85		CHE 382.20		GDR 379.10		4. JPN 375.45 5. HUN 369.80 6. USA 369.75
BALANCE BEAM	URS 19.650 NATALYA KUCHINSKAYA		CHE 19.575 VERA ČÁSLAVSKÁ		URS 19.250 LARISSA PETRIK		4. GDR Karin Janz 19.225 4. USA Linda Metheny 19.225 6. GDR Erika Zuchold 19.150
FLOOR EXERCISES	URS 19.675 LARISSA PETRIK CHE 19.675 VERA ČÁSLAVSKÁ				URS 19.650 NATALYA KUCHINSKAYA		4. URS Zinaida Voronina 19.550 5. URS Olga Karasseva 19.325 5. CHE Bohumila Řimnácová 19.325
HORSE VAULT	CHE 19.775 VERA ČÁSLAVSKÁ		GDR 19.625 ERIKA ZUCHOLD		URS 19.500 ZINAIDA VORONINA		4. CHE Maria Krajčirova 19.475 5. URS Natalya Kutschinskaya 19.375 6. CHE Miroslava Skleničková 19.325
UNEVEN BARS	CHE 19.650 VERA ČÁSLAVSKÁ		GDR 19.500 KARIN JANZ		URS 19.425 ZINAIDA VORONINA		4. CHE Bohumila Řimnácová 19.350 5. GDR Erika Zuchold 19.325 6. CHE Miroslava Skleničková 18.200

MODERN PENTATHLON

	①		②		③		
INDIVIDUAL	SWE 4,964 BJÖRN FERM		HUN 4,953 ANDRÁS BALCZÓ		URS 4,795 PAVEL LEDNEV		4. GDR Karl-Heinz Kutschke 4,764 5. URS Boris Onischenko 4,756 6. FRA Raoul Gueguen 4,756
TEAM	HUN 14,325 ANDRÁS BALCZÓ ISTVÁN MÓNA FERENC TÖRÖK		URS 14,248 PAVEL LEDNEV BORIS ONISCHENKO STASIS SCHAPARNIS		FRA 13,289 RAOUL GUEGUEN LUCIEN GUIGUET JEAN-PIERRE GIUDICELLI		4. USA Moore/Beck/ Lough 13,280 5. FIN Aho/Ketelä/ Hotanen 13,238 6. GDR Kutschke/Tscherner/ Lüderitz 13,167

159

ROWING

Event	Gold	Silver	Bronze	4th–6th		
SINGLE SCULLS	NED 7:47.80 HENRI JAN WIENESE	FRG 7:52.00 JOCHEN MEISSNER	ARG 7:57.19 ALBERTO DEMIDDI	4. USA John Van Blom 5. GDR Achim Hill 6. GBR Kenneth Dwan	8:00.51 8:06.09 8:13.76	
DOUBLE SCULLS	URS 6:51.82 ANATOLY SASS ALEKSANDR TIMOSHININ	NED 6:52.80 L. FRANS VAN DIS HENRICUS DROOG	USA 6:54.21 WILLIAM MAHER JOHN NUNN	4. BUL Schelev/Valtschev 5. GDR Schmied/Haake 6. FRG Glock/Hild	6:58.48 7:04.92 7:12.20	
PAIR-OARED SHELL WITHOUT COXSWAIN	GDR 7:26.56 JÖRG LUCKE HANS-JÜRGEN BOTHE	USA 7:26.71 LAWRENCE HOUGH PHILIP JOHNSON	DEN 7:31.84 PETER CHRISTIANSEN IB IVAN LARSEN	4. AUT Ebner/Losert 5. SUI Rüssli/Zwimpfer 6. NED Luynenburg/Stokvis	7:41.80 7:46.79 —	
PAIR-OARED SHELL WITH COXSWAIN	ITA 8:04.81 PRIMO BARAN RENZO SAMBO BRUNO CIPOLLA (COX)	NED 8:06.80 HERMAN SUSELBEEK HADRIAAN VAN NES RODERICK RIJNDERS (COX)	DEN 8:08.07 JÖRN KRAB HARRY JÖRGENSEN PREBEN KRAB (COX)	4. GDR Wollmann/Gunkel/ Neubert 5. USA Hobbs/Edmunds/ MacDonald 6. FRG Hiesinger/Hartung/ Benter	8:08.22 8:12.60 8:41.51	
FOUR-OARED SHELL WITHOUT COXSWAIN	GDR 6:39.18 FRANK FORBERGER DIETER GRAHN FRANK RÜHLE DIETER SCHUBERT	HUN 6:41.64 ZOLTÁN MELIS GYÖRGY SARLÓS JÓZSEF CSERMELY ANTAL MELIS	ITA 6:44.01 TULLIO BARAGLIA RENATO BOSATTA P. ANGELO CONTI MANZINI ABRAMO ALBINI	4. SUI Altenburger/Gobet/ Rentsch/Meister 5. USA Raymond/Wright/ Hamlin/Terry 6. FRG Hitzbleck/Weinreich/ Buchter/Heck	6:45.78 6:47.70 7:08.22	
FOUR-OARED SHELL WITH COXSWAIN	NZL 6:45.62	GDR 6:48.20	SUI 6:49.04	4. ITA 5. USA 6. URS	6:49.54 6:51.41 7:00.00	
EIGHT-OARED SHELL WITH COXSWAIN	FRG 6:07.00	AUS 6:07.98	URS 6:09.11	4. NZL 5. CHE 6. USA	6:10.43 6:12.17 6:14.34	

SHOOTING

Event	Gold	Silver	Bronze	4th–6th		
RAPID-FIRE PISTOL	POL 593 JÓZEF ZAPĘDZKI	ROM 591/147 MARCEL ROŞCA	URS 591/146/148 RENART SULEIMANOV	4. GDR Christian Düring 591/146/147 5. FRG Erich Masurat 590 6. GDR Gerhard Dommrich 589		
FREE PISTOL	URS 562/30 GRIGORY KOSSYKH	FRG 562/26 HEINZ MERTEL	GDR 560 HARALD VOLLMAR	4. USA Arnold Vitarbo 559 5. POL Pawel Malek 556 6. GDR Helmut Artelt 555		
SMALL-BORE RIFLE PRONE	CHE 598 JAN KURKA	HUN 598 LÁSZLÓ HAMMERL	NZL 597 IAN BALLINGER	4. ROM Nicolae Rotaru 597 5. GBR John Palin 596 6. FRA Jean Loret 596		
SMALL-BORE RIFLE THREE POSITIONS	FRG 1,157 BERND KLINGNER	USA 1,156 JOHN WRITER	URS 1,154 VIKTOR PARKHIMOVICH	4. USA John Foster 1,153 5. MEX José Gonzales 1,152 6. CAN Gerald Ouellette 1,151		
FREE RIFLE THREE POSITIONS	USA 1,157 GARY ANDERSON	URS 1,151 VLADIMIR KORNEV	SUI 1,148 KURT MÜLLER	4. URS Shota Kveliashvili 1,142 5. SUI Erwin Vogt 1,140 6. FRG Hartmut Sommer 1,140		
TRAP	GBR 198 JOHN BRAITHWAITE	USA 196/25/25 THOMAS GARRIGUS	GDR 196/25/23 KURT CZEKALLA	4. URS Pavel Senichev 196/22 5. FRA Pierre Candelo 195 6. POL Adam Smelczyński 195		
SKEET	URS 198/25 YEVGENY PETROV	ITA 198/24/25 ROMANO GARAGNANI	FRG 198/24/23 KONRAD WIRNHIER	4. URS Yuri Tsuranov 196 5. PER Pedro Gianella 194 6. CHI Nicolas Atalah 194		

SWIMMING

Event	Gold	Silver	Bronze	4th–6th		
100-METER FREESTYLE	AUS 52.2 MICHAEL WENDEN	USA 52.8 KENNETH WALSH	USA 53.0 MARK SPITZ	4. GBR Robert McGregor 53.5 5. URS Leonid Ilyichev 53.8 6. URS Georgy Kulikov 53.8		
200-METER FREESTYLE	AUS 1:55.2 MICHAEL WENDEN	USA 1:55.8 DONALD SCHOLLANDER	USA 1:58.1 JOHN NELSON	4. CAN Ralph Hutton 1:58.6 5. FRA Alain Mosconi 1:59.1 6. AUS Robert Windle 2:00.9		

Event	Gold	Silver	Bronze	4th / 5th / 6th	
400-METER FREESTYLE	USA 4:09.0 MICHAEL BURTON	CAN 4:11.7 RALPH HUTTON	FRA 4:13.3 ALAIN MOSCONI	4. AUS Gregory Brough 5. AUS Graham White 6. USA John Nelson	4:15.9 4:16.7 4:17.2
1,500-METER FREESTYLE	USA 16:38.9 MICHAEL BURTON	USA 16:57.3 JOHN KINSELLA	AUS 17:04.7 GREGORY BROUGH	4. AUS Graham White 5. CAN Ralph Hutton 6. MEX Guillermo Echevarria	17:08.0 17:15.6 17:36.4
100-METER BACKSTROKE	GDR 58.7 ROLAND MATTHES	USA 1:00.2 CHARLES HICKCOX	USA 1:00.5 RONALD MILLS	4. USA Larry Barbiere 5. CAN James Shaw 6. NED Bob Schoutsen	1:01.1 1:01.4 1:01.8
200-METER BACKSTROKE	GDR 2:09.6 ROLAND MATTHES	USA 2:10.6 MITCHELL IVEY	USA 2:10.9 JACK HORSLEY	4. USA Gary Hall 5. ESP Santiago Esteva 6. URS Leonid Dobrosskokin	2:12.6 2:12.9 2:15.4
100-METER BREASTSTROKE	USA 1:07.7 DONALD McKENZIE	URS 1:08.0 VLADIMIR KOSSINSKY	URS 1:08.0 NIKOLAI PANKIN	4. BRA José Sylvio Fiolo 5. URS Yevgeny Mikhailov 6. AUS Ian O'Brien	1:08.1 1:08.4 1:08.6
200-METER BREASTSTROKE	MEX 2:28.7 FELIPE MUÑOZ	URS 2:29.2 VLADIMIR KOSSINSKY	USA 2:29.9 BRIAN JOB	4. URS Nikolai Pankin 5. URS Yevgeny Mikhailov 6. GDR Egon Henninger	2:30.3 2:32.8 2:33.2
100-METER BUTTERFLY	USA 55.9 DOUGLAS RUSSELL	USA 56.4 MARK SPITZ	USA 57.2 ROSS WALES	4. URS Vladimir Nemshilov 5. JPN Satoshi Maruya 6. URS Yuri Suzdaltsev	58.1 58.6 58.8
200-METER BUTTERFLY	USA 2:08.7 CARL ROBIE	GBR 2:09.0 MARTIN WOODROFFE	USA 2:09.3 JOHN FERRIS	4. URS Valentin Kuzmin 5. SWE Peter Feil 6. FRG Folkert Meeuw	2:10.6 2:10.9 2:11.5
200-METER INDIVIDUAL MEDLEY	USA 2:12.0 CHARLES HICKCOX	USA 2:13.0 GREGORY BUCKINGHAM	USA 2:13.3 JOHN FERRIS	4. PER Juan Bello 5. CAN George Smith 6. CAN John Gilchrist	2:13.7 2:15.9 2:16.6
400-METER INDIVIDUAL MEDLEY	USA 4:48.4 CHARLES HICKCOX	USA 4:48.7 GARY HALL	FRG 4:51.4 MICHAEL HOLTHAUS	4. USA Gregory Buckingham 5. CAN John Gilchrist 6. FRG Reinhard Merkel	4:51.4 4:56.7 4:59.8
4 x 100-METER FREESTYLE RELAY	USA 3:31.7 ZACHARY ZORN STEPHEN RERYCH MARK SPITZ KENNETH WALSH	URS 3:34.2 SEMYON BELITS-GEIMAN VIKTOR MAZANOV GEORGY KULIKOV LEONID ILYICHEV	AUS 3:34.7 GREGORY ROGERS ROBERT WINDLE ROBERT CUSACK MICHAEL WENDEN	4. GBR Turner/Hembrow/ McGregor/Jarvis 5. GDR Wiegand/Poser/ Gregor/Gericke 6. FRG Kremer/von Schilling/ Schorning/Fassnacht	3:38.4 3:38.8 3:39.0
4 x 200-METER FREESTYLE RELAY	USA 7:52.30 JOHN NELSON STEPHEN RERYCH MARK SPITZ DONALD SCHOLLANDER	AUS 7:53.70 GREGORY ROGERS GRAHAM WHITE ROBERT WINDLE MICHAEL WENDEN	URS 8:01.60 VLADIMIR BURE SEMYON BELITS-GEIMAN GEORGY KULIKOV LEONID ILYICHEV	4. CAN Smith/Jacks/ Gilchrist/Hutton 5. FRA Rousseau/Letast/ Luyce/Mosconi 6. FRG Fassnacht/Kremer/ Meeuw/von Schilling	8:03.22 8:03.77 8:04.33
4 x 100-METER MEDLEY RELAY	USA 3:54.9 CHARLES HICKCOX DONALD McKENZIE DOUGLAS RUSSELL KENNETH WALSH	GDR 3:57.5 ROLAND MATTHES EGON HENNINGER HORST-GÜNTHER GREGOR FRANK WIEGAND	URS 4:00.7 YURI GROMAK VLADIMIR KOSSINSKY VLADIMIR NEMSHILOV LEONID ILYICHEV	4. AUS Byrom/O'Brien/ Cusack/Wenden 5. JPN Tanaka/Taguchi/ Maruya/Iwasaki 6. FRG Blechert/Betz/ Stoklasa/Kremer	4:00.8 4:01.8 4:05.4
100-METER FREESTYLE	USA 1:00.0 JAN HENNE	USA 1:00.3 SUSAN PEDERSEN	USA 1:00.3 LINDA GUSTAVSON	4. CAN Marion Lay 5. GDR Martina Grunert 6. GBR Alexandra Jackson	1:00.5 1:01.0 1:01.0
200-METER FREESTYLE	USA 2:10.5 DEBBIE MEYER	USA 2:11.0 JAN HENNE	USA 2:11.2 JANE BARKMAN	4. GDR Gabriele Wetzko 5. YUG Mirjana Segrt 6. FRA Claude Mandonnaud	2:12.3 2:13.3 2:14.9
400-METER FREESTYLE	USA 4:31.8 DEBBIE MEYER	USA 4:35.5 LINDA GUSTAVSON	AUS 4:37.0 KAREN MORAS	4. USA Pamela Kruse 5. GDR Gabriele Wetzko 6. MEX Maria Teresa Ramirez	4:37.2 4:40.2 4:42.2
800-METER FREESTYLE	USA 9:24.0 DEBBIE MEYER	USA 9:35.7 PAMELA KRUSE	MEX 9:38.5 MARIA TERESA RAMIREZ	4. AUS Karen Moras 5. USA Patricia Caretto 6. CAN Angela Coughlaw	9:38.6 9:51.3 9:56.4
100-METER BACKSTROKE	USA 1:06.2 KAYE HALL	CAN 1:06.7 ELAINE TANNER	USA 1:08.1 JANE SWAGERTY	4. USA Kendis Moore 5. HUN Andrea Gyarmati 6. AUS Lynette Watson	1:08.3 1:09.1 1:09.1
200-METER BACKSTROKE	USA 2:24.8 LILLIAN WATSON	CAN 2:27.4 ELAINE TANNER	USA 2:28.9 KAYE HALL	4. AUS Lynette Watson 5. GBR Wendy Burrell 6. YUG Zdenka Gasparac	2:29.5 2:32.3 2:33.5
100-METER BREASTSTROKE	YUG 1:15.8 DJURDJICA BJEDOV	URS 1:15.9 G. PROZUMENSHIKOVA	USA 1:16.1 SHARON WICHMAN	4. FRG Uta Frommater 5. USA Catie Ball 6. JPN Kyoe Nakagawa	1:16.2 1:16.7 1:17.0

200-METER BREASTSTROKE	USA 2:44.4 SHARON WICHMAN	YUG 2:46.4 DJURDJICA BJEDOV	URS 2:47.0 G. PROZUMENSHIKOVA	4. URS Alla Grebennikova 2:47.1 5. USA Cathy Jamison 2:48.4 6. URS Svetlana Babanina 2:48.4
100-METER BUTTERFLY	AUS 1:05.5 LYNETTE McCLEMENTS	USA 1:05.8 ELLIE DANIEL	USA 1:06.2 SUSAN SHIELDS	4. NED Ada Kok 1:06.2 5. HUN Andréa Gyarmati 1:06.8 6. FRG Heike Hustede 1:06.9
200-METER BUTTERFLY	NED 2:24.7 ADA KOK	GDR 2:24.8 HELGA LINDNER	USA 2:25.9 ELLIE DANIEL	4. USA Toni Hewitt 2:26.2 5. FRG Heike Hustede 2:27.9 6. USA Diane Giebel 2:31.7
200-METER INDIVIDUAL MEDLEY	USA 2:24.7 CLAUDIA KOLB	USA 2:28.8 SUSAN PEDERSEN	USA 2:31.4 JAN HENNE	4. GDR Sabine Steinbach 2:31.4 5. JPN Yoshimi Nishigawa 2:33.7 6. GDR Marianne Seyedl 2:33.7
400-METER INDIVIDUAL MEDLEY	USA 5:08.5 CLAUDIA KOLB	USA 5:22.2 LYNN VIDALI	GDR 5:25.3 SABINE STEINBACH	4. USA Susan Pedersen 5:25.8 5. GBR Shelagh Ratcliffe 5:30.5 6. GDR Marianne Seydel 5:32.0
4 x 100-METER FREESTYLE RELAY	USA 4:02.5 JANE BARKMAN LINDA GUSTAVSON SUSAN PEDERSEN JAN HENNE	GDR 4:05.7 MARTINA GRUNERT UTA SCHMUCK ROSWITHA KRAUSE GABRIELE WETZKO	CAN 4:07.2 ANGELA COUGHLAW MARILYN CORSON ELAINE TANNER MARION LAY	4. AUS Steinbeck/Eddy/ Watson/Bell 4:08.7 5. HUN Kovács/Patoh/ Gyarmati/Turóczy 4:11.0 6. JPN Kawanishi/Nishigawa/ Fujii/Kobayashi 4:13.6
4 x 100-METER MEDLEY RELAY	USA 4:28.3 KAYE HALL CATIE BALL ELLIE DANIEL SUSAN PEDERSEN	AUS 4:30.0 LYNETTE WATSON JUDY PLAYFAIR LYNETTE McCLEMENTS JANET STEINBECK	FRG 4:36.4 ANGELIKA KRAUS UTA FROMMATER HEIKE HUSTEDE HEIDEMARIE REINECK	4. URS Lekveishvili/Grebets/ Devyatova/Grebennikova 4:37.0 5. GDR Grunert/Wittke/ Lindner/Schmuck 4:38.0 6. GBR Burrell/Harrison/ Auton/Jackson 4:38.3

VOLLEYBALL

FINAL STANDINGS	URS	JPN	CHE	4. GDR 5. POL 6. BUL
FINAL STANDINGS	URS	JPN	POL	4. PER 5. KOR 6. CHE

WATER POLO

FINAL STANDINGS	YUG	URS	HUN	4. ITA 5. USA 6. GDR

WEIGHT LIFTING

BANTAMWEIGHT 123 lbs. (56 kg)	IRI 367.5 S. MOHAMMAD NASSIRI	HUN 367.5 IMRE FÖLDI	POL 357.5 HENRYK TREBICKI	4. URS Gennady Chetin 352.5 5. JPN Shiro Ichinoseki 350.0 6. PUR Fernando Baez Cruz 345.0
FEATHERWEIGHT 132 lbs. (60 kg)	JPN 392.5 YOSHINOBU MIYAKE	URS 387.5 DITO SHANIDZE	JPN 385.0 YOSHIYUKI MIYAKE	4. POL Jan Wojnowski 382.5 5. POL Mieczyslaw Nowak 375.0 6. IRI Nasrollah Dehnavi 365.0
LIGHTWEIGHT 148.75 lbs. (67.5 kg)	POL 437.5 WALDEMAR BASZANOWSKI	IRI 422.5 PARVIZ JALAYER	POL 420.0 MARIAN ZIELIŃSKI	4. JPN Nobuyuki Hatta 417.5 5. KOR Shin-Hee Won 415.0 6. HUN János Bagócs 412.5
MIDDLEWEIGHT 165 lbs. (75 kg)	URS 475.0 VIKTOR KURENTSOV	JPN 455.0 MASASHI OUCHI	HUN 440.0 KÁROLY BAKOS	4. USA Russell Knipp 437.5 5. KOR Chun-Sik Lee 437.5 6. GDR Werner Dittrich 435.0
LIGHT HEAVYWEIGHT 181.5 lbs. (82.5 kg)	URS 485.0 BORIS SELITSKY	URS 485.0 VLADIMIR BELYAYEV	POL 472.5 NORBERT OZIMEK	4. HUN Gyözö Veres 472.5 5. GDR Karl Arnold 467.5 6. CHE Hans Zdražila 462.5
MIDDLE HEAVYWEIGHT 198.25 lbs. (90 kg)	FIN 517.5 KAARLO KANGASNIEMI	URS 507.5 JAN TAITS	POL 495.0 MAREK GOLĄB	4. SWE Bo Johansson 492.5 5. FIN Jaako Kailajärvi 485.0 6. HUN Árpád Nemessányi 482.5
SUPER HEAVYWEIGHT unlimited weight	URS 572.5 LEONID ZHABOTINSKY	BEL 555.0 SERGE REDING	USA 555.0 JOSEPH DUBE	4. GDR Manfred Rieger 532.5 5. FRG Rudolf Mang 525.0 6. FIN Mauno Lindroos 495.0

WRESTLING, FREESTYLE

Event	Gold	Silver	Bronze	Others
FLYWEIGHT 114.5 lbs. (52 kg)	JPN SHIGEO NAKATA	USA RICHARD SANDERS	MGL SURENJAV SUKHBAATAR	4. URS Nazar Albaryan 5. ITA Vincenzo Grassi 6. IND Sudesh Kumar
BANTAMWEIGHT 125.5 lbs. (57 kg)	JPN YOJIRO UETAKE	USA DONALD BEHM	IRI ABUTALEB GORGORI	4. URS Ali Aliyev 5. BUL Ivan Shavov 6. POL Zbigniew Zedzicki
FEATHERWEIGHT 136.5 lbs. (62 kg)	JPN MASAAKI KANEKO	BUL ENYU TODOROV	IRI S. SEYED-ABASSY	4. GRE Nicolaos Karypidis 5. ROM Petre Coman 6. URS Yeikan Tedeyev
LIGHTWEIGHT 149.5 lbs. (68 kg)	IRI ABDOLLAH MOVAHED	BUL ENYU DIMOV-VULCHEV	MGL SEREETER DANZANDARJAA	4. USA Wayne Wells 5. URS Zarbeg Beriashvili 6. IND Udey Chand
WELTERWEIGHT 163 lbs. (74 kg)	TUR MAHMUT ATALAY	FRA DANIEL ROBIN	MGL DAGVASUREN PUREV	4. IRI Ali-Mohamad Momeni 5. JPN Tatsuo Sasaki 6. URS Yuri Schakmuradov
MIDDLEWEIGHT 181 lbs. (82 kg)	URS BORIS GUREVITCH	MGL MUNKBAT JIGJID	BUL PRODAN GARDZHEV	4. USA Thomas Beckham 5. TUR Hüseyin Gürsoy 6. GDR Peter Döring
LIGHT HEAVYWEIGHT 198.5 lbs. (90 kg)	TUR AHMET AYIK	URS SCHOTA LOMIDZE	HUN JÓZSEF CSATÁRI	4. BUL Said Mustafov 5. MGL Khorloo Baianmunkh 6. USA Jess Lewis
SUPER HEAVYWEIGHT unlimited weight	URS ALEKSANDR MEDVED	BUL OSMAN DURALIEV	FRG WILFRIED DIETRICH	4. ROM Ştefan Ştîngu 5. USA Larry Kristoff 6. IRI Abolfazi Anvari

WRESTLING, GRECO-ROMAN

Event	Gold	Silver	Bronze	Others
FLYWEIGHT 114.5 lbs. (52 kg)	BUL PETER KIROV	URS VLADIMIR BAKULIN	CHE MIROSLAV ZEMAN	4. HUN Imre Alker 5. FRG Rolf Lacour 6. FIN Jussi Vesterinen
BANTAMWEIGHT 125.5 lbs. (57 kg)	HUN JÁNOS VARGA	ROM ION BACIU	URS IVAN KOCHERGIN	4. GRE Othon Moschidis 5. JPN Koji Sakurama 6. two-way tie
FEATHERWEIGHT 136.5 lbs. (62 kg)	URS ROMAN RURUA	JPN HIDEO FUJIMOTO	ROM SIMEON POPESCU	4. BUL Dimiter Galinchev 5. TUR Hizir Alakoc 6. FIN Martti Laakso
LIGHTWEIGHT 150 lbs. (68 kg)	JPN MUNJI MUMEMURA	YUG STEVAN HORVAT	GRE PETROS GALAKTOPOULOS	4. FRG Klaus Rost 5. FIN Eero Tapio 6. two-way tie
WELTERWEIGHT 163 lbs. (74 kg)	GDR RUDOLF VESPER	FRA DANIEL ROBIN	HUN KÁROLY BAJKÓ	4. BUL Metodi Zarev 5. ROM Ion Tăranu 6. SWE Jan-Ivar Karström
MIDDLEWEIGHT 181 lbs. (82 kg)	GDR LOTHAR METZ	URS VALENTIN OLENIK	YUG BRANISLAV SIMIČ	4. ROM Nicolae Neguţ 5. USA Richard Wayne Baughman 5. BUL Peter Krumov
LIGHT HEAVYWEIGHT 198.5 lbs. (90 kg)	BUL BOYAN RADEV	URS NIKOLAI YAKOVENKO	ROM NICOLAE MARTINESCU	4. SWE Per Svensson 5. NOR Tore Hem 6. three-way tie
SUPER HEAVYWEIGHT unlimited weight	HUN ISTVÁN KOZMA	URS ANATOLY ROSHIN	CHE PETR KMENT	4. SWE Sten Ragnar Svensson 5. ROM Constantin Buşiu 6. BUL Stefan Petrov

YACHTING

Event	Gold	Silver	Bronze	Others
FINN MONOTYPE	URS 11.7 VALENTIN MANKIN	AUT 53.4 HUBERT RAUDASCHL	ITA 55.1 FABIO ALBARELLI	4. GBR William Roberts 46.87 5. CAN William Fritz 47.8 6. CAN John Loaring 48.2
5.5-METER CLASS	SWE 8.0 ULF SUNDELIN JÖRGEN SUNDELIN PETER SUNDELIN	SUI 32.0 LOUIS NOVERRAZ BERNHARD DUNAND MARCEL STERN	GBR 39.8 ROBIN AISHER ADRIAN JARDINE PAUL ANDERSON	4. FRG Harmstorf/Stolze/ Stein 47.4 5. ITA Zucchinetti/Carattino/ Carattino 51.1 6. CAN Leibel/Weiss/ Hasen 68.0

DRAGON CLASS	○ USA 6.0 GEORGE FRIEDRICHS BARTON JAHNCKE GERALD SCHRECK	○ DEN 26.4 AAGE BIRCH POUL HÖJ JENSEN NIELS MARKUSSEN	● GDR 32.7 PAUL BOROWSKI KONRAD WEICHERT KARL-HEINZ THUN	4. CAN Tupper/Miller/Irwin 64.1 5. AUS Cuneo/Anderson/ Ferguson 65.0 6. SWE Broberg/Eisner/Hanson 71.4
STAR CLASS	○ USA 14.4 LOWELL NORTH PETER BARRETT	○ NOR 43.7 PEDER LUNDE PER OLAV WIKEN	● TA 44.7 FRANCO CAVALLO CAMILO GARGANO	4. DEN Elvström/Mik-Meyer 50.4 5. BAH Knowles/Knowles 63.4 6. AUS Forbes/Williamson 68.7
FLYING DUTCHMAN	○ GBR 3.0 RODNEY PATTISSON IAIN MACDONALD-SMITH	○ FRG 43.7 ULLRICH LIBOR PETER NAUMANN	● BRA 48.4 REINALDO CONRAD BURKHARD CORDES	4. AUS Ryves/Sargeant 49.1 5. NOR Lofteröd/Lofteröd 52.4 6. FRA Cheret/Trouble 68.0

NATIONAL MEDAL COUNT

COMPETITORS COUNTRIES: 111 ATHLETES: 5,531 MEN: 4,750 WOMEN: 781

	GOLD	SILVER	BRONZE	TOTAL		GOLD	SILVER	BRONZE	TOTAL		GOLD	SILVER	BRONZE	TOTAL		GOLD	SILVER	BRONZE	TOTAL
USA	45	28	34	107	CHE	7	2	4	13	SWE	2	1	1	4	BEL		1	1	2
URS	29	32	30	91	GBR	5	5	3	13	FIN	1	2	1	4	KOR		1	1	2
HUN	10	10	12	32	KEN	3	4	2	9	CUB		4		4	UGA		1	1	2
FRG	5	11	10	26	MEX	3	3	3	9	AUT		2	2	4	ARG			2	2
JPN	11	7	7	25	BUL	2	4	3	9	MGL		1	3	4	PAK	1			1
GDR	9	9	7	25	YUG	3	3	2	8	NZL	1		2	3	VEN	1			1
POL	5	2	11	18	DEN	1	4	3	8	BRA		1	2	3	TPE			1	1
AUS	5	7	5	17	NED	3	3	1	7	TUR	2			2	IND			1	1
ITA	3	4	9	16	IRN	2	1	2	5	NOR	1	1		2	GRE			1	1
FRA	7	3	5	15	CAN	1	3	1	5	ETH	1	1		2					
ROM	4	6	5	15	SUI		1	4	5	TUN	1		1	2					

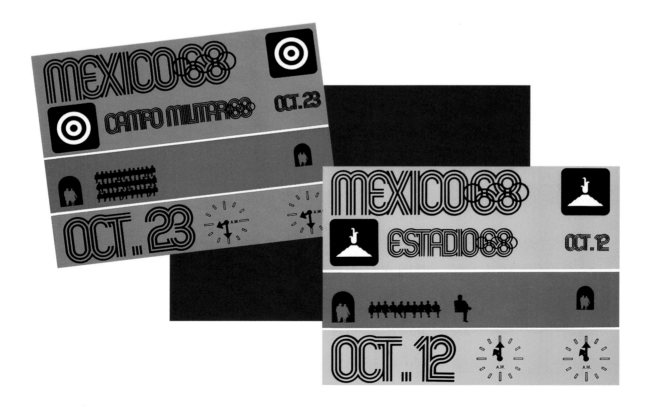

SAPPORO 1972 PROGRAM OF EVENTS

Thursday, FEBRUARY 3

AM	EVENT	VENUE
11:00	OPENING CEREMONY	Makomanai Speed-Skating Rink

PM	EVENT	VENUE
4:00	HOCKEY	Makomanai Indoor Skating Rink
7:30	HOCKEY	Makomanai Indoor Skating Rink

Friday, FEBRUARY 4

AM	EVENT	VENUE
8:30	BOBSLED	Mt. Teine Bobled Course
	two-man, 1st and 2nd runs	
9:00	SPEED SKATING	Makomanai Speed-Skating Rink
	5,000 meters	
	NORDIC SKIING	Makomanai Cross-Country Courses
	30 kilometers	
	LUGE	Mt. Teine Luge Course
	• singles, 1st and 2nd runs	
	• women's singles, 1st and 2nd runs	
10:00	FIGURE SKATING	Mikaho Indoor Skating Rink
	women's compulsory figures	
	NORDIC SKIING	Miyanomori Jump Hill
	combined (jumping)	

PM	EVENT	VENUE
1:30	ALPINE SKIING	Mt. Eniwa
	women's downhill, training	
2:00	HOCKEY	Makomanai Indoor Skating Rink
7:00	HOCKEY	Makomanai Indoor Skating Rink, Tsukisamu Indoor Skating Rink

Saturday, FEBRUARY 5

AM	EVENT	VENUE
8:30	BOBSLED	Mt. Teine Bobled Course
	two-man, 3rd and 4th runs	
9:00	NORDIC SKIING	Makomanai Cross-Country Courses
	combined (cross-country)	
10:00	SPEED SKATING	Makomanai Speed-Skating Rink
	500 meters	
	FIGURE SKATING	Mikaho Indoor Skating Rink
	women's compulsory figures	
	HOCKEY	Makomanai Indoor Skating Rink

PM	EVENT	VENUE
1:30	ALPINE SKIING	Mt. Eniwa
	women's downhill	

	EVENT	VENUE
2:00	HOCKEY	Makomanai Indoor Skating Rink
6:00	LUGE	Mt. Teine Luge Course
	women's singles, 3rd run	
7:00	HOCKEY	Makomanai Indoor Skating Rink

Sunday, FEBRUARY 6

AM	EVENT	VENUE
9:00	NORDIC SKIING	Makomanai Cross-Country Courses
	women's 10 kilometers	
10:00	SKI JUMPING	Miyanomori Jump Hill
	small hill	
	SPEED SKATING	Makomanai Speed-Skating Rink
	1,500 meters	

PM	EVENT	VENUE
12:30	HOCKEY	Tsukisamu Indoor Skating Rink
1:30	ALPINE SKIING	Mt. Eniwa
	downhill, training	
3:00	FIGURE SKATING	Makomanai Speed-Skating Rink
	pairs compulsory figures	
4:00	HOCKEY	Tsukisamu Indoor Skating Rink

Monday, FEBRUARY 7

AM	EVENT	VENUE
8:30	LUGE	Mt. Teine Luge Course
	singles, 3rd run	
9:00	NORDIC SKIING	Makomanai Cross-Country Courses
	15 kilometers	
	SPEED SKATING	Makomanai Speed-Skating Rink
	10,000 meters	
11:30	HOCKEY	Makomanai Indoor Skating Rink

PM	EVENT	VENUE
12:30	HOCKEY	Tsukisamu Indoor Skating Rink
1:30	ALPINE SKIING	Mt. Eniwa
	downhill	
2:45	HOCKEY	Makomanai Indoor Skating Rink
4:00	HOCKEY	Tsukisamu Indoor Skating Rink
6:00	LUGE	Mt. Teine Luge Course
	• singles, 4th run	
	• women's singles, 4th run	
	FIGURE SKATING	Makomanai Indoor Skating Rink
	women's free skate	
7:30	HOCKEY	Tsukisamu Indoor Skating Rink

Tuesday, FEBRUARY 8

AM	EVENT	VENUE
9:00	FIGURE SKATING	Mikaho Indoor Skating Rink
	compulsory figures	

PM	EVENT	VENUE
1:30	ALPINE SKIING	Mt. Teine
	women's giant slalom	
2:00	HOCKEY	Makomanai Indoor Skating Rink
6:00	FIGURE SKATING	Makomanai Indoor Skating Rink
	pairs free skate	

Wednesday, FEBRUARY 9

AM	EVENT	VENUE
9:00	NORDIC SKIING	Makomanai Cross-Country Courses
	women's 5 kilometers	
	BIATHLON	Makomanai Biathlon Course
	20 kilometers	
9:30	FIGURE SKATING	Mikaho Indoor Skating Rink
	compulsory figures	
10:00	SPEED SKATING	Makomanai Speed-Skating Rink
	women's 1,500 meters	
	HOCKEY	Makomanai Indoor Skating Rink

PM	EVENT	VENUE
1:30	ALPINE SKIING	Mt. Teine
	giant slalom, 1st race	
2:00	HOCKEY	Makomanai Indoor Skating Rink, Tsukisamu Indoor Skating Rink
7:00	HOCKEY	Makomanai Indoor Skating Rink

Thursday, FEBRUARY 10

AM	EVENT	VENUE
8:30	NORDIC SKIING	Makomanai Cross-Country Courses
	50 kilometers	
10:00	SPEED SKATING	Makomanai Speed-Skating Rink
	women's 500 meters	
	HOCKEY	Makomanai Indoor Skating Rink

PM	EVENT	VENUE
1:30	ALPINE SKIING	Mt. Teine
	giant slalom, 2nd race	
2:00	HOCKEY	Makomanai Indoor Skating Rink, Tsukisamu Indoor Skating Rink
4:15	LUGE	Mt. Teine Luge Course
	two-seater, 1st and 2nd runs	
7:00	HOCKEY	Makomanai Indoor Skating Rink, Tsukisamu Indoor Skating Rink

Friday, FEBRUARY 11

AM	EVENT	VENUE
8:30	BOBSLED	Mt. Teine Bobled Course
	four-man, 1st and 2nd run	
9:00	BIATHLON	Makomanai Biathlon Course
	4 x 7.5-kilometer relay	
10:00	SKI JUMPING	Okurayama Jump Hill
	large hill	
	SPEED SKATING	Makomanai Speed-Skating Rink
	women's 1,000 meters	
11:00	ALPINE SKIING	Mt. Eniwa
	women's slalom	

PM	EVENT	VENUE
6:00	FIGURE SKATING	Makomanai Indoor Skating Rink
	free skate	

Saturday, FEBRUARY 12

AM	EVENT	VENUE
8:30	BOBSLED	Mt. Teine Bobled Course
	four-man, 3rd and 4th runs	
9:00	NORDIC SKIING	Makomanai Cross-Country Courses
	women's 3 x 5-kilometer relay	
10:00	SPEED SKATING	Makomanai Speed-Skating Rink
	women's 3,000 meters	
11:00	ALPINE SKIING	Mt. Eniwa
	slalom, eliminations	

PM	EVENT	VENUE
2:00	HOCKEY	Tsukisamu Indoor Skating Rink
4:00	HOCKEY	Makomanai Indoor Skating Rink
7:30	HOCKEY	Makomanai Indoor Skating Rink

Sunday, FEBRUARY 13

AM	EVENT	VENUE
9:00	NORDIC SKIING	Makomanai Cross-Country Courses
	4 x 10-kilometer relay	
	HOCKEY	Makomanai Indoor Skating Rink
11:00	ALPINE SKIING	Mt. Eniwa
	slalom, final	

PM	EVENT	VENUE
12:30	HOCKEY	Makomanai Indoor Skating Rink
6:00	CLOSING CEREMONY	Makomanai Indoor Skating Rink

SAPPORO 1972
11TH OLYMPIC WINTER GAMES

LEGEND   MEN'S EVENT   WOMEN'S EVENT   MIXED EVENT   OLYMPIC RECORD   WORLD RECORD

DNF = Did Not Finish   DQ = Disqualified   est = estimated   NR = No Result   * refer to end maps for country codes

BIATHLON

20 KILOMETERS
 NOR 1:15:55.50 *MAGNAR SOLBERG*   **GDR** 1:16:07.60 *HANSJÖRG KNAUTHE*   **SWE** 1:16:27.03 *LARS-GÖRAN ARWIDSON*

4. URS	Aleksandr Tikhonov	1:16:48.65
5. FIN	Yrjö Salpakari	1:16:51.43
6. FIN	Esko Saira	1:17:34.80

4 x 7.5-KILOMETER RELAY
 URS 1:51:44.92 *ALEKSANDR TIKHONOV / RINNAT SAFINE / IVAN BIAKOV / VICTOR MAMATOV*   **FIN** 1:54:37.25 *ESKO SAIRA / JUHANI SUUTARINEN / HEIKKI IKOLA / MAURI RÖPPÄNEN*   **GDR** 1:54:57.67 *HANSJÖRG KNAUTHE / JOACHIM MEISCHNER / DIETER SPEER / HORST KOSCHKA*

4. NOR	Hovda/Nordkild/ Svendsberget/Solberg	1:56:24.41
5. SWE	Arwidson/Olsson/ Wadman/Petrusson	1:56:57.40
6. USA	Karns/Morse/ Donahue/Bowerman	1:57:24.32

BOBSLED

TWO-MAN
 FRG 4:57.07 *WOLFGANG ZIMMERER / PETER UTZSCHNEIDER*   **FRG** 4:58.84 *HORST FLOTH / PEPI BADER*   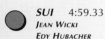 **SUI** 4:59.33 *JEAN WICKI / EDY HUBACHER*

4. ITA	Gaspari/Armano	5:00.45
5. ROM	Panţuru/Zangor	5:00.53
6. SWE	Eriksson/Johansson	5:01.40

FOUR-MAN
 SUI 4:43.07 *JEAN WICKI / HANS LEUTENEGGER / WERNER CARMICHEL / EDY HUBACHER*   **ITA** 4:43.83 *NEVIO DE ZORDO / ADRIANO FRASSINELLI / CORRADO DAL FABBRO / GIANNI BONICHON*   **FRG** 4:43.92 *WOLFGANG ZIMMERER / STEFAN GAISREITER / WALTER STEINBAUER / PETER UTZSCHNEIDER*

4. SUI	Candrian/Schenker/ Juon/Beeli	4:44.56
5. FRG	Floth/Bader/ Ertel/Gilik	4:45.09
6. AUT	Gruber/Oberhauser/ Chwalla/Eder	4:45.77

FIGURE SKATING

SINGLES
 TCH 9 2,739.1 *ONDREJ NEPELA*   **URS** 20 2,672.4 *SERGEI CHETVEROUKHIN*   **FRA** 28 2,653.1 *PATRICK PERA*

4. USA	Kenneth Shelley	43	2,596.0
5. USA	John Petkevich	47	2,591.5
6. GDR	Jan Hoffmann	55	2,567.6

SINGLES
 AUT 9 2,751.5 *BEATRIX SCHUBA*   **CAN** 23 2,673.2 *KAREN MAGNUSSEN*   **USA** 27 2,663.1 *JANET LYNN*

4. USA	Julie Holmes	39	2,627.0
5. HUN	Zsuzsa Almássy	47	2,592.4
6. GDR	S.Morgenstern	53	2,579.4

PAIRS
 URS 12 420.4 *IRINA RODNINA / ALEKSEI ULANOV*   **URS** 15 419.4 *LYUDMILA SMIRNOVA / ANDREI SURAIKIN*   **GDR** 29 411.8 *MANUELA GROSS / UWE KAGELMANN*

4. USA	Starbuck/Shelley	35	406.8
5. FRG	Lehmann/Wiesinger	52	399.8
6. URS	Chernieva/Blagov	52	399.1

HOCKEY

FINAL STANDINGS
 URS   **USA**   **TCH**

4. SWE
5. FIN
6. POL

LUGE

SINGLE
 GDR 3:27.58 *WOLFGANG SCHEIDEL*   **GDR** 3:28.39 *HARALD EHRIG*   **GDR** 3:28.73 *WOLFRAM FIEDLER*

4. GDR	Klaus Bonsack	3:29.16
5. FRG	Leonhard Nagenrauft	3:29.67
6. FRG	Josef Fendt	3:30.03

TWO-SEATER
 ITA 1:28.35 *PAUL HILDGARTNER / WALTER PLAIKNER*   **GDR** 1:28.35 *HORST HÖRNLEIN / REINHARD BREDOW*   **GDR** 1:29.16 *KLAUS BONSACK / WOLFRAM FIEDLER*

4. JPN	Arai/Kobayashi	1:29.63
5. FRG	Brandner/Schwarm	1:29.66
5. POL	Więckowski/Kubik	1:29.66

SINGLE		GDR 2:59.18 ANNA-MARIA MÜLLER		GDR 2:59.49 UTE RÜHROLD		GDR 2:59.54 MARGIT SCHUMANN	4. FRG Elisabeth Demleitner 3:00.80 5. JPN Yuko Otaka 3:00.98 6. two-way tie 3:02.33

SKIING, ALPINE

		1st		2nd		3rd	4th–6th
DOWNHILL	⃝	SUI 1:51.43 BERNHARD RUSSI	⃝	SWE 1:52.07 ROLAND COLLOMBIN	⃝	AUT 1:52.40 HEINRICH MESSNER	4. SUI Andreas Sprecher 1:53.11 5. NOR Erik Håker 1:53.16 6. SUI Walter Tresch 1:53.19
SLALOM	⃝	ESP 1:49.27 F. FERNANDEZ OCHOA	⃝	ITA 1:50.28 GUSTAV THÖNI	⃝	ITA 1:50.30 ROLAND THÖNI	4. FRA Henri Duvillard 1:50.45 5. FRA Jean-Noël Augert 1:50.51 6. ITA Eberhard Schmalzl 1:50.83
GIANT SLALOM	⃝	ITA 3:09.62 GUSTAV THÖNI	⃝	SUI 3:10.75 EDMUND BRUGGMANN	⃝	SWE 3:10.99 WERNER MATTLE	4. FRG Alfred Hagn 3:11.16 5. FRA Jean-Noël Augert 3:11.84 6. FRG Max Rieger 3:11.96
DOWNHILL	⃝	SUI 1:36.68 MARIE-THERES NADIG	⃝	AUT 1:37.00 ANNEMARIE PRÖLL	⃝	USA 1:37.68 SUSAN CORROCK	4. FRA Isabelle Mir 1:38.62 5. FRG Rosi Speiser 1:39.10 6. FRG Rosi Mittermaier 1:39.32
SLALOM	⃝	USA 1:31.24 BARBARA COCHRAN	⃝	FRA 1:31.26 DANIÈLLE DEBERNARD	⃝	FRA 1:32.69 FLORENCE STEURER	4. CAN Judy Crawford 1:33.95 5. AUT Annemarie Pröll 1:34.03 6. FRG Pamela Behr 1:34.27
GIANT SLALOM	⃝	SUI 1:29.90 MARIE-THERES NADIG	⃝	AUT 1:30.75 ANNEMARIE PRÖLL	⃝	AUT 1:32.35 WILTRUD DREXEL	4. CAN Laurie Kreiner 1:32.48 5. FRG Rosi Speiser 1:32.56 6. FRA Florence Steurer 1:32.59

SKIING, NORDIC

		1st		2nd		3rd	4th–6th
15 KILOMETERS, CLASSICAL	⃝	SWE 45:28.24 SVEN-ÅKE LUNDBÄCK	⃝	URS 46:00.84 FEDOR SIMASHOV	⃝	NOR 46:02.68 IVAR FORMO	4. FIN Juha Mieto 46:02.74 5. URS Yuri Skobov 46:04.59 6. GDR Axel Lesser 46:17.01
30 KILOMETERS, CLASSICAL	⃝	URS 1:36:31.15 VYACHESLAV VEDENINE	⃝	NOR 1:37:25.30 PÅL TYLDUM	⃝	NOR 1:37:32.44 JOHS HARVIKEN	4. SWE Gunnar Larsson 1:37:33.72 5. FRG Walter Demel 1:37:45.33 6. URS Fedor Simachev 1:38:22.50
50 KILOMETERS, CLASSICAL	⃝	NOR 2:43:14.75 PÅL TYLDUM	⃝	NOR 2:43:29.45 MAGNE MYRMO	⃝	URS 2:44:00.19 VYACHESLAV VEDENINE	4. NOR Reidar Hjermstad 2:44:14.51 5. FRG Walter Demel 2:44:32.67 6. SUI Werner Geeser 2:44:34.13
4 x 10-KILOMETER RELAY	⃝	URS 2:04:47.94 VLADIMIR VORONKOV YURI SKOBOV FEDOR SIMACHEV VYACHESLAV VEDENINE	⃝	NOR 2:04:57.06 PÅL TYLDUM ODDVAR BRÅ IVAR FORMO JOHS HARVIKEN	⃝	SUI 2:07:00.06 ALFRED KÄLIN ALBERT GIGER ALOIS KÄLIN EDUARD HAUSER	4. SWE Magnusson/Åslund/ 2:07:03.60 Larsson/Lundbäck 5. FIN Taipale/Mieto/ 2:07:50.19 Repo/Karjalainen 6. GDR Hessler/Lesser/ 2:10:03.73 Grimmer/Klause
COMBINED	⃝	GDR 413.340 ULRICH WEHLING	⃝	FIN 405.505 RAUNO MIETTINEN	⃝	GDR 398.800 KARL-HEINZ LUCK	4. FIN Erkki Kilpinen 391.845 5. JPN Yuji Katsuro 390.200 6. TCH Tomáš Kučera 387.935
5 KILOMETERS, CLASSICAL	⃝	URS 17:00.50 GALINA KULAKOVA	⃝	FIN 17:05.50 MARJATTA KAJOSMAA	⃝	TCH 17:07.32 HELENA ŠIKOLOVÁ	4. URS Alevtina Olunina 17:07.40 5. FIN Hilkka Kuntola 17:11.67 6. URS L. Moukhatcheva 17:12.08
10 KILOMETERS, CLASSICAL	⃝	URS 34:17.82 GALINA KULAKOVA	⃝	URS 34:54.11 ALEVTINA OLUNINA	⃝	FIN 34:56.45 MARJATTA KAJOSMAA	4. URS L. Moukhatcheva 34:58.56 5. FIN Helena Takalo 35:06.34 6. NOR Aslaug Dahl 35:18.84
3 x 5-KILOMETER RELAY	⃝	URS 48:16.15 ALEVTINA OLUNINA LYUBOV MOUKHATCHEVA GALINA KULAKOVA	⃝	FIN 49:19.37 HELENA TAKALO HILKKA KUNTOLA MARJATTA KAJOSMAA	⃝	NOR 49:51.49 INGER AUFLES ASLAUG DAHL BERIT MÖRDRE- LAMMEDAL	4. FRG Mrklas/Rothfuss/ 50:25.61 Enler 5. GDR Haupt/Fischer/ 50:28.45 Unger 6. TCH Bartušová/Šikolová/ 51:16.16 Cillerová

SKI JUMPING

		1st		2nd		3rd	4th–6th
SMALL HILL	⃝	JPN 244.2 YUKIO KASAYA	⃝	JPN 234.8 AKITSUGU KONNO	⃝	JPN 229.5 SEIJI AOCHI	4. NOR Ingolf Mork 225.5 5. TCH Jiří Raška 224.8 6. POL Wojciech Fortuna 222.0
LARGE HILL	⃝	POL 219.9 WOJCIECH FORTUNA	⃝	SUI 219.8 WALTER STEINER	⃝	GDR 219.3 RAINER SCHMIDT	4. FIN Tauno Käyhkö 219.2 5. GDR Manfred Wolf 215.1 6. URS Garii Napalkov 210.1

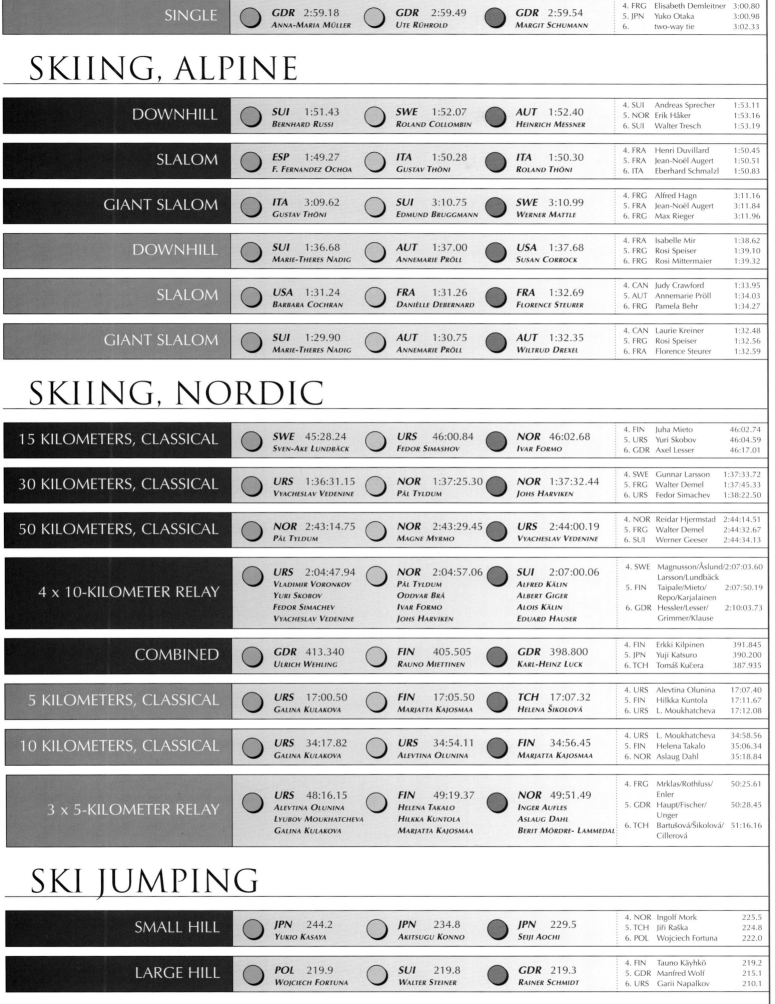

SPEED SKATING

500 METERS		FRG 39.44 ERHARD KELLER		SWE 39.69 HASSE BÖRJES		URS 39.80 VALERY MURATOV	4. NOR Per Björang 39.91 5. FIN Seppo Hänninen 40.12 6. FIN Leo Linkovesi 40.14
1,500 METERS		HOL 2:02.96 ADRIANUS SCHENK		NOR 2:04.26 ROAR GRÖNVOLD		SWE 2:05.89 GÖRAN CLAESSON	4. NOR Björn Tveter 2:05.94 5. HOL Jan Bols 2:06.58 6. URS Valery Lavrouchkin 2:07.16
5,000 METERS		HOL 7:23.61 ADRIANUS SCHENK		NOR 7:28.18 ROAR GRÖNVOLD		NOR 7:33.39 STEN STENSEN	4. SWE Göran Claeson 7:36.17 5. NOR Willy Olsen 7:36.47 6. HOL Cornelis Verkerk 7:39.17
10,000 METERS		HOL 15:01.35 ADRIANUS SCHENK		HOL 15:04.70 CORNELIS VERKERK		NOR 15:07.08 STEN STENSEN	4. HOL Jan Bols 15:17.99 5. URS Valery Lavrouchkin 15:20.08 6. SWE Göran Claeson 15:30.19
500 METERS		USA 43.33 ANNE HENNING		URS 44.01 VERA KRASNOVA		URS 44.45 LYUDMILA TITOVA	4. USA Sheila Young 44.53 5. FRG Monika Pflug 44.75 6. HOL Atje Keulen-Deelstra 44.89
1,000 METERS		FRG 1:31.40 MONIKA PFLUG		HOL 1:31.61 ATJE KEULEN-DEELSTRA		USA 1:31.62 ANNE HENNING	4. URS Lyudmila Titova 1:31.85 5. URS Nina Statkevitch 1:32.21 6. USA Dianne Holum 1:32.41
1,500 METERS		USA 2:20.85 DIANNE HOLUM		HOL 2:21.05 CHRISTINA BAAS-KAISER		HOL 2:22.05 ATJE KEULEN-DEELSTRA	4. HOL E. van den Brom 2:22.27 5. GDR Rosemarie Taupadel 2:22.35 6. URS Nina Statkevitch 2:23.19
3,000 METERS		HOL 4:52.14 CHRISTINA BAAS-KAISER		USA 4:58.67 DIANNE HOLUM		HOL 4:59.91 ATJE KEULEN-DEELSTRA	4. HOL Sippie Tigelaar 5:01.67 5. URS Nina Statkevitch 5:01.79 6. URS Kapitolina Sereguina 5:01.88

NATIONAL MEDAL COUNT

COMPETITORS COUNTRIES: 49   ATHLETES: 1,274   MEN: 1,000   WOMEN: 274

	GOLD	SILVER	BRONZE	TOTAL
URS	6	10	9	25
GDR	9	9	6	24
FIN	4	3	6	13
NOR	3	2	4	9
USA	4	4		8

	GOLD	SILVER	BRONZE	TOTAL
SWE	4	2	2	8
TCH		2	4	6
SUI	2	2	1	5
FRG	2	1	1	4
CAN	2	1	1	4

	GOLD	SILVER	BRONZE	TOTAL
FRA		1	2	3
ITA	2			2
LIE			2	2
GBR	1			1
JPN		1		1

	GOLD	SILVER	BRONZE	TOTAL
YUG		1		1
AUT			1	1

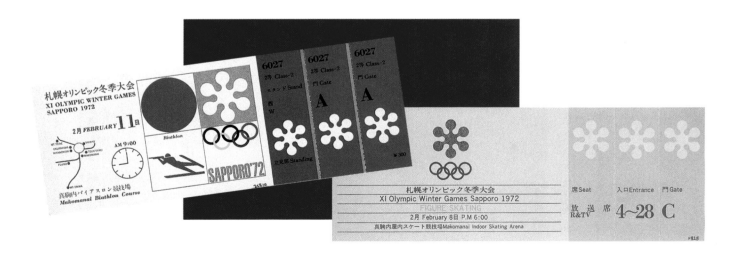

RECORD OF THE XIX OLYMPIAD

OCTOBER 12, 1968-AUGUST 25, 1972

OFFICERS OF THE INTERNATIONAL OLYMPIC COMMITTEE

Avery Brundage — President
Constantin Andrianov — Vice President
José de J. Clark Flores — Vice President
The Lord Killanin — Vice President

Other Executive Members:
Sheik Gabriel Gemayel
Marquess of Exeter
Syed Wajid Ali
Count Jean de Beaumont
Jonkheer Herman A. Van Karnebeek

INTERNATIONAL OLYMPIC COMMITTEE MEMBERSHIP DURING THE XIX OLYMPIAD

ARRIVALS: 18

—— 1968 ——

October 10	Agustin Carlos Arroyo	Ecuador
	José Beracasa	Venezuela
	Abdel Mohamed Halim	Sudan
	Hamengku Buwono IX	Indonesia
	René Rakotobe	Madagascar

—— 1969 ——

June 6	Cecil Lancelot Cross	New Zealand
	Raymond Gafner	Switzerland
	Louis N'Daye Guirandou	Ivory Coast
	Masaji Kiyokawa	Japan
	Virgilio de Leon	Panama
	Rudolf Nemetschke	Austria

—— 1970 ——

May 12	Maurice Herzog	France
	Sven Thofelt	Sweden
	Henry Hsu	Taiwan

—— 1971——

September 15	Prabhas Charusathiara	Thailand
	Vitaly Smirnov	USSR
	Ydnekatchew Tessema	Ethiopia

—— 1972 ——

| February 1 | Berthold Beitz | FRG |

DEPARTURES: 12

—— 1968 ——

| November 30 | John Jewett Garland* | USA |
| December 6 | Albert Mayer* | Switzerland |

—— 1969 ——

March 23	Amadou Barry*	Senegal
June 6	Manfred Mautner-Markhof	Austria
August 31	Miguel Moenck*	Cuba

—— 1970 ——

| May 12 | Gustaf Dyrssen | Sweden |

—— 1971——

| April 8 | Armand Massard* | France |

April 17	José de Clark*	Mexico
July 17	Alexei Romanov	USSR
July 25	René Rakotobe*	Madagascar
August 14	Georg von Opel*	FRG
September 15	Georg Wilhelm von Hanover	FRG

* Died in office; all others resigned

Total IOC membership by end of XIX OLYMPIAD: 75

Net increase in the IOC membership: 2

OFFICERS OF THE UNITED STATES OLYMPIC COMMITTEE

12th USOC Quadrennial, November 29, 1965, to April 19, 1969

Douglas F. Roby

Roby was elected USOC president November 29, 1965. His term spanned the XVIII and XIX Olympiads.

Other elected officers were:
Franklin L. Orth, First Vice President
Dr. Merritt H. Stiles, Second Vice President
Robert J. Kane, Secretary
Julian K. Roosevelt, Treasurer
Patrick H. Sullivan, Counselor
Arthur G. Lentz, Executive Director *
Everett D. Barnes, Executive Director

* Served as acting director, June 1-December 1, 1968

13th USOC Quadrennial, April 19, 1969, to February 9, 1973

Franklin L. Orth

Orth was elected USOC president April 29, 1969. His term was to span the XIX and XX Olympiads, but he died on March 29, 1970.

Other elected officers:

Clifford H. Buck, First Vice President
Philip O. Krumm, Second Vice President
Robert J. Kane, Secretary
Julian K. Roosevelt, Treasurer
Patrick H. Sullivan, Counselor
Arthur G. Lentz, Executive Director

HONORARY PRESIDENTS OF THE UNITED STATES OLYMPIC COMMITTEE

During the XIX Olympiad, President Lyndon Baines Johnson served as honorary president of the USOC until he left office on January 20, 1969. Richard M. Nixon assumed the role when he was sworn in as the United States president on the same date.

OLYMPIC AWARDS

OLYMPIC DIPLOMA OF MERIT

The Olympic Diploma of Merit, created in 1905 during the III Olympic Congress in Brussels, was awarded to an individual who had been active in the service of sport and/or had contributed substantially to the Olympic movement.

RECIPIENTS:

1968	Vernon Morgan	Great Britain
1969	Francisco Nobre Guedes	Portugal
1970	Jean-François Brisson	France
1971	Gaston Meyer	France
1972	Andres Merce Varela	Spain

SIR THOMAS FEARNLEY CUP

The Fearnley Cup, donated in 1950 by Sir Thomas Fearnley, former member of the International Olympic Committee in Norway from 1927 to 1950, was awarded to a sports club or a local sports association practicing meritorious achievement in the service of the Olympic movement.

RECIPIENTS:

| 1967 | Club Atletico Sudamericana | Argentina |
| 1972 | The Guayas Sports Federation | Ecuador |

THE OLYMPIC CUP

Beginning in 1906, the Olympic Cup was awarded annually to a person, institution, or association that had contributed significantly to sport or to the development of the Olympic movement. The Olympic Cup was kept at the IOC; honorees received a reproduction. The award was originally conceived by Baron Pierre de Coubertin.

RECIPIENTS

City of Mexico, awarded June 1969 for the year 1968.

Polish Olympic Committee, awarded June 1969 for the year 1969.

Organizing Committee of the Asian Games in Bankok, awarded September 1971 for the year 1970.

Organizing Committee of the Pan-American Games, City of Cali, Colombia, awarded September 1971 for the year 1971.

National Olympic Committee of Turkey, awarded January /February 1972 for the year 1972.

City of Sapporo, awarded August/September 1972 for the year 1972.

THE MOHAMED TAHER TROPHY

The Mohamed Taher Trophy was donated in 1950 by His Excellency Mohamed Taher Pasha, former member of the International Olympic Committee in Egypt from 1934 to 1968. The award went to an amateur athlete, Olympian, or otherwise, whose excellence merited special recognition.

RECIPIENTS:

1971 Rowing Team of New Zealand

THE COUNT ALBERTO BONACOSSA TROPHY

The Count Alberto Bonacossa Trophy, presented in 1954 by the Italian National Olympic Committee in honor of Count Alberto Bonacossa, former member of the International Olympic Committee in Italy from 1925 to 1953, was awarded to the national Olympic committee that had done outstanding work in furthering the Olympic movement during the preceding year.

1971 Greek National Olympic Committee

OFFICIAL PUBLICATIONS OF THE INTERNATIONAL OLYMPIC COMMITTEE

THE OLYMPIC CHARTER

The Olympic Charter provides the official rules, procedures, and protocols of the IOC, which are periodically updated by vote of the membership at an IOC Session. One edition was issued during the XIX Olympiad.

Edition 16   Issued September 1971
             (In French and English)

THE OLYMPIC REVIEW

Information Letter (Lettre d'Information) - Beginning in October 1967, the IOC began to publish the *Information Letter*, a monthly newsletter to keep members informed of IOC business. Produced in Lausanne, the *Information Letter* became the 10th version of the *Olympic Review* and had its own sequential numbering system.

#13-#14	October-November 1968
#15	December 1968
#16	January 1969
#17	February 1969
#18	March 1969
#19	April 1969
#20-#21	May-June 1969
#22	July 1969
#23-#24	August-September 1969
#25	October 1969
#26-#27	November-December 1969

Olympic Review (Revue Olympique) - Dissatisfied with the *Information Letter*, the IOC began to produce a much more informative monthly called the *Olympic Revue* in January 1970. It is the 11th and most recent permutation of the monthly Olympic magazine that is published today. Printed in English and French, the *Olympic Review* uses the same numbering system as the *Information Letter*.

#28	January 1970
#29	February 1970
#30-#31	March-April 1970
#32	May 1970
#33	June 1970
#34-#35	July-August 1970
#36	September 1970
#37	October 1970
#38-#39	November-December 1970
#40-#41	January-February 1971

#42	March 1971
#43	April 1971
#44	May 1971
#45	June 1971
#46	July 1971
#47	August 1971
#48	September 1971
#49	October 1971
#50-#51	November-December 1971
#52	January 1972
#53-#54	February-March 1972
#55	April 1972
#56-#57	May-June 1972
#58	July 1972

THE IOC HANDBOOK

This publication lists the names and addresses of the members of the IOC, the NOCs, and the IFs, as well as information on Olympic-related associations. The IOC decided in 1967 that the IOC Handbook would be published after each IOC Session. Issues during the XIX Olympiad included:

1968 IOC Handbook
1969 IOC Handbook
1970 IOC Handbook
1971 IOC Handbook

ACKNOWLEDGMENTS

The publisher would like to thank the following for their invaluable assistance to 1st Century Project and World Sport Research & Publications: Gov. Francisco G. Almeda (Philippine Olympic Committee, Manila); Sheik Fahad Al-Ahmad Al-Sabah (Olympic Committee of Kuwait); Don Anthony; Maj. Gen. Charouck Arirachakaran (Olympic Committee of Thailand, Bangkok); Bibliothèque National de France (Paris); Marie-Charlotte Bolot (University of the Sorbonne Cultural Library and Archives, Paris); Boston Public Library; British Museum and Library (London); Gail Britton; Richard L. Coe; Anita DeFrantz (IOC Member in the United States); Margi Denton; Carl and Lieselott Diem - Archives/Olympic Research Institute of the German Sport University Cologne; Edward L. Doheny, Jr. Library (University of Southern California, Los Angeles); Robert G. Engel; Miguel Fuentes (Olympic Committee of Chile, Santiago); National Library of Greece (Athens); Hollee Hazwell (Columbiana Collection, Columbia University, New York); Rebecca S. Jabbour and Bill Roberts (Bancroft Library, University of California at Berkeley); Diane Kaplan (Manuscripts and Archives, Sterling Library, Yale University, New Haven); David Kelly (Sport Specialist, Library of Congress, Washington, D.C.); Fékrou Kidane (International Olympic Committee, Lausanne); Peter Knight; Dr. John A. Lucas; Los Angeles Public Library; Blaine Marshall; Joachaim Mester, President of the German Sport University Cologne; Ed Mosk; Geoffroy de Navacelle; New York Public Library; Olympic Committee of India (New Delhi); Richard Palmer (British Olympic Association, London); C. Robert Paul; University of Rome Library and Archives; Margaret M.

Sherry (Rare Books and Special Collections, Firestone Library, Princeton University); Dr. Ruth Sparhawk; Gisela Terrell (Special Collections, Irwin Library, Butler University, Indianapolis); Walter Teutenberg; The Officers, Directors and Staff (United States Olympic Committee, Colorado Springs); University Research Library, (University of California at Los Angeles); John Vernon (National Archives, Washington, DC); Emily C. Walhout (Houghton Library; Harvard University); Herb Weinberg; Dr. Wayne Wilson, Michael Salmon, Shirley Ito (Paul Ziffren Sports Resource Center Library, Amateur Athletic Foundation of Los Angeles); Patricia Henry Yeomans; Nanci A. Young (Seeley G. Mudd Manuscript Library, Princeton University Archives); Dr. Karel Wendl, Michéle Veillard, Patricia Eckert, Simon Mandl, Ruth Perrenoud, Nikolay Guerguiev, Fani Kakridi-Enz, Laura Leslie Pearman, and Christine Sklentzas (International Olympic Committee Olympic Studies and Research Center, Lausanne); and Pat White (Special Collections, Stanford University Library, Palo Alto).

The publishers recognize with gratitude the special contributions made for Volume 17 by Ian Blackwell, Andrew Wrighting (Popperfoto, Overstone); Val Ching (Allsport, Pacific Palisades); Peter Csanadi (Adidas, Herzogenaurach); Marjet Dirks (Netherlands Sports Museum, Lelystad); Deborah Goodsite (The Corbis-Bettmann Archive, New York City); Violeta Zorrilla Hidalgo (Ramírez Vázquez y Asociados, S. A. De C. V., Pedredal de San Angel); Eileen Kennedy (Museum of the City of New York, New York City); Ken Kishimoto, Shigeaki Matsubara (Photo Kishimoto, Tokyo);

Andy Kiss (Duomo, New York City); Lappe Laubscher; Prem Kalliat (Sports Illustrated Picture Sales, New York City); Mihaela Liptez-Penes (Romanian Olympic Committee, Bucuresti); Jackie Loos, A. Fanarof (South African Library, Cape Town); Alexandra Leclef Mandl (The International Olympic Committee, Lausanne); David Ment, Bette Weneck (The Milbank Memorial Library, Teachers College Columbia University, New York City); Jan Mraz (Slovak Olympic Committee, Bratislava); John Nixon (Long Photography, Los Angeles); Patricia Olkiewicz (United States Olympic Committee, Colorado Springs); Jim Parker (Colorado State Archives, Denver); Michael Shulman (Archive Photos, New York City); Mary Ternes (D.C. Public Library, Washington D.C.); and Beatrice Trueblood.

The Publishers would also like to thank the following individuals, institutions and foundations for providing initial funding for the project: The Amelior Foundation (Morristown, New Jersey); Roy and Mary Cullen (Houston); The English, Bonter, Mitchell Foundation (Ft. Wayne, Indiana); Adrian French (Los Angeles); The Knight Foundation (Miami); The Levy Foundation (Philadelphia); and, Jonah Shacknai (New York). And for completion funding: Michael McKie, Optimax Securities, Inc. (Toronto); Graham Turner, Fraser & Beatty (Toronto); and Century of Sport Partnership (Toronto).

And a special thanks to Barron Pittenger (Assistant Executive Director, United States Olympic Committee, September 1981 to August 1987 and Executive Director, August 1987 to Dectmber 1989).

BIBLIOGRAPHY

Agostini, Mike. "My Take-Home Pay as an Amateur Sprinter." *Sports Illustrated*, January 30, 1961.

Allen, Neil. "Pay up, Pay up, and they'll play the game." *World Sports*, February 1972.

Anonymous. "Amateurism's Pros and Cons." *Newsweek*, February 14, 1972.

Anonymous. "Shamateurism." *Time*, February 7, 1972.

Anonymous. "Showdown at Sapporo." *Time*, February 14, 1972.

Anonymous. "Say Sayonara, Mr. Brundage." *World Sport*, March 1972.

Bonventre, Peter. "The Olympics: Fire and Ice in Japan." *Newsweek*, February 14, 1972.

Brasher, Christopher. *Munich 72*. London: Stanley Paul, 1972.

Brokhin, Yuri. *The Big Red Machine*. New York: Random House, 1977.

Buchanan, Ian. *British Olympians*. Enfield, Middlesex: Guiness, 1991.

Carlson, Lewis H. and John J. Fogarty. *Tales of Gold*. Chicago: Contemporary Books, Inc., 1987.

Condon, Robert J. *Great Women Athletes of the 20th Century*, Jefferson, North Carolina: McFarland & Company, Inc., 1991.

Crossman, Colonel Jim. *Olympic Shooting*. Washington, DC: National Rifle Association, 1978.

Duncanson, Neil. *The Fastest Men on Earth*. London: Willow Books, 1988.

Espy, Richard. *The Politics of the Olympic Games*. Berkeley: University of California Press, 1979.

Fry, John. "On Age and the Greening of the Olympics." *Ski*, February 1972.

Fry, John. "Report from Japan." *Ski*. March 1972.

Gilbert, Bill. "Problems in a Turned-On World." *Sports Illustrated*, June 23, 1969.

Gilbert, Doug. *The Miracle Machine*. New York: Coward, McCann & Geoghegan, Inc., 1980.

Goodbody, John. *The Illustrated History of Gymnastics*. London: Stanley Paul, 1982.

Gordon, Harry. *Australia and the Olympic Games*. St. Lucia, Queensland: University of Queensland Press, 1994.

Green, Nancy and Jack Batten, *Nancy Greene: An Autobiography*. Don Mills, Ontario: General Publishing Co., Ltd., 1968.

Guttman, Allen. *The Games Must Go On: Avery Brundage and the Olympic Movement*. New York: Columbia University Press, 1984.

Guttman, Allen. *The Olympics: A History of the Modern Games*. Urbana and Chicago: University of Illinois Press, 1992.

Hano, Arnold. "The Black Rebel who 'Whitelists' the Olympics." *New York Times Magazine*, May 12, 1968.

Hayes, Bob and Robert Pack. *Run, Bullet, Run.* New York: Harper & Row, Publishers 1990.

Hemery, David. *Another Hurdle: The Making of an Olympic Champion.* New York: Taplinger Pubishing Co., 1976.

Henry, Bill. *An Approved History of the Olympic Games.* Los Angeles: The Southern California Committee for the Olympic Games, 1981.

Hill, Christopher R. *Olympic Politics.* Manchester: Manchester University Press, 1992.

Hollander, Phyllis. *100 Greatest Women in Sports.* New York: Grosset & Dunlap, 1976.

Howell, Reet & Max. *Aussie Gold.* Melbourne: Brooks/Waterloo, 1988.

Jerome, John. "The Cochran Cartel." *Skiing*, December 1971.

Jerome, John. "Sapporo: Can this be ski racing?" *Skiing*, September 1972.

Johnson, William O. "The Name is the Name of the Game." *Sports Illustrated*, March 9, 1970.

Johnson, William O. "Go East Young Olympian." *Sports Illustrated*, November 15, 1971.

Johnson, William O. "Defender of the Faith." *Sports Illustrated*, July 24, 1972.

Johnson, William O. "The Big Man Lowers His Olympic Boom." *Sports Illustrated*, January 17, 1972.

Johnson, William O. "Games of the Rainbow." *Sports Illustrated*, February 14, 1972.

Johnson, William O. "The Go-Go Girls of Sapporo." *Sports Illustrated*, February 21, 1972.

Johnson, William O. "Babe: An Unreal Pro." *Sports Illustrated*, October 13, 1975.

LaChance, Dr. Leo E. "Trixi Schuba: A Champion Revisited." *Skating*, January 1993.

Larsen, John. "A Family Affair." *World Sports*, August 1968.

The Lord Killanin and John Rodda. *The Olympic Games: 80 Years of People, Events and Records.* New York: Collier Books, 1976.

McCallum, Jack. "The Regilding of a Legend." *Sports Illustrated*, October 25, 1982.

Miller, Geoffrey. *Behind the Olympic Rings.* Lynn, MA: H.O. Zimman, Inc., 1981.

Moore, Kenny. "A Courageous Stand." *Sports Illustrated*, August 5, 1991.

Moore, Kenny. "The Eye of the Storm." *Sports Illustrated*, August 12, 1991.

Moore, Kenny. "Giants on the Earth." *Sports Illustrated*, June 29, 1987.

Nelson, Cordner & Roberto Quercetani. *Runners and Races: 1,500M./Mile.* Los Altos, CA: TAFNews Press, 1973.

Olsen, Jack. "The Cruel Deception." *Sports Illustrated*, July 1, 1968.

Parker, John L. Jr. "The Miler Moves On." *Runner's World*, January 1986.

Pfeiffer, Doug. " Big Excite' at Sapporo." *Skiing*, January 1972.

Prokop, Dave. *The African Running Revolution.* London: World Publications, 1975.

Quick, Shayne P. "Black Knight Checks White King." *The Canadian Journal of History of Sport*, Vol. XXI, No. 2. December, 1990.

Ramsamy, Sam. *Apartheid: The Real Hurdle.* London: International Defence and Aid Fund for Southern Africa, 1982.

Report of the Commission of Inquiry into the Use of Drugs and Banned Practices Intended to Increase Athletic Performance, 1990.

Ress, Paul and Gwilym S. Brown. "A Tale of Two Idols." *Sports Illustrated*, March 18, 1968.

Ryun, Jim with Mike Phillips. *In Quest of Gold: The Jim Ryun Story.* San Francisco: Harper & Row, 1984.

Schaap, Dick. *The Perfect Jump.* New York: Signet Books, 1976.

Segrave, Jeffrey O. and Donald Chu (ed.), *The Olympic Games in Transition.* Champaign, IL: Human Kinetics Books, 1988.

Shaplen, Robert. "Amateur." *New Yorker*, July 23, 1960.

Simson, Vyv and Andrew Jennings. *The Lords of the Rings: Power, Money and Drugs in the Modern Olympics.* London: Simon & Schuster, 1992.

Smith, Beverly. *Figure Skating: A Celebration.* Toronto: McClelland & Stewart Inc., 1994.

Spivey, Donald (ed.). *Sport in America: New Historical Perspectives.* Westport, CT: Greenwood Press, 1985.

Stambler, Irwin. *Women in Sports.* Garden City: Doubleday & Company, Inc., 1975.

Steinbach, Valeri. *638 Olympic Champions: Three Decades in the Olympic Movement.* Moscow: Raduga Publishers, 1984.

Thayer, Charles W. "A Question of the Soul." *Sports Illustrated*, August 15, 1960.

The Associated Press. *Pursuit of Excellence: The Olympic Story.* Danbury, CT: Grolier Enterprises, Inc., 1979.

Tomlinson, Alan and Gary Whannel (ed.), *Five-ring circus: Money, Power and Politics at the Olympic Games.* London: Pluto Press, 1984.

Track and Field News, October/November 1968.

Underwood, John. "Lost Laughter." *Sports Illustrated*, September 30, 1968.

Underwood, John. "No Goody Two-Shoes." *Sports Illustrated*, March 10, 1969.

Verschoth, Anita. "Attack of the Killer Queen." *Sports Illustrated*, February 11, 1980.

Wallechinsky, David. *The Complete Book of the Olympics.* Boston: Little, Brown & Company, 1991.

Ward-Smith, A.J. "Altitude and wind effects on long jump performance with particular reference to the world record established by Bob Beamon." *Journal of Sports Sciences*, 1986.

Wenn, Stephen R. *A History of the International Olympic Committee and Television, 1939-1980.* Ph.D. Thesis, The Pennslyvania State University, 1993.

Wiggins, David K. " The Year of Awakening': Black Athletes, Racial Unrest and the Civil Rights Movement of 1968." *The International Journal of the History of Sport*, April 1992.

Women's Track and Field World, November/December 1968.

Wright, Benjamin T. *Skating Around the World: 1892-1992.* Davos: The One Hundredth Anniversary History of the International Skating Union, 1992.

Zrala, Lenka. "20 Years Later: Vera Caslavska, gymnastics artist of the '60s, is still at it today." *International Gymnast*, August 1989.

Exerpts from the following newspapers:
The Chicago Tribune
The London Times
The New York Herald Tribune
The Los Angeles Times

PHOTO CREDITS

Every effort has been made to locate the holders of the rights to the pictures in this book.

Adidas/*Leichtathletik* No. 38, September 17, 1968 33(top)
Allsport 75
Allsport/MSI 79
AP/Wide World Photos 15 (bottom)
Archive Photos 63
Archive Photos/Express Newspapers 62
Archives of the International Olympic Committee cover, 3, 9 (right), 16, 80, 95, 98, 111, 119, 121, 124 (top center), 125 (right), 164 (left), 168
© Brian Lanker 1991 41
© Long Photography, Inc. 1967/*Sports Illustrated* Volume 27, No. 3 64
© Washington Post, reprinted by permission of D. C. Public Library 43
Colorado State Archives 102
Diem-Archives, Deutsche Sporthochschule Köln 89

Duomo 124 (top left), 130, 145, 146-147
Foto dpa 34-35, 101, 114-115, 116
Foto Votava 127
Jim Greensfelder 135
Neil Leifer/Sports Illustrated 44
Photo Archive of Pedro Ramírez Vázquez, Architect 9 (left), 18, 19, 22, 29, 33 (bottom), 39, 42, 46, 49, 54 (top left), 54 (top center), 54 (top right), 56 (top), 56 (bottom left), 56-57, 57 (top), 57 (bottom right), 58, 60 (right), 60 (left), 66, 84, 88, 90-91, 103, 105 (top), 105 (bottom), 164 (right)
Photo Kishimoto 30 (bottom), 47, 48, 69, 72, 78, 109, 120 (top), 123, 124 (top right), 125 (left), 126 (top), 128, 129 (top), 131, 132, 133, 134, 137 (bottom), 138, 139, 140, 143, 144, 148
Popperfoto 23, 74, 85, 129 (bottom), 136 (left), 136-137
Pressens Bild 61

Private Collection 141
Rich Clarkson © 1965 59
Rich Clarkson © 1967 50
Romanian Olympic Committee 81
South African Library, Cape Town: Cape Times Collection 92, 96-97, 97 (top)
The Corbis-Bettmann Archive 118
***The Revolt of the Black Athlete*, Harry Edwards, The Free Press, New York 1969** 25
The Sapporo City Official Report of the 11th Winter Olympic Games 120 (bottom)
United States Olympic Committee Photo Library 4-5, 6, 12, 17, 21, 30-31, 36, 68 (bottom), 73, 76, 77, 83, 86, 87, 126 (bottom)
UPI/Corbis-Bettmann 10, 11, 13, 15 (top), 20, 26, 38 (top), 38 (bottom), 40, 52, 68 (top), 70-71, 99, 106, 113, 142 (top), 142 (bottom)

INDEX

THE OLYMPIC WORLD
SAPPORO 1972 WINTER GAMES

PARTICIPATING COUNTRIES

North America

CAN . . . . CANADA
USA UNITED STATES OF AMERICA

South America

ARG . . . . ARGENTINA

Europe

AUT . . . . AUSTRIA		
BEL . . . . BELGIUM		
BUL . . . . BULGARIA		
CHE . . . . CZECHOSLOVAKIA	**GDR** . GERMAN DEMOCRATIC REP.	**NOR** . . . . NORWAY
ESP . . . . SPAIN	**GRE** . . . . GREECE	**POL** . . . . POLAND
FIN . . . . FINLAND	**HOL** . . . . THE NETHERLANDS	**ROM** . . . . ROMANIA
FRA . . . . FRANCE	**HUN** . . . . HUNGARY	**SUI** . . . . SWITZERLAND
FRG . FEDERAL REP. OF GERMANY	**ITA** . . . . ITALY	**SWE** . . . . SWEDEN
GBR . . . . GREAT BRITAIN	**LIE** . . . . LIECHTENSTEIN	**URS** . . . . USSR